GOING UP IN THE WORLD

BRYAN KESSELMAN

All rights reserved, no part of this publication may be reproduced or transmitted by any means whatsoever without the prior permission of the publisher.

Edited by Julia Krzyzanowska

Cover image public domain
ISBN: 978-1-916756-09-0

Veneficia Publications
January 2024

VENEFICIA PUBLICATIONS UK
veneficiapublications.com

CONTENTS

PART 1 1

CHAPTER ONE 3
CHAPTER TWO 19
CHAPTER THREE 35
CHAPTER FOUR 47
CHAPTER FIVE 55
CHAPTER SIX 63
CHAPTER SEVEN 72
CHAPTER EIGHT 76
CHAPTER NINE 81
CHAPTER TEN 92
CHAPTER ELEVEN 101
CHAPTER TWELVE 103
CHAPTER THIRTEEN 111
CHAPTER FOURTEEN 118
CHAPTER FIFTEEN 125
CHAPTER SIXTEEN 128
CHAPTER SEVENTEEN 139
CHAPTER EIGHTEEN 144
CHAPTER NINETEEN 147
CHAPTER TWENTY 156

CHAPTER TWENTY-ONE 159
CHAPTER TWENTY-TWO 164
CHAPTER TWENTY-FOUR 166
CHAPTER TWENTY-FIVE 173
CHAPTER TWENTY-SIX 175

PART 2 181

CHAPTER ONE 183
CHAPTER TWO 187
CHAPTER THREE 195
CHAPTER FOUR 199
CHAPTER FIVE 203
CHAPTER SIX 208
CHAPTER SEVEN 211
CHAPTER EIGHT 215
CHAPTER NINE 222
CHAPTER TEN 226
CHAPTER ELEVEN 233
CHAPTER TWELVE 245
CHAPTER THIRTEEN 252
CHAPTER FOURTEEN 256
CHAPTER FIFTEEN 259
CHAPTER SIXTEEN 263
CHAPTER SEVENTEEN 267

PART 3 277

CHAPTER ONE 281
CHAPTER TWO 286
CHAPTER THREE 294
CHAPTER FOUR 298
CHAPTER FIVE 304
CHAPTER SIX 309
CHAPTER SEVEN 312
CHAPTER EIGHT 318
CHAPTER NINE 322
CHAPTER TEN 330
CHAPTER ELEVEN 336
CHAPTER TWELVE 339

PART 1
THE
HOTEL LIFTS

CHAPTER ONE

Lord and Lady Tongue sit facing each other, each at one end of a long, oaken refectory table, eating a miserable breakfast of thin gruel served to them by Lord Tongue's faithful steward Groves. A tortoiseshell cat sits near the door drinking milk from a saucer. Lord Tongue, whose name has become a byword for miserliness, sits on the edge of his chair, for were he to attempt the process of reclining comfortably back, the chair would certainly collapse. It has become very unstable as a result of the ill use given it by its occupant in the long-distant, reckless days of his youth, when he would leap upon it to address, with warm words, the assembled company at banquets given by his late elder brother, the previous Marquess of Tongue.

Lady Tongue, with her birds-nest hair, picks daintily at her sugared gruel, passing each morsel through pursed lips into her mouth, where she thoughtfully considers the flavour—a flavour which mixes with the already present, ever-present, pungent taste of well- matured, burnt tobacco. Everyone who has received confidences from Lady Tongue is familiar with the scent of stale cigar smoke.

Lord Tongue mops up his bowl with a slice of pumpernickel—dry, brown, and as bitter as his wife's cheap Havanas, her only luxury. In silence they began their meal, and in silence they finish. As Groves begins to tidy the breakfast things away, Lord Tongue rises and walks, a little unsteadily, towards the far end of the table where sits his spouse.

Eventually, when he gets there, he will assist her to arise and then escort her to the garden, since the day promises to be a fair one. If it were not a fine morning, or in winter, they would proceed slowly to their small sitting-room, but now, the garden awaits, overgrown and untended, yes, but oh, what memories it holds in its tangled grasp! Each thorn clutches greedily to the air and to life. Each sucker sucks at the life-essences in the ground like a thirsty babe at its mother's breast. In the centre of the garden stands a mighty cedar tree: the only thing of beauty left in all the grounds of Mandible Hall, Westmorland.

Once, Lord and Lady Tongue were young lovers. Once, Groves was able to dash here and there carrying urgent messages between them. Now, he is as crabbed as they. His head twitches now and then, and his toupee is always sadly awry.

Young lovers, yes. Handsome and beautiful, no. Lord Tongue has always been extremely short-sighted, and he has always worn spectacles with the thickest lenses which, even in his youth, kept the world in a haze, so that he was unable to see that his beloved was no Venus. Lady Tongue, in her youth, knew that Lord Tongue was no Adonis but, knowing herself to be no Venus, allowed herself to fall in love as quickly as possible. Nor had their union been unblessed, for they had a daughter, Alice, the bright jewel of their existence.

Alice, child of their later years, now thirty-three, unmarried, short-sighted as her father, awaits them in the garden sitting by a small table at which she has breakfasted on water and air. Rake-thin, she sits primly sipping her water. Her hair has been scraped back from her forehead and assembled into a tight bun on the back of her head. Wisps of hair have escaped the bun and blow in the gentle breeze that plays occasionally about the garden. The old people greet their daughter and sit by her.

Every day, the scene is exactly the same. Here is today's conversation (the stilted language is reported accurately).

"Alice, my love."

"Yes, father."

"Alice, your mother and I have decided that the time has come for a change in your circumstances. In short, m'dear, that you should marry."

Alice blushed. She was under no misapprehension of her charms. This unhappy creature had willingly kept herself apart from the rest of mankind. Sadly, she looked at her parents.

"I don't think that…"

"You don't need to think," said her mother. "What we have decided will come to pass. Tomorrow, your intended arrives."

"My intended!" gasped Alice.

"My child," said her father, "it is time that you knew the truth."

"Don't excite yourself, Father."

"Alice," said her mother, "you are to marry Sir Arthur Winsome, and he will be here tomorrow."

"My love," murmured Lord Tongue to his wife, "you have arrived at the conclusion somewhat quickly, don't you think? I was going to tell Alice in a more..."

"Oh, how you waffle! Enough of this pontification! What do you say, Alice?"

"But Sir Arthur is, according to my magazine, the most handsome man in the county. Why should he wish to marry me?"

"Well...," said her father.

"Well...," said her mother. "For your..."

"For your..."

"Inheritance!" they both declared simultaneously, clapping their hands together. And then, linking arms, and pulling Alice to her feet, all three danced (somewhat haltingly, if the truth be known), laughing all the while, round the cedar tree.

Nighttime.

Alice, alone once more, was in despair over the need to make a favourable impression on her suitor. She was determined to make herself as attractive as possible for the moment when she would receive him for the first time and, as a result of her extreme nervousness, could not sleep. She tossed and turned in her bed, unable to find a comfortable position, and eventually sat up, turned on her small bedside light and picked up the novel she had been reading. She had left her reading glasses on the sideboard in the dining room, and so, in slippered feet, she slipped downstairs to retrieve them.

All was darkness except for the area at the foot of the stairs, which was dimly lit by the moonlight that shone through the circular window above the front door. Mandible Hall was silent, and, though Alice had lived there all her life, there was something unnerving about the pattern on the hall carpet. In the half-light, it seemed to be made up of several dark snakes slowly twisting themselves around each other.

On returning to her room with her glasses, she felt unable to concentrate on her book after all, so she took out her diary and began to write in it—though not an account of recent events. Alice was writing a melodrama and, as a pianist of rather vague talent, planned to set the text to music. Since it will be relevant to the events that follow, the script of the first two scenes is inserted here. It was titled:

MANDEVILLE'S MIND

Characters

Sir Robert Mandeville (Bart.)
Julia (his ward—in love with Anthony Goodpoint)
Rev. Anthony Goodpoint (a young curate in love with Julia)
Harewood Ruskin (Sir Robert's elderly servant)

Time: Mid-19th Century.

A stormy autumn day. Late afternoon.

Place: A country residence in Shropshire.

SCENE ONE

[A large study room. Wooden wainscoting. Large ornate fireplace with no fire burning. Bookshelves. Desk. Chairs. A shotgun mounted on the wall.]

Sir Rob: When I was young and had no cares, I spent my days in sordid vice.
 Now, alone with thoughts of death, my loathsome guilt must pay the price.

Julia: Uncle, why so sad? Peace you'd surely find, if to our curate you would tell all that troubles your mind.

Sir Rob: My dear, you'll drive me mad with all your little kindnesses.
 Leave me to my sorrows.

[Enter: Ruskin]

Ruskin: Sir. At the front door young Goodpoint stands.

Sir Rob: (Ah, yes. He with humble hands.) Show him in.
 (How I detest his servile ways.)

Julia:' Tis he. My mind is in a daze.
Ruskin: *[Announcing]* Reverend *Goodpoint*.

Julia: (And soon I may be free of this place, if God wills it.)

Goodpoint: *[Entering]* (Amen to that.) Sir Robert, I trust you are in the best of health.

Sir Rob: And you, sir?

Goodpoint: A slight cold, but that is all.

Sir Rob: Take care, these illnesses may work their worst.

Goodpoint: Mens sana in corpore sano.

Sir Rob: (Cheeky pup, what does he mean by that?) Come, sir, a glass of sherry, the finest to be had.

Goodpoint: Thanks, I'll not refuse.
 Many a time when I was a boy, I passed this house while going to school where first I met your niece...

Sir Rob: Enough of that. What brings you here on such a day as this?

Goodpoint: Just this: the villagers would have you open their fair next month. *[Becoming eloquent]* When summer spreads her golden wings...

Sir Rob: *[Interrupting]* Why, what's this? You're a poet, sir. Save your verses for another who may like 'em more... What need have they of me? Tell them to leave me alone As I do them.

Goodpoint: *[Aside to Julia]* Julia, get to the back door. I'll meet you there.

Julia: *[Aside to Goodpoint]* Take care. He is craftier than the devil.

Sir Rob: *[Overhearing wrongly]* (Mandeville! What does she mean by uttering my family name?)
 [To Goodpoint] Come with me, sir, we'll discuss this further.
 [To Ruskin] Watch her!

[Exit Sir Robert and Goodpoint. Julia sits in an armchair. Ruskin watches her. The scene ends.]

SCENE TWO

[The same study. Some hours later. Julia alone.]

Julia: Watching and waiting, it seems so long.
 When will he come? I'm impatient to be gone from this dreadful place.

[Enter: Goodpoint]

Goodpoint: At last, my love, I am here. Your uncle went to bed with a headache. Now, let us be gone from this place.

[Enter: Ruskin]

Ruskin: Caught you! Now you're done for! Now you'll be for it! Two birds in a trap—a cage of your own making.

[Enter: Sir Robert]

Sir Rob: Julia, get to bed.
[To Goodpoint]   Now, sir, you cannot move, you are helpless.
So, you would steal from me the one bright jewel of my life.

Goodpoint: What is this? I am unable to stir. Frozen by some magic power.

Sir Rob: Mind over matter, my dear sir, Nothing more.
My teacher was a pupil of that Mesmer of fame and high renown. And now the agonies may begin.

[Sir Robert makes sweeping passes with his hands.]

Goodpoint: Ah! What pain, what torment, what sorrow.

Sir Rob: Suffer in body as I do in mind!

Julia: Free him, sir.

Sir Rob: Niece, get to bed.

Julia: *[To Ruskin]* Help us.

Ruskin: *[Undecided]* I am powerless.

Julia: Free him.

Sir Rob: To bed.

Julia: Help us.

Ruskin: I cannot. *[Holding Sir Robert despite his comment.]*
    [To Julia and Goodpoint] Run!

Sir Rob: Traitor. Die!

[Julia and Goodpoint escape. Ruskin falls to the floor. Sir Robert takes the shotgun from the wall and hurries out.]

Naturally, Alice had cast herself, in her mind, as Julia—not that her life was anything like that, but she enjoyed letting her imagination run wild. And now, the thought of being carried away by the handsome Sir Arthur Winsome, even if he was only after her inheritance, made her hug herself with a tremulousness that surprised her.

The following morning, Alice rose early. She had not slept well and was glad to be up. After putting on her dressing gown, she began to attend to matters of her beauty. She was rather unsure of how to make the best of herself, and so she asked her maid to advise her.
    "What should I do with my hair, Clara?"
    "Why, Miss, I should leave it loose today." (Clara always wanted to do whatever was easiest.)
    "Brush it for me."
    "That I will, Miss." Much brushing.
    "What shall I do with my face, Clara?"

"Why, some foundation, Miss, always helps—perhaps, if I may advise some cover cream…" (Much applying of makeup.)

"What shall I wear, Clara?"

"Why, your white gown, of course, Miss." (Much dressing.)

"My hair is not quite right, Clara."

"Well, Miss, perhaps we should put it up after all." (Further dressing of hair.)

"My face is not quite right, Clara." (Further application of makeup.)

"Oh, Clara, I look a fright!"

"Let's start again, Miss."

And so on—all morning long. Every so often, Alice stopped Clara so that she could hold her glasses to her eyes to look at herself in the mirror.

Alice was by now in a nervous agony of anticipation. She spoke quite sharply to Clara more than once, which was unusual for her because she was rather afraid of Clara.

Clara was silent, tight-lipped, and had sore fingers from so much buttoning, unbuttoning and re-buttoning; she felt herself to be on the verge of resigning, and would have done so, were it not for the fat bonus she felt sure would soon be coming her way.

Mandible Hall stood on the top of a gentle hill overlooking both the sea and a long winding path that made its way from the local railway station to the garden gate. From the place where she usually sat, Alice had a clear view of any visitors who might approach. Gazing at this scene through a pair of binoculars was usually one of Alice's favourite occupations. Now, she could hardly bear to look in case her suitor should arrive.

After breakfast, which followed pretty much along the lines of that of the previous day, Lord and Lady Tongue sat in the small sitting room silently awaiting the arrival of the bridegroom; Alice stood by the mantelpiece and stared at the clock. Ten o'clock was the appointed time, but it came and went, and the seconds ticked slowly by. Alice was used to being busy. She always had something on the go, someone to see, an appointment to keep, charitable works that needed to be done, so this waiting around was not only dull, but it was wasting her time, and she was beginning to resent that.

Half past ten came and went, and then eleven. The three of them waited still. Groves, immensely tall, though with bandy legs, entered creakily at eleven thirty.

"Hm-hm, Sir Arthur Winsome," he bellowed hoarsely.

Lord and Lady Tongue helped each other rise rather crookedly, while Alice flushed a delicate pink and wished to be, "...somewhere else, anywhere, but not here!"

In bounded the healthiest individual imaginable. His ginger hair and moustache, together with a florid complexion and rather large waistline, made him seem far too big for the room.

"Here at last. A bit late. Sorry. No time to explain. Motor's parked outside. Anyone for a jaunt? Let's go!"

All four were stuffed in no time into an open-topped Aston Martin Lagonda. Sir Arthur at the wheel put foot to floor, and they were off. Corners and bends taken at over fifteen miles per hour. Lady Tongue, holding onto her hat, which she had had the presence of mind to grab as she passed it in the hall, was nearly sick.

Lord Tongue, hanging over the other side of the car, was sick. But Alice sat in the passenger seat next to Sir Arthur, and could not take her eyes off him, though he was somewhat out of focus as she had made certain not to be wearing her glasses.

"Isn't he wonderful?" she breathed.

"Good goer isn't she?" shouted Sir Arthur. "The car I mean. Only got her yesterday... haven't paid for her yet." he added as they disembarked on arrival back at Mandible Hall.

"Oh, well, I'm sure we could erm..." started Lord Tongue.

It had certainly seemed to Alice and her mother, who strained their ears in vain at the study door that afternoon trying to hear the conversation between the Marquess and Sir Arthur, that there was much amity between the two men. But they could not actually hear any words.

After a good hour or so, during which time all that could be heard from the hall was guffawing and occasional lapses into attempts at singing snatches of the latest musical comedy hits, mother and daughter gave up and went into the drawing room where tea was served to them by a rather sulky Clara.

Inside the study, however, negotiations had proceeded most satisfactorily.

To begin with, there had been some idle talk over tumblers of whisky and expensive cigars reserved for special occasions. And then, the serious business started.

"By the way," said Lord Tongue, "are you still interested in my daughter?"

"Yes, indeed," replied the young(ish) man, "but, if I may ask, why would you want me to... er... do this? I mean to say, my reason is evident, and I have made no secret of it. To put it plainly... I need the money that you have agreed to settle upon her when she marries. Question is... what do you get out of it?"

"True," remarked the Marquess, "it may be hard for you to understand, and we haven't really been as open with you as perhaps we should have been. You will, of course, have noticed that Alice is not everyone's idea of a catch, except financially, of course—and there lies the first reason. She needs to be settled with someone. Lady Tongue and I are not getting younger, and we want to know that Alice's future is secure." As he said this, he proffered the whisky bottle to Arthur, who waved his hand slightly in polite refusal. "Then there is the matter of grandchildren, which, of course we would like to have... but I have not really answered your question, have I? You see, my boy, my wife and I read the newspapers avidly. Avidly. And you have been noticed. That is to say, we can see that you show great promise in one particular field."

"Well, really," said Arthur, "I cannot for the life of me think what you could be talking about."

"Your father, my boy, he was..."

"Something of a rascal, I'm afraid. The family tend not to talk about him."

"You have his tools of trade, I think."

"Why, yes, he left them to me in his will. How curious that you should mention them, I was only looking at them the other evening."

"And have you ever used them? Come, come, we have no need, I think, to hedge. Your father was a jewel thief, and you are in need of money."

"If you will allow me to say, sir..."

"You think that we ourselves have no need of money. What then could be my interest? But... my boy! Don't you see? To put it plainly... we are bored. We want to try a new pastime."

"And Alice..."

"...knows nothing of this—it will be our secret."

"Does Lady Tongue know?"

"Why, it was her idea! A symbiotic relationship. We supply you with the opportunity, you get on with the practical side of things."

A few minutes later, Lord Tongue and Sir Arthur Winsome entered the drawing room where Alice sat tinkling the piano keys while her mother stared at *The Times* crossword puzzle.

Lord Tongue winked at his wife knowingly, and she winked back, though, short sighted as he was, he missed her wink. Alice, who had not noticed the winks, stopped playing and looked mistily at Arthur. Her face was pink with shyness, but Arthur walked over to her with a smiling face, took her hand and, without a word, led her through the French windows into the rose garden just outside. There, he formally proposed and was accepted.

Now, it must not be supposed that Lord and Lady Tongue had bad intentions towards their daughter, or that they were not perfectly nice people. In truth, they cared about her deeply, and were most concerned that she should be happy. But they felt that Alice's sheltered upbringing had been unexciting to say the least, and when they remembered the circumstances of their own meeting, they felt that an experience as extraordinary as had happened to them should also be granted to their daughter.

This is not the place to go into that Venetian affair—we reserve that for another occasion—but the great happiness they had been granted for the years they had been together was, in no small measure, due to that wonderful time.

At five o'clock, it was time for Arthur Winsome to leave, though he would return later that week so that all arrangements for the wedding could be made. He sprang into his car after shaking Lord and Lady Tongue by the hand and giving Alice an affectionate kiss on her cheek.

"Bye!" shouted Sir Arthur as the car sped away.

CHAPTER TWO

We move away from the Tongues and Sir Arthur to a seaside town on the south coast of England, about three months later: to a luxury hotel with all modern conveniences, as well as an ornamental south-facing garden with palm trees and a rather dysfunctional staff. It is Friday the 2nd of October, 1931. The days are growing colder, though some still struggle on with warmer moments.

The foyer of the Hotel Splendide, in a town that glorified itself with the name Paunceton-sur-la-Mer, was large and well-appointed, with cushioned sofas and chairs upholstered with Liberty-patterned covers. At the far end of the foyer, beyond the reception desk, were two lifts side by side. Opposite the two lifts were two more lifts, for the hotel was a large one with two separate wings. The lifts themselves had manual control handles and were operated by a team of four people, and it is to this merry crew that we must now be introduced.

Ben was forty. He had behaved like a forty-year-old since he had been twenty. He was unassuming in appearance, the sort of man that people might look at for some time but then find themselves at a loss to describe. He had worked in the hotel longer than any of the others employed there and had never been able to get any further advanced than his position of Senior Lift Operator. He had been engaged to Angela, one of the other lift operators, for some years, and they had been waiting for Ben to make something of himself before they got married. Angela was quite pretty, and she had made up her mind some years before that she was not really going to wait long for Ben to get on with things, but that she would improve her own lot and then see if she still wanted to marry him. But she was still in the same job, and not too happy about it.

The other two lift operators need to be introduced carefully. Their names were Andrew and Mary, and they were both twenty-five. They were, in point of fact, brother and sister— twins, but though Ben and Angela knew this, it was kept secret from Mr Horniman, the hotel manager. That was important, as it was company policy not to employ two people from the same family. Their relationship with each other was, as is often the case with siblings, affectionate and difficult at the same time.

Mr Horniman was a pompous individual, though he had no self- confidence. He was engaged to be married to the daughter of a local bank manager, an engagement which was proving to be something of a problem.

The other person who should be mentioned at this juncture is a certain Mrs Garthwaite, who owned the hotel and spent several weeks at a time occupying one or other of the more luxurious suites, but without paying for staying, despite the fact that, by rights, she should have done so, as it made Mr Horniman's task of balancing the books very difficult (he insisted on doing the books himself).

The morning had been unremarkable, though busy. At nine o'clock, Lift 2 arrived on the ground floor, and Andrew stepped out, followed by four large people. He went back into the lift, carried out four heavy suitcases, loaded them onto a trolley and then wheeled the trolley to the reception desk, followed by the departing guests. He stood nearby as they paid their bills but realised very quickly that no tip would be forthcoming from any of them. He pulled a face (secretly) and returned to his lift in a sour mood. At that moment, Lift 1 arrived, and out stepped Ben followed by his "passengers". Ben, likewise, received no tip. While this was happening, Lifts 3 and 4 arrived, and out stepped Mary and Angela. Each was given a tip as their passengers walked by, a fact which did not go unnoticed by the men.

"I'm never going to get out of here," sighed Andrew. "I'll still be a lift boy when I'm eighty!"

"I thought so too when I was your age," said Ben encouragingly.

"And what happened?" This from Angela.

"I'm still here!"

"You're not eighty," said Mary.

"I feel it, though," replied Ben. "Excuse me..." he added, as a buzzing noise came from inside his lift, and he went in to answer the call. The others watched the dial above the lift door as Ben's lift ascended.

"Fourth floor", said Andrew, "I expect that'll be Mrs G. She probably wants him to run an errand—hardly ever uses the lift".

"Claustrophobia," said Angela, "she's a martyr to it; she told me so herself."

Mary showed her tip money to her brother:

"You can share mine if you like."

"No thanks, Sis," said Andrew, "you keep it."

At that moment, Andrew's lift buzzed, and Andrew disappeared into it, leaving Mary and Angela alone.

It was not really allowed for the lift operators to stand about engaged in idle gossip, but at that particular moment, all had suddenly become quiet in the foyer, and the only person visible was Philippa, the efficient (not to say redoubtable) young receptionist, and she had her back turned and was busy sorting pencil stubs by size. Still, Mary and Angela had to keep their voices low so as not to be overheard.

"Why do you always offer him your money?" asked Angela.

"Because he never takes it. Listen, Angela, I've got something to tell you."

"Oh good; I love secrets."

"Yes," said Mary, "but please keep this one. I don't know why I tell you these things, you never keep them to yourself."

"Because I'm your best friend."

"Some friend!" replied Mary with a giggle.

"What is it then?"

"I've been offered a new job."

"You're going to leave?" said Angela looking rather surprised.

"Of course not, silly. It's here."

"In the hotel?"

"I'm being promoted. It's still a bit hush-hush, but I just had to tell someone."

"What about your brother?"

The receptionist looked up sharply; Mary took Angela by the hand and pulled her into her own lift where they could not be seen.

"For goodness' sake, don't tell Andrew, he always spoils everything. My mother told him to keep an eye on me for some reason, and he follows me everywhere. I've lost three jobs in the last two years because of him."

"Have you told Mr Horniman he's your brother yet?"

"What do you take me for? You know Mr Horniman hates Andrew. Ever since Andy saw him kissing Philippa, he's been looking for any excuse to sack him."

"Yes, I know," said Angela with a smile, "Horniman's been running round like a scared rabbit since then."

"He's been trying to keep that revolting incident from his fiancée."

"Have you ever seen her?" asked Angela.

"No, have you?"

"No one ever has. She's a…a…a…" Angela managed to stifle a sneeze.

"A legend?"

"A- a- apocryphal!"

"Is that a mythological monster?"

"Perhaps," said Angela, "but you haven't told me what the job is yet."

"Hotel Receptionist," said Mary.

"How did that happen?"

"Well, apparently Philippa has to leave… suddenly… I don't know why, and Mr Horniman just offered it to me."

"How wonderful for you!" said Angela.

"I'm to have an assistant, I'll recommend you if you like."

"How wonderful!"

"I think he likes me… Mr Horniman."

"Oh! ...How wonderful!"

A moment here while we listen in to Angela's thoughts on hearing Mary's news.

Angela: [thinking] He said he liked me—that job should be mine!

Angela's lift buzzed and she hurried out of Mary's and into her own. As she ascended, Andrew's lift arrived on the ground floor, and an elderly man exited hurriedly. Mary and Andrew watched him, and then, just as Andrew was about to say something to her, Mary's lift buzzed, and she ascended to higher regions.

Ben arrived in his lift. No passengers. Mrs Garthwaite had kept him occupied for some time on the fourth floor.

"What did Mrs G want?" asked Andrew.

"To look at me, I think," replied Ben in a gloomy voice. "Every day she calls me up, and every day I go up and move things around for her. General dogsbody, that's me!"

"Listen, Ben," said Andrew, changing the subject, "can you keep a secret?"

"You can trust me."

"I've got a new job."

"I thought you said you'd be a lift boy till you're eighty."

"That was for Mary's sake. She follows me everywhere I go. I've lost three jobs this year because of her interfering. Our mother told her to keep an eye on me. I don't know why, I'm older than Mary. She should have asked *me* to keep an eye on *her*!"

"You're only older by a few minutes, Andy. Does Mr Horniman know she's your sister?"

"Mercifully not. Imagine what would happen if he did. I'd never know a moment's peace until I'd acted as Cupid for him. He's been walking around in a daze ever since he met her."

"So that's why you told Mary about Horniman being engaged."

"And that he plays around… yes, to put her off. She's silly enough to think that he's a good catch."

"Oh, I see. What's the job?"

"Assistant Receptionist," said Andrew. "It means having to work with that awful Philippa, but at least Mary won't be cramping my style all the time."

"Well done! How did you get that?"

"Mr Horniman noticed my efficiency."

"I thought you said he didn't like you."

"I'm just trying to put Mary off the scent. She's like a bloodhound with an old bone."

A moment here while we listen in to Ben's thoughts on hearing Andrew's news.

Ben: [thinking] I've been here for years. Where's my promotion? That job should be mine!

And now you can see the state of affairs that exists in the hotel. Each person has his or her own itinerary, each one has his or her own secret, and each one spreads the seeds of disinformation to one or more of the others.

Mr Horniman himself suddenly came into view, or rather, his stomach did, for he tended to promenade, hands behind his back, in an irritating, self-important manner with arched back, chin up, and with eyes that looked down at his inferiors.

"Good morning, Andrew... Ben," he said in rotund tones.

"Silly old goat!" whispered Ben to Andrew.

Andrew, though, had more sense.

"Good morning, sir," he replied in a rather oily fashion. Could you tell me when I start at the desk?"

"This afternoon. Get your new uniform from stores, don't forget to give them a deposit, and then report back at one. I think you might take the rest of the morning off."

"Yes, sir, thank you very much."

Andrew gave a knowing look to Ben, hung an "Out of Service" sign by his lift and made his exit. Horniman looked at himself in a full-length mirror nearby with satisfaction while straightening his tie. Ben looked disgusted but quickly changed his expression, when Horniman looked up, into one of subservience.

"Excuse me, sir," said Ben.

"Yes, yes, can't it wait? What is it?

"I... erm... Andrew's a splendid fellow, don't you think?"

"Indeed, he is. Just what this hotel needs—enthusiastic people like Andrew."

"He's very young, though, isn't he?"

"Indeed, he is. Just what this hotel needs—youth."

"He hasn't been here very long, though."

"Indeed not. And promoted already. That young fellow will go far."

"I sometimes wonder," remarked Ben, "if experience isn't more important than youth."

"After all is said and done, when you have finally achieved your goals in life, there is only one thing missing."

"And that is?" asked Ben.

"Youth," replied Horniman. "It is the most important thing of all, and we must do our best not to resent those who have it, while we do not."

This remark showed that Horniman had more understanding of life (and of Ben) than one might at first have given him credit for.

Ben's lift buzzed.

"Have a good day, Ben," said Mr Horniman.

"Thank you, sir…" said Ben as he walked into his lift, and then, as the doors closed upon him (under his breath), "…very much for nothing!"

Mary and Angela arrived onto the ground floor in their lifts simultaneously. Both were tipped, both thanked their passengers, looked at each other and laughed.

"A photo finish again." They spoke together, as it was a formula they had hit on to amuse themselves. Mary noticed Horniman.

"Excuse me, sir," she said.

"That's quite all right, my dear," said Horniman patronisingly.

Angela interrupted, which was, perhaps, just as well as the expression of adoration on Horniman's face made Mary turn away to hide her reaction to it.

"Mary's been telling me about her good fortune," said Angela.

"Now, now, Mary, discretion, you know," said Horniman cryptically.

Mary understood Horniman's suggestiveness. It worried her, but she chose to ignore it.

"When do I start, sir?"

"I think you should start today. Why don't you take the rest of the morning off, and report at the desk at one."

So, Mary hung an "Out of Service" notice by her lift, just as her brother had done not long before, and left the foyer.

Horniman was pompous enough to apostrophise audibly when the mood struck him, not that he really expected to be overheard. However, in a tangled sort of way, he liked the idea of being thought to be so far above the common man that he could utter dramatic thoughts aloud and be admired by those around him.

He looked at Mary as she went and said aloud, but to himself, "Charming. Quite charming!"

Angela, who was standing close by, naturally overheard and, therefore, startled him when she said, almost as if in reply,

"They make a lovely couple, don't you think?"

"Who do you mean?" asked Horniman.

"Mary and Andrew, of course. They've known each other for years." Horniman stared at her.

"Have they?" he said. Angela's lift buzzed.

"Oh yes, didn't you know?" chirped Angela as the lift doors closed on her. Mr Horniman stared after her.

Angela giggled to herself while imagining Horniman's disappointment on hearing that Andrew and Mary might be romantically involved with each other.

Horniman, meanwhile, mused to himself as he turned on his heels to walk towards his office: "Still, maturity and security may yet win the day."

In the early afternoon, an unaccustomed hush pervaded the atmosphere in the foyer. Two of the hotel guests were seated at low coffee tables with newspapers spread before them. Other guests were either out or seated in the dining room for lunch. The reception desk was deserted, and only Lift 1, if any had looked inside, showed any sign of action. For Angela and Ben had set up a small, collapsible table there, and, seated on stools, they were eating lunch: supplied by the kitchen in paper bags. They had been charged for them, a situation to which both strongly objected. For as long as Ben could remember, the hotel had never let any employees have anything for nothing.

Shortly before one o'clock, Andrew appeared behind the reception counter and began to polish the desktop. He was wearing his new uniform, which was not actually new, and for which he had had to pay a deposit, and was keen to look as busy as possible so as to make a good impression on Philippa, though he was surprised that she was not there.

One o'clock was briefly announced by the single bell-strike of the small desk-clock, and at that moment, Mary arrived and walked into the area behind the desk. The two looked at each other, and then each spoke at exactly the same time:

"What are you doing here? I work here," they both said.

Mary was quicker on the uptake than her brother.

"Are you the new Assistant Receptionist?" she asked.

"Yes, I am," said Andrew. "Have you seen Philippa?"

"Um! She doesn't work here anymore, and... this is going to be fun... I'm your new boss."

"Don't say it," said Andrew, aghast.

"Yes, I'm the new Head Receptionist. So don't make a fuss. The boot's on the other foot now, isn't it? You'll be taking your orders from me!"

"Says who?"

"Mr Horniman gave me this job," declared Mary primly, "and I'm going to make the most of it."

"Why do you follow me everywhere, Mary?"

"You know very well that I'm supposed to be looking after you."

"And who's looking after you?"

"Well, not that it's any of your business, but a certain Hotel Manager seems to be very interested in a certain young lady not a million miles away from here."

"Mary, you wouldn't. Not Horniman?"

"Perhaps not—he's too stingy, and he chases every pretty girl that he sees."

"And catches them sometimes," said Andrew, thinking of how he had spotted Horniman kissing Philippa when he thought no one could see.

"Yes, that's why Philippa left so suddenly. Mrs Garthwaite seemed to suspect something, and Horniman's terrified of her—I keep my ear to the ground."

"So I see," remarked Andrew. "But he hasn't a hope with you, has he?"

"Not as far as I'm concerned," said Mary, "anyway, he's engaged." Andrew stifled a laugh.

"What's so funny?" demanded Mary. "Have you seen his fiancée?"

"Has anyone?"

"Ah, that's just it, no one has…except…"

"Oh, you're always so mysterious. Have you seen her? What's she like?"

"That would be telling."

"Oh, you're infuriating! And just as I thought I was one up on you, you come up with a mystery like this. Go and sharpen the pencils!"

"Yes, miss," said Andrew with exaggerated humility. And both moved to opposite ends of the desk, Andrew to look at the pencils, and Mary to take possession of the hotel register.

A little later that afternoon, a lady of imposing proportions sailed over to the reception desk and addressed herself to Andrew who, until then, had been gazing into space in a world of his own.

"Excuse me, young man," said Mrs Garthwaite, for it was she, "sorry to interrupt your pipedream, and all that. Could you tell me what the latest dollar-pound exchange rate is today?"

"I really don't know. I'll try to find out for you."

"Why don't you know? Aren't you interested in banking? I mean, if you are not interested in banking, then why are you working here?"

"This isn't a bank, Mrs Garthwaite."

"Don't be impertinent! I know very well this isn't a bank. Fetch Mr Horniman!"

"I'm sure I can find out what you would like to know without disturbing him."

"Is something wrong?" asked Mary who, at that moment, came out of the small office behind the reception desk.

"I want to see the manager."

Mr Horniman, who always had the knack of being somewhere just when he was not wanted, suddenly seemed to appear out of nowhere.

"Yes, Mrs Garthwaite, how can I be of assistance?"

"This young man has been extremely impertinent."

"What?" said Andrew, "but I…"

"Quiet, Andrew!" said Mr Horniman. "Go on."

"He refused to help me, then spoke to me as if I were an idiot. And such language…"

"I assure you, I…"

"Be quiet, Andrew!"

"It's not true."

"That's enough," said Horniman. "Thank you for bringing this to my attention, Mrs Garthwaite, I'll deal with it." And then, fixing Andrew with a beady-eyed stare, "So this is how you repay my confidence in you. You will return to your lift at once!" Then, turning to Mrs Garthwaite and leading her into his office to recuperate from her deep emotions, "I'm very sorry about this, I assure you it shan't happen again, please, make yourself comfortable." He turned round to Mary as he stood in the doorway, "I think you'll be better off without an assistant for now."

The postman arrived with the second post and gave a small bundle of letters to Mary.

"A bit late, aren't you?" she said.

The postman shrugged and pulled a face.

"No appreciation!" he muttered gloomily as he left.

In Horniman's office, Mrs Garthwaite had seated herself in an armchair and had poured herself a tumbler of brandy, which she was sipping in a flustered way. Horniman left her there and walked back to Mary.

"Tell me," he said, "have you known that young man long?"

"What do you mean?"

"Ah, Mary, I'm afraid you can't keep secrets from me. I know everything."

"Oh! Does it make any difference?"

Horniman got a little closer.

"Not necessarily, it all depends."

"On what?"

"On you."

"Me?"

"Well, now you're here, we'll be working together much more closely."

"Will we?"

"Yes, and I was thinking…"

"I don't think that would be very wise, sir… mixing business with pleasure. I think, if I may, I'd be better off doing my old job in the lift."

Mary walked over to Lift 3 and removed the "Out of Service" sign before walking inside.

Mr Horniman, left alone, began to apostrophise more, this time addressing a large aspidistra that stood to one side of the reception desk.

"Oh dear, oh dear, I did hope that I had found a soulmate at last Mary is delightful; her brother is a pain. What? I'm not supposed to know? Ah, but I know everything that happens in this hotel, particularly when I have such efficient and loyal informants as Angela and Ben. Every secret is an open book to me. Perhaps I'll try her again tomorrow." And he started sorting the letters which Mary had left on the desk, placing them into pigeon-holes for the hotel guests, while humming in a self-satisfied way.

CHAPTER THREE

The wedding took place in late September; the honeymoon was not a success.

Arthur Winsome and his new wife had been all smiles during the ceremony, but it took only a short while for each to realise that this was, potentially, a disaster in the making. Alice had changed from her white wedding dress into her going-away outfit. She walked shyly towards Arthur's car where all the luggage had been stowed. Arthur could hardly bear to look at her. He was already deep in the throes of regret and, for thirty minutes after they had departed the scene, did not say a word.

Lady Tongue had watched the car as it sped away, with tears in her eyes. She was comforted by her husband, who also had mixed feelings about the whole thing: on the one hand he was going to miss his daughter, on the other he was relieved that someone else would now have the burden of her sulky moods. It has not been mentioned before, but it now has to be said that Alice had two distinct moods: ecstatically happy or very sulky. She had been very happy, but as she looked at her husband of two hours, her mood began to change.

"Aren't you going to say something, darling?" she said.

Bearing in mind the arrangement, which was not one of love, this was certainly not calculated to get a polite reply, but Arthur still said nothing. Alice pursed her lips and began counting the sheep or cows in each field that they passed.

This was the model for the next few days. Arthur hardly said a word unless he had to; Alice muttered occasional endearments which were ignored. Matters in the bedroom were no better. For, while Alice had imagined a knight on a charger carrying her off to exotic lands, Arthur had booked a bed-and-breakfast house in the poky Midlands town of Upper Murford for their honeymoon. It had taken the best part of a day to get there, and he was very tired, tired of the whole damn business! She still had her head in the clouds, but by the time she had made herself as pretty as she could on the first evening, he was lying on the bed, fully dressed and fast asleep with his shoes still on his feet. He had been steadily drinking scotch, and nothing Alice did could wake him. "Still," she thought, with implausible romantic thoughts running through her head, "there's always tomorrow night." And she herself went to bed and dreamed all night long about masked balls. The days were dull, and this went on for nearly a week: six nights of the same routine. Alice, ever hopeful, told herself the same thing each evening: "there's always tomorrow night."

But the seventh night never came. When Alice awoke, Arthur was not in the room; Arthur was not in the hotel; Arthur and his car were not in Upper Murford at all. The bill had been paid in advance, so there was no trouble there, and Alice was not, in any case, short of money. But she did feel a great sense of shame, for how could she, as a (deserted) wife of less than a week, bring herself to return to her parents?

But Alice was thirty-three years old, not a baby. She was not stupid, just naive, and she had some of her mother's character when it came to overcoming the odds. She had breakfast, packed her things into her suitcase, and then asked the landlady to phone for a taxi to take her to the nearest railway station.

Outside the station stood a man in his late middle-ages and a shabby raincoat. Several strands of hair were ineffectively and incompetently plastered down over his bald pate. In one hand he held a petrol cigarette lighter, in the other, a tatty paper carrier bag.

"Excuse me, miss," said the man to Alice in a hesitant, almost embarrassed voice, "excuse me."

Thinking that he was about to ask directions to some destination, Alice stopped and looked enquiringly at the man while waiting for him to speak again. She did not have to wait long. The man cleared his throat awkwardly.

"I wonder, erm, I haven't got enough money to buy a ticket home…"

"Oh, no!" thought Alice, "here we go again! Why do they always choose me?"

"…so would you buy this lighter for five bob?"

"I'm afraid," replied Alice, "I haven't any change."

There was something seedy and unwholesome about the man. As Alice went to pass him and enter the ticket office, he made a feeble attempt to stop her.

"What?" he said reproachfully and sadly, "not even five shillings?" This last remark was made as though he had a God-given right to as much of Alice's money as he liked, and it was accompanied by a small, but unmistakably threatening, gesture.

"I'm afraid not," said Alice hurriedly.

She walked on, bought her ticket, and continued past the barrier, down the steps and onto the platform to wait for her train. There were a few other people waiting. Alice put her glasses on and looked at the timetable. She saw that it would be another ten minutes before the next train arrived.

"Probably longer," she murmured to herself, "knowing what the trains are like nowadays."

She occupied her time by walking slowly up and down the platform. When she had done this two or three times, she glanced up and noticed that the man with the lighter was now in the station, standing train-side of the barrier at the top of the steps.

"I wonder if he sold the lighter," Alice thought. She had been feeling a little guilty because she did have enough change to give him now that she had bought her ticket and had been considering going back out of the station to give it to him.

"When he comes down, I'll tell him I'm glad to see that he got enough money for his fare."

But the man stood there for a long time. A young man came down the steps and onto the platform.

"I wonder if he bought the lighter," thought Alice.

Other people arrived. Still the man stayed at the top; Alice thought his behaviour most strange.

"Perhaps he saw me waiting here and doesn't want to come near. It does seem odd, though."

The man moved to a place halfway down the steps and stopped there. Alice walked slowly away and then turned back. As she neared the steps once more, she heard a jingling sound.

"I knew it! I knew it!" She felt triumphant at making a deduction, feeling almost as if she were Sherlock Holmes.

Alice sat on a bench from where she could see the man's body but not his face, which was hidden by a large sign suspended from the roof. This meant that he would not be able to see that he was being watched.

She felt that her suspicions were confirmed when she saw him counting money, taking coins out of various pockets in his coat and putting them into a ladies' purse that might once have been pink.

"I bet that carrier-bag is stuffed full of lighters! I wonder how he got them—not honestly, that's certain."

A train arrived on the opposite platform. People got off and started to walk up the steps. The man climbed back to the top where he could easily intercept them. As the people passed him, Alice could see that he tried to stop one or two. His hard-luck story met with no success, though, as everyone ignored him.

"What a sauce he has! He can see now that I'm watching him; he knows that I know what his game is, and he's still trying it on!" Alice was amused by the whole incident.

She gave up her observation at that point as the train was about to arrive. She stood next to a lady who smiled at her and said, "Did you see that man waiting on the steps?"

Alice told her what she had seen.

"Yes," replied the other, "he tried to stop me too—but I've seen him here before. He lives not too far away. I know because he sat opposite me on the train once and spoke to me. He said, 'I've been very lonely since my wife died; you wouldn't like to come out with me tonight, would you?' I said I didn't think my husband would like it very much. I told my husband about it. Said someone had asked me out. He said, "Short-sighted, was he?"

"That was nice of him!" said Alice, and they both laughed.

The train had now arrived, and both women boarded. Alice's new acquaintance got out at the next station, and Alice settled back to enjoy the scenery.

Alice took the train to the south coast and the seaside town of Paunceton-sur-la-Mer, for she remembered happy holidays there as a child. There were two changes of train, and the journey took three hours: ample time to reflect on what she should do next. The second change was at the town of Paunceton Muffet. Since she would have to wait there an hour before her connection, she left the station to stretch her legs. There were a number of small, dowdy shops in a row just opposite the station entrance, including a bookshop. Feeling in need of something to read, she walked over to it and went inside.

The shop was dark and had a damp smell. Alice went straight over to the spotty youth who was sitting on a stool behind the till, for she had no intention of finding the book she wanted herself.

"I'd like to buy a copy of Great Expectations, please." The spotty youth looked up from his crossword puzzle book and took the pencil that he had been chewing out of his mouth.

"What version would you like?" he muttered indistinctly, for that book existed in a number of editions, some illustrated, and several were in stock.

"What do you mean, 'virgin!?'" demanded Alice, taken aback.

"N-no," stammered the lad, "version, version. Which version would you like?"

This says something about Alice's frame of mind, for she was easily offended, and did not like to think she was being insulted.

Book bought; Alice travelled on to her destination.

"I shall compare the writing of dear Dickens with that of my own," she said to herself.

Paunceton-sur-la-Mer appeared on maps until 1901 as Paunceton. But that year, the new King had visited and not awarded the town the title of Regis. The mayor and councillors had taken great umbrage at a perceived insult and voted unanimously to change its name not to Paunceton on Sea, or super-Mare, but to something more exotic. The mayor's wife had been born in Paris, though she had been brought up in London and spoke with a strong Cockney accent, and so the town became Paunceton-sur-la-Mer to honour her birthplace.

Once Alice had arrived at the station, she had her luggage taken to the Hotel Splendide, but since the day was bright, and she had ascertained that the hotel was a mere twenty minutes' walk through the ornamental gardens and along the front, she decided to use shanks' pony and make her own way.

The air was clean and fresh, and the scent of the pine trees made her slow her walk through the gardens. The path sloped gently down towards the sea front. A gap in the bushes ahead gave her a sudden view of the sea, which looked grey-green in the mid-afternoon sunlight. She gave a sigh of contentment, "I haven't got to rush to be anywhere, I have no one to see, I can do as I wish."

On reaching the hotel, she went to the reception desk, which at that moment was being manned by the Hotel Manager as he had, one way or another, lost three receptionists in a day. There were rooms available at all prices, but Alice was sensible that she must not spend too much money as she did not know exactly how long she would need to be independent. She took a mid-priced room on the third floor and had her bags, which were waiting for her, taken up.

"Could I order some tea in my room?" she asked.

"Certainly, Mrs er...Winsome," said Horniman, squinting at the register that Alice had just signed, but which was upside-down to him. He took a fountain pen from his breast pocket and made a mark in purple ink next to Alice's name.

Alice, who had always felt insecure about herself, suddenly felt confident. Perhaps it was due to the considerable improvement in her appearance over the last few weeks. Her maid had given her much help, encouraging her to let her hair hang loose about her shoulders rather than tying it up. Her hair was probably her best feature—mousy in colour, yes, but sleek and glossy with a gentle natural curl. She wrote a letter to her parents, feeling that she ought to let them know where she was, and put it in the hotel post-box, then she went to her room. Tea was brought to her there together with some delicate sandwiches, and after eating them, she lay on the bed for an hour.

Horniman, meanwhile, was busily devising means to pay attention to all the ladies in his life without letting any of them know about the others.

To begin with, there was his fiancée (the bank manager's daughter), then there was the delightfully cheeky Mary, and Angela, and Philippa, of course—he would have to take special care to attend to her needs, for though she no longer worked for the hotel, she would still be living nearby, and she was now in the family way. He did not feel particularly guilty about this indiscretion, but he knew he would have to play it safe. Then there was Mrs Garthwaite, or "The Dragon", as he liked to think of her. She was a thorn in his side as she knew about his fiancée and was trying to get him to break off his engagement and take up with her instead. Horniman was not bothered by the fact of Mrs Garthwaite, but he was bothered by the thought that if he should decide not to marry the bank manager's daughter, the inevitable Breach of Promise case would follow, and he was not in a position to think about paying damages. He owed his bookmaker a considerable amount of money, and the nauseating fellow was not only dunning him at every opportunity but had taken to uttering threats in a most unnerving fashion.

It was now four o'clock, and Horniman strolled thoughtfully around the foyer. He primped the flower in his buttonhole when he caught sight of his reflection in one of the mirrors, he nodded at one of the guests who was going out, and at another who was coming in. His stroll inevitably took him to the lift area.

For the last few minutes, Mary and Andrew had been talking in low voices just by Mary's lift.

"Don't be depressed," she said, "something will turn up."

"Don't count on it."

"Did he really have a go at you?"

"I think I'll have to stay out of his way for a few days. I don't know what's come over him, he's always been difficult, but now... look out, here he comes! I'm not hanging around here. Follow me up. I'll see you on the roof in about five minutes."

Andrew ascended in his lift. Horniman arrived just as the lift doors closed.

"Where's he off to in a hurry?"

"He's just been buzzed," said Mary.

"He's lucky he still works here. Mrs Garthwaite wanted to sack him, but I persuaded her that it would hardly be fair for a first offence. Besides, I think of him just like a son."

"Why should her opinion matter?" asked Mary, returning to the subject of Mrs Garthwaite.

"Mary—she owns the hotel, or most of it anyway."

"I thought you owned it."

"No, indeed, I wish I did. Mary, won't you reconsider my offer?"

"What offer was that?"

"Why, Mary, I look on that lad as a son, as I think I mentioned. I look on you as... as... as..."

"Yes?"

"As a father to a daughter. A daddy, if you like."

"Oh," said Mary, "I see..."

But before she could make any retort to Horniman's "sugar daddy" implications, the conversation was interrupted by the arrival of Lift 1. The doors opened. Mr Horniman stared; his moustache bristled.

"What the devil is going on in here?" he demanded.

Mary took this opportunity to make her escape in her lift up to the roof.

Inside the lift, something Mr Horniman had never seen before was taking place. A small table was set for tea with beautiful napery, and two people, Ben and Angela, were sitting at it. Ben's jacket was draped around his stool, and Ben was sitting on it—actually sitting on his uniform jacket! and holding a teacup. His top button was undone, and he was not wearing his tie. Angela was cutting a slice of Madeira cake.

The two looked guiltily round at Mr Horniman.

"Sorry, sir," said Ben, "we were just..."

"I can see what you were doing. What do you think this is, a teashop? No, sir! It's a hotel lift." He took the cup from Ben. "Smarten yourself up. What have you got here? Earl Grey! What else have you got in there? Cucumber sandwiches, buttered teacakes, strawberry jam, a kettle and... and... and... a primus stove! I've never seen anything like it in my life. Is this how you always work, Angela?"

"I like to make myself comfortable," replied Angela.

"Comfortable? This is Sybaritic!"

"Oh, thank you, sir," said Angela, "you can join us if you like."

"I want to see both of you in my office. Now. Follow me, please."

The interview over, Ben and Angela meekly left the office, and Horniman went back to reception. Alice was waiting for him there. She had tried to phone down to order a newspaper for the following morning but, since there had been no reply, had come to make the order in person. Order made, she booked a table for supper in the restaurant, and then went to the local cinema, missing only the first ten minutes of the main feature.

PRINCES CINEMA
PAUNCETON-SUR-LA-MER
Week Commencing Monday September 28th, 1931,
Ronald Coleman with Loretta Young
in
"THE DEVIL TO PAY"
Perfect Entertainment
With full supporting programme
Times of showing 4.10pm, 7.30pm
Prices 1/10, 1/6, 1/3, 9d and 6d

CHAPTER FOUR

Mrs Garthwaite sat in the hotel's conservatory surrounded by potted Kentia palm trees and purple plumbago flowers. On a table to one side of her was a reading lamp that, since the sky outside was overcast, she had turned on so that she could read her Financial Times, which she always did in the afternoon, while drinking a cup of tea into which she would pour a little nip of something stronger. She chose to do this in the conservatory, which was on the second floor, because she knew that she would be undisturbed by anyone else. The hotel library might have been a more logical place, and that too was on the second floor, but she liked to look out over the hotel gardens. The library did not offer such a view, but the conservatory did.

She was in her middle-ages, a widow, stoutish, but not unpleasant to look at. She did, however, have a fearsome temper and could demolish the members of the staff (both female and male) in her own house with a look.

Mrs Garthwaite adjusted her position on the wicker chair and stretched. It was nearly time for her five o'clock walk. Glancing through the window at the sky made her decide to go for her walk straight away. "It's getting cloudy and dark," she thought, "I'll go now." She got up and walked down the corridor to the two lifts that operated in that wing of the hotel.

She pressed the button of Lift 3 and waited. "I'll pop to the chemist and get some bismuth tablets; I feel a little indigestion coming on."

The lift arrived, and Mrs Garthwaite entered it. This was unusual, as her dislike of enclosed spaces meant that she usually only took the lift on upward journeys. Mary took her down to the ground floor, and she got out. As she passed the reception desk where Mr Horniman was vainly trying to locate the pencil sharpener that was, at that moment, in Andrew's pocket, while at the same time taking Alice's newspaper order, Mrs Garthwaite suddenly felt a little dizzy, perhaps the lift journey had been unwise after all. Alice finished making the order and turned away from the desk. Mrs Garthwaite sat down in an armchair and called weakly to Horniman.

"Ralph," (pronounced Rafe), Horniman looked up. "Ralph, I'm afraid I'm not feeling very well..."

She shut her eyes.

Mr Horniman was good in a crisis.

"I'll call the doctor," he said.

The doctor arrived shortly after.

"I think it's indigestion," he said. Mrs Garthwaite moaned. She looked very pale.

"Let's get her to the hospital," said the doctor, and so an ambulance was summoned.

Meanwhile, Mary had gone up in her lift to the roof where her brother was waiting.

"Where have you been?" said Andrew as soon as he saw her. "I've been waiting here for ages."

"First, I had to get away from you-know-who, he's such a bore," said Mary, "and then Mrs G called the lift. She didn't look very well; I hope she's all right."

"Anyway," said Andrew, "what do you say we call a truce?"

"Done!"

"What now? We've got to find some way of getting further on. I want to go up in the world—and I don't just mean in a lift either—or at least to get rich quickly."

"Well, this job was your idea, wasn't it?"

"I don't know, it seems as if however hard I try, all my plans go wrong."

"Yes, I know about your plans, and that's exactly why Mummy wanted me to keep an eye on you."

"All right, I admit it," said Andrew, "I thought that if I was working in a place like this, I might follow in the family tradition: acquire a few sundry objects from guests when they weren't looking."

"Like Uncle Jim? He went to prison."

"Ah, yes, but that's because he didn't have method—that is, he had method, but it was a very bad method."

"And you have one that will work, I suppose."

"My idea is to be in a position where I can get hold of all the room keys and make copies. And I was so close..." Andrew broke off; Mary was holding out her hand, and in it was a key.

"Do you know what this is?" she asked. He shook his head, and Mary continued, "It's a copy of the master key."

"Clever girl! You didn't waste any time, did you? Look, we've done our best to throw Ben and Angela off the scent by inventing our argument..."

"Oh, the argument's been real enough," said Mary, pointedly.

"Yes, well that's your fault. Anyway, there's only one fly in the ointment."

"...Horniman!"

"I just can't shake him off," said Mary. "Wherever I go, whenever I turn around, he's always there."

Andrew thought for a moment, then grinned. "Well, why not? What a marvellous idea!"

"If you're thinking what I think you're thinking, then you're mad. It really is too fantastic. I'm not making up to Horniman. What would everybody say?"

"But don't you see? It's just the distraction we need. Ben and Angela will be too busy gossiping about it, Horniman will be going around with that sickly moonfaced expression of his, only twice as much, you'll get a massive promotion, and I'll be free to roam the corridors with the key to all the rooms safely in my pocket."

"A massive promotion is what I'm afraid of!"

"Oh, don't be such a scaredy!"

"Well, I'm in. It'll be rather fun, wont it? Trying to keep Horniman out of the way while you're playing Raffles. Fifty-fifty?"

"Of course, as always."

At this moment they became aware of frantic buzzing from their lifts, and both returned to being humble lift operators, though a grinning Andrew had the master key in his pocket, while Mary was looking thoughtful.

"See you on the mezzanine at ten," called Andrew as the lift doors shut.

Mrs Garthwaite lay on her bed in a private hospital ward. She was propped up with three pillows and writing a "to-do" list in her memorandum book. Occasionally, she stopped to sip tea from the cup on the high table next to her.

    1.   Will
    2.   Diet
    3.   Manager
    4.   Valuation
    5.   Play

These items may seem to be meaningless, but the explanation of each is not hard to deduce.
    1.   Will—she had not made a will, but she intended to do so soon.
    2.   Diet—she realised that she needed to lose some weight.
    3.   Manager—she wished to know exactly what to do about Mr Horniman. What were his intentions? How could she interest him further, (this brought up, again, the diet). If she could not get his romantic interest, could she and should she replace him, and if so, with whom?
    4.   Valuation—she had some items which she would like valued by a jeweller. This related to the will.
    5.   Play—she would like to find a new play which she could produce at a local theatre, preferably a play with a starring role in it that she herself could assume, which brings us back, again, to the need to lose weight.

The doctor who examined her had recommended that she stay in hospital overnight. She had reluctantly agreed to this, but she had sent to the hotel for some of her things and intended to make the best of it. As a result, the hospital staff were all busily trying to keep as far from her room as possible.

Back at the hotel, Mr Horniman was busy making himself look important by walking through all the public rooms on the ground floor and giving everything a general inspection. The staff were, therefore, all trying to work as smartly as they could, and everything was running smoothly.

Andrew, on the other hand, was doing his best to avoid operating his lift by every devious method he could, taking as much time as possible in moving from floor to floor. This meant that Ben was doing the lion's share of lift work on that side of the hotel. Angela and Mary were working their lifts in their usual efficient fashion.

By that time, many of the hotel staff knew that Mrs Garthwaite would be away overnight. Her room was on the fourth floor. At about nine o'clock, when many of the hotel guests were either downstairs in the restaurant or out for the evening, Andrew left his lift on the third floor, walked up to the fourth, and, using his master key, slipped into Mrs Garthwaite's room. He did not intend to rob her there and then; there was almost certainly no time to do that, merely to make a reconnaissance so that he could return on another occasion if there was something worth returning for. The room was in darkness. Andrew turned on the bedside light, checked the time on his watch, and began to look around.

There are certain rules one has to follow when conducting an operation of this sort. Andrew knew them, and he also knew that he had already broken at least three of his own rules. He should not have turned on the light, he should have given himself more time, and he should have made sure of a better alibi if his absence from duty was noticed. But he was a fast worker, and he took in all that he needed to know very quickly. To begin with, the room safe was locked, which implied that something was probably inside. He would need a different master key to open the safe. Next, Mrs Garthwaite was evidently a very neat person. All her clothes were beautifully folded in the chest of drawers or carefully hung in the wardrobe, and there were no valuables of any sort kept in either of those places. His search was as thorough as the short time he had given himself would allow, and it included the bathroom and the bed.

Andrew was also able to find other pieces of information about Mrs Garthwaite; she liked detective novels (one was on the table by her bed with a bookmark at the halfway point), and she kept a diary. Not an appointment diary, but a journal written in a childish hand. It was not a large book, and Andrew put it inside his waistcoat in such a way that the shape would be hidden by his jacket. Then he turned off the light and left. The entire operation had taken seven minutes.

HOTEL SPLENDIDE

Supper Menu
Friday 2ND October

Hors d'ouvres
Tomato Juice

Grapefruit cocktail

Egg Mayonnaise

Starters
Tomato Soup

Consommé Froid

Pea Soup

Fish
Fillet of Plaice

Haddock with Poached Egg

Grilled Sole

Entrees
Escalope of Veal

Fillet Steak

Lamb Cutlets and Mint Sauce

Vegetables
Mashed or Sautéed Potatoes

Cabbage

Peas or Runner beans

Russian Salad

Desserts
Meringue Glacée

Peach Melba

Fruit Salad and Cream

Cheese and Biscuits

Coffee

CHAPTER FIVE

Alice had supper in the hotel restaurant: a rather plain meal consisting of plaice and boiled vegetables done in the traditional English fashion. There were not many people eating there at that time: an elderly married couple in one corner eating slowly, a young lady with dark skin and a pleasant smile who sat by herself reading a book as she ate, and a middle-aged husband and wife with their son and daughter who were all laughing at something one of them had said.

Once Alice had eaten, she stood up from the table, left the restaurant and went to the lifts so that she could be taken up to her room; she was very tired. Lift 1 arrived to take her up to the third floor. Ben had been working his lift all day, and he too was tired. Tomorrow he would have to work until after midnight. Today, he finished at ten p.m. During the night, only one lift would be left in operation. Lift 3 was usually the one used, and those who really needed 1 or 2 after ten p.m. would have to walk around the balcony which connected the two wings in a rather inconvenient way on each floor. Just as Alice was closing the door of her room, she looked along the corridor and saw a man coming down the stairs and entering Lift 2.

There was nothing, at first sight, that should have set alarm bells ringing in Alice's mind, and yet, something seemed not quite right. It wasn't the fact that Andrew, for it was he that she had seen, had not summoned the lift to whichever floor he had started from, nor the fact that Andrew was wearing a hotel staff uniform, and not even the way that he had appeared to glide down the stairs and into the lift. As Alice closed her room door behind her and walked over to the dressing table, she could not rid herself of the thought that there was more to this than met the eye. And then it dawned on her. There was a familiarity about the movement and the lithe figure of the young man. The corridor was not very well lit, and if it had been, she would not have seen his face clearly at that distance without her glasses, perhaps even if she had been wearing them. But vanity was creeping up on her with age, and she endeavoured to do without them at every opportunity. Tired though she was, her curiosity overcame the desire for an early night. She fumbled for a moment inside the depths of her capacious handbag, located her glasses and put them on.

"What a relief," she thought, "perhaps, after all, though I hate wearing them, it's better to be able to see clearly." And she hurried from the room, went to the lift area and pressed the down button.

Lift 1 arrived. Ben was still operating it, and it would be some minutes yet before he would be able to leave his post. Alice was most disappointed, for she had hoped that the other lift would arrive instead. However, she stepped inside and was conveyed to the ground floor. Her feet were hurting as her shoes were too tight, and she tottered over to one of the sofas in the reception area. A member of the bar staff appeared, and she ordered some hot chocolate. Then she sat and watched the lifts. Her patience was rewarded, for

Andrew's lift arrived a few minutes later, and Andrew himself stepped out to have a short conversation with Ben.

"I knew it!" Alice said to herself, and she quivered with a strange excitement.

It was by now ten minutes to ten. Andrew was looking forward to meeting his sister on the mezzanine floor; Mary was already waiting for him there. Ben was looking forward to his bed, and Mrs Garthwaite was already asleep in her hospital bed. Angela was with Mr Horniman in his office, and the door was locked. They had been carrying on an 'innocent' little intrigue for a few weeks, and this was another reason that Horniman had wanted to remove Philippa from the hotel, as she had been becoming too possessive and rather jealous, not to say suspicious.

Alice, once back in her room, was thinking hard. She had recognised the gliding lift operator from a stay in a different hotel the year before. A number of strange things had happened during that holiday. Things went missing. In particular, she had missed a pair of gold earrings; other guests had also mislaid items.

Ten o'clock chimed on the little clock in reception. Ben abruptly left his lift and walked out into the street to smoke a cigarette. Angela peered around the door of Mr Horniman's office, and she stepped out unnoticed. She went into the staff area and directly to her own bedroom. Mr Horniman, still in his office, took a telephone call from his fiancée and promised to go for lunch to her house the following day (Saturday).

Andrew arrived on the mezzanine floor; Mary was waiting for him in their usual quiet corner. "What's cooking?" she asked in a low voice.

"That Garthwaite woman's got something in her safe, and it's locked."

"Don't worry, I have a key to the safe too," said Mary, dangling it before Andrew's eyes.

"Why didn't you say so before?"

"Why do you think? And we may not get another chance quite so easily after tonight."

"You mean we should go back there?"

"Why not? Let's change into mufti and then meet back here at eleven."

So are plans made, which seem simple at the time, but which can become complicated when they don't go as expected. How could they have known, for example, that Alice Winsome, short-sighted though she was, had decided to take matters into her own hands and keep a watchful, if myopic, eye on the comings and goings in the hotel?

This, and other possibilities, did not occur to them. They were practiced, though not very successful thieves and, in their small way, enjoyed the thrill of the chase, the new identities they might adopt if necessary, the thoughts of funds they might accrue in foreign bank accounts, and they looked forward to easy, independent lives free from the necessity of work.

Alice amazed herself. She had always thought of herself as timid, unadventurous; the sort of person who would never have any kind of adventure. But something had taken hold of her: something completely unexpected and marvellous. She could not explain it.

This remarkable change was not only in her attitude to life but also in her appearance.

Her cheeks had acquired a healthy glow; the dull pallor was gone. Her eyes shone with an almost luminous quality.

"Surely I'm dreaming," she thought to herself as she gazed into the mirror on the back of her bedroom door. But she felt that there was no doubt. "I'm a real Cinderella," she said out loud. She put her hands to her cheeks. They seemed to be unnaturally hot and her heart was beating with excitement.

It might have been a delusion, a fantasy that only she could see. Does magic exist? Something that seemed new to her was at work.

She opened the door and looked out into the darkening corridor. The circle pattern on the carpet reminded her of dark, serpent-like coils. She tried to keep her breathing steady as she pushed the door so that it was only open by the smallest crack and began to watch.

Time passed slowly. It was tiring work, and she began to doubt her new adventurous spirit really existed. "Suppose I was mistaken, and no change has taken place?" She was on the verge of giving up, when she saw the shadows of two people moving silently up the stairwell by the lifts from the floor below to the one above. Alice bit her lip for a moment, and then began to follow.

She was light as a feather and glided gracefully after her quarry. Ahead, Mary and Andrew were also keeping as quiet as they could. From somewhere below, in the depths of the hotel, muffled sounds of activity came wafting up the stairs, but no one came near the three people who were moving onto the fourth floor; there was nothing but silence. It was as if some spell had been cast on the hotel, as if an enchantment had stopped time itself.

From a distance, Alice saw the two who were ahead of her move towards a door. It was Mrs Garthwaite's, of course. Andrew unlocked the door, and he and Mary entered closing the door behind them. Alice, without thinking of the possibility of discovery or danger, moved closer and waited a moment before putting her hand on the doorknob, turning it silently and gently opening it about three inches wide.

Then, suddenly, the door was grabbed from the other side and pulled open, and Alice found herself dragged into the room and facing the two would-be thieves.

No one said a thing for some moments; no one knew what to say. Alice, in her mind, had never got as far as to work out what she would do under these circumstances, and the others were not violent types.

"Just what are you doing here?" Mary asked eventually.

"I like that! You've no right to be here either."

"This is our room," said Andrew.

"Nonsense!" said Alice, "it belongs to that large lady who wasn't feeling well earlier. You're up to no good, and I know exactly what to do about it!" Mary and Andrew looked concerned. "I'm going to take charge," said Alice decisively.

"Take charge?" said Mary.

"Of what?" said Andrew.

"Of you two," replied Alice. It's obvious you haven't got the slightest idea how to carry out an operation like this."

"Oh, and you do!" said Mary sarcastically.

"Well, for a start, I wouldn't be working in the place I was planning to rob."

"That's all you know," declared Andrew. "It just so happens that this is an inside job!"

"It's rubbish!" said Alice, "I know all about it."

Alice's knowledge came from reading detective fiction—hardly the most reliable source of instruction for criminals, but her air of confidence made the others fall silent. She said nothing, though, about recognising Andrew, because she was no longer certain she had been correct.

And so it was that Alice became the leader of a small band of thieves. This was her first job. After opening the safe, removing a pearl necklace from Mrs Garthwaite's jewellery case and then removing all traces of their activity, the three of them reconvened in Alice's room. The necklace was put into a brown paper bag and placed behind the large radiator by the window.

"We'll deal with it tomorrow," said Alice to the others, while at the same time trying to devise a way of returning the loot to Mrs Garthwaite without being noticed, for she had no intention of becoming a criminal and had in fact decided to reform Andrew and Mary.

CHAPTER SIX

"Welcome back," said Mr Horniman to Mrs Garthwaite the following morning as she stepped through the hotel door. "I trust you had a comfortable night."

Mr Horniman had not had a comfortable night himself; he was very worried. Several thousand pounds had disappeared from the hotel's accounts, and they would need to be replaced. He was particularly concerned because it was he who had abstracted the money, and, unfortunately, he had spent it all. It had been spent, in part, on presents for his fiancée and, in part, on horses. He had lost a considerable sum; his bookmaker was a constant thorn in his side. All night long, Horniman had lain awake trying to work out how to take back the gifts he had made to his "beloved", without arousing suspicion, so that he might begin the process of making good. But he knew that even if he did this, it would not cover either the shortfall in the hotel's books or the amount he had lost by backing the wrong horses.

"But I'll have to get the necklace back, at least," he thought.

He had given his fiancée a pearl necklace, the most expensive thing he had bought her, costing even more than the engagement ring. He would have liked to be able to get that back too, in fact, he'd like to get out of the whole thing. He thoroughly regretted having got engaged to someone who needed such proofs of his devotion.

Hearing his greeting, Mrs Garthwaite stared at Mr Horniman with a haughty expression.

"Really," she uttered, "I don't think you can have anything to say to me!" And without any explanation, she rolled on past the hotel manager, leaving him lost for words. Mr Horniman could not think what might have brought on such a remark. Feeling guilty about his own deceitful behaviour, though, he began to analyse everything he had done to see if there might be a possibility that Mrs Garthwaite had caught on to any of his financial misdemeanours. But he was certain that he had covered all his tracks thoroughly, at least as far as she was concerned. Mrs Garthwaite, though, knew a little more than he thought was the case.

Earlier that morning, as she was leaving the hospital, she was handed a letter addressed to her.

"But really," she said, "no one knows I'm here."

The letter was from ex-receptionist Philippa, and as Mrs Garthwaite sat in a taxi which took her back to the hotel, she read it. What she read made her white with fury.

Dear Mrs Garthwaite,

My apologies for writing to you in this way, but as you know I recently left the hotel and did not have a chance to see you before I went. I have been having some difficulty with Mr Horniman, and wanted to tell you earlier, but somehow couldn't bring myself to do it, though I tried a few times. I need to tell you as from one woman to another, and I know you won't judge me too harshly, my reason for leaving. It was not of my own choice, but the condition I find myself in meant that Mr Horniman has behaved most unfairly, though everything was his fault as much as mine. Well, he promised to do the right thing by me, but now will not speak to me or answer any letter I send. So, I have no choice but to write to you to ask you to speak with him on my behalf. I have no one to turn to.

Sincerely,

P. Potter (Miss)

Mrs Garthwaite had drawn all the correct conclusions from this poorly written missive, and though by the time she had reached the hotel her anger had abated a little, she still could hardly bring herself to look at Mr Horniman, let alone hold a conversation with him.

Mr Horniman shrugged as Mrs Garthwaite walked away and decided that, for the moment, he would lay this new problem to one side and concentrate on the other matters which occupied him. Lunchtime was approaching, and he would need to leave for his appointment with the banker, the banker's wife and their daughter. He decided to concentrate all his thoughts on the problem of the necklace.

Leaving the hotel a few minutes later, he walked towards the house where he was expected. The route took him through the park, and he had plenty of time to think. He rolled his upper lip up to his nose and exhaled, a habit of his when alone. The day was overcast, and he had put on a lined raincoat to keep himself warm and dry. His shoes shone as if they were new; in one hand he carried a small box of chocolates, and in the other a large black umbrella with a very unusual wooden handle carved into the shape of a lion's head. On his head he wore a bowler hat.

The front door was already open when Mr Horniman arrived. His fiancée's elder brother was just leaving. The two men nodded as they passed on the path, but having little liking for each other, their conversation was limited to one grunt each. A servant held the door open as Horniman entered and took his coat, hat and umbrella with an oily subservience.

"Miss Zoë asked if you would go into the music room when you arrived," said the servant.

"Thank you, George," said Mr Horniman, and they both proceeded down the hall towards a door from behind which could be heard the gentle strains of Mozart sung by a fluttery singing voice. He paused outside until a suitable break occurred and then went in. George, who had an uncanny ability to appear or disappear from sight at inconvenient times, vanished from Horniman's view, sliding himself into the kitchen to have a word with the cook.

Zoë was sitting at a boudoir grand piano accompanying her own singing, while her mother sat by the window with her eyes closed and a smile on her lips.

"Ralph, you're here," said Zoë, and, though the remark tended to state the obvious, Horniman affected not to notice, but stepped forward holding the chocolate box before him as if proffering it to a goddess.

"Why have you stopped?" said Zoë's mother.

"Ralph is here, mother," said Zoë, taking the chocolate box as she spoke. She smiled, and it was as if the sun had come out from behind the clouds. There was no doubt that she was quite delightful.

Zoë Giddins was the kind of person who brings everything to a standstill when she enters a room. It was not that she was beautiful, though many would say that she was, nor that she had a devastating personality, though she was remarkably clever and very well-spoken. No, it was all due to a radiance that seemed to emanate from her. You may ask why and how it was that she had become affianced to the middle-aged, pompous Ralph Horniman. And here, perhaps, is the moment to mention that Horniman himself had an indefinable magnetic quality that attracted many to him, though not his employees (with the possible exception of Angela who professed to find him abhorrent when with the others but had a different reaction to Horniman when she was alone with him). Horniman, though, belonged to a class of individuals who present a very convincing front but who are, in fact, only out to help themselves.

Mrs Giddins opened her eyes. She had, of course, known perfectly well why her daughter had stopped singing, but pretended that Horniman's presence in the room was a complete surprise.

"Good afternoon, Ralph," she said, "you are on time as always. Do sit, Zoë was just about to sing Abendempfindung, one of my favourites."

One of Horniman's great shortcomings was that he had no ear for music at all. In fact, he found the whole thing rather dull. He did enjoy going to the music hall if there was a lively show with plenty of saucy girls swivelling their hips, but he did not relish the idea of listening to Abendempfindung and was on the point of finding some reason for the private concert to stop, when Zoë forestalled him by saying,

"Really, mother, it must be time for lunch now, and father will be cross if it's delayed."

Mrs Giddins stood, and the three of them moved from the music room directly into the dining room through a pair of sliding doors. As they went in, a door opened at the far end, and Mr Giddins, bank manager, entered. He was about the same age as his future son-in-law, both being around fifty, but there the similarity stopped. On the one hand, Horniman was stoutish, and had a moustache which he tried to tame unsuccessfully with wax. He also tried to behave with his friends as if he were an experienced man-about-town, jolly and generous (though he was none of those things). On the other hand, Mr Giddins was slim, clean-shaven, very respectable and had a limited sense of humour and no sense of fun. Horniman sometimes wondered how Zoë's parents had agreed to let him become engaged to her, although he often wished that they had not done so. Giddins, on the other hand was in no hurry to see his daughter swept away by some fly-by-night only after her money. He, easily fooled, liked the respectability he perceived in Horniman. They all sat down to lunch, which was served by George who insinuated himself beautifully around the table with a smile on his face and an air that reminded Horniman of cooking sherry.

The meal was not a great event. The food was not hot; the conversation was intermittent and colder than the ices which were served for dessert. George observed all from his position by the dumb waiter on the wall, not far from the door by which Mr Giddins had entered. From the kitchen down below, the cook's voice could be heard wafting up the dumb waiter shaft, huskily berating the kitchen maid for some misdemeanour or other, and this lent an uncomfortable air to the frosty atmosphere. Mr Giddins, always a hard man to please, picked at his food and gave accusing looks to his wife as if the poor meal was her fault. Mrs Giddins looked embarrassed and glanced every so often at their guest to see if he had noticed that anything was amiss. Zoë Giddins stared dreamily into space without a thought on her mind and hardly touched the food on her plate. Horniman, who was hungry, did his best with the meal, though his mind was fixed on thoughts of the pearl necklace that he had, in a moment of weakness, given to Zoë. He tried not to stare at her, a difficult task because she was actually wearing the necklace at that moment.

George, being a silent type, remained where he was most of the time, stepping forward only when necessary, and his presence went largely unnoticed. If anyone had looked at him, they might have seen that his grin had been replaced with the suggestion of a sneer under his nose, for he was a superior type and felt his position in life was not what it ought to be. Down below, the noise from the kitchen became harder to ignore, until finally, Mrs Giddins looked at George and asked him to step downstairs to put an end to the war which seemed to have broken out. George left to attend to this task. The fire burning cheerlessly in the fireplace began suddenly to smoke, and the room now acquired an uncomfortable closeness.

The meal seemed to have come to a natural end. Mr Horniman was desperate to leave, even though he had not managed to find an opportunity to recover the pearl necklace. All four stood up from the table, and though Mrs Giddins insisted he should stay a while, Horniman took his departure. He and Zoë went into the hall where, in the absence of George who was in the kitchen, he found his own coat, took his hat from the hall table, put them both on, then kissed Zoë on the cheek in an absent-minded kind of way and left.

Once he had departed, Zoë returned to the dining room and looked reproachfully at her parents who were once again sitting at the table. "Don't look at us like that, young lady," said her father, rather as if he were addressing a rude teenager.

"Well, really, Daddy," she replied, "I do think you could have been more welcoming to Ralph. What has he done to annoy you? I thought you liked him."

"Of course he does, we both do," said Mrs Giddins, "don't we, dear?" and she looked at her husband with a crocodile-like grin.

"Yes, of course," he said, answering his wife's grin with a fixed one of his own.

"He's very respectable," said Zoë, "you told me so yourself."

But even she had some doubts about him, and these seemed reinforced by the attitude of her parents. She looked puzzled and was just going to express herself more forcibly on the subject with the statement that, after all, it was they who had encouraged her to bring Horniman to make a proposal of marriage to her, when she was interrupted by a knock at the door. This was followed by the entry into the room of George who was carrying an umbrella.

"I beg your pardon, madam," he said, addressing the lady of the house, "but the gentleman left this in the hall when he left."

"I'm sure he will be able to collect it next time he comes," said Mrs Giddins.

Zoë thought she might take it round to the hotel herself, though she did not say so.

She had to go out in any case as she had an important purchase to make, which had to be done that afternoon. After her father had left the room, she turned to her mother, "I have to get Daddy a birthday present," she said.

"Well, really, you've left it a bit late, don't you think?"

"I know exactly what to get him, I won't be long." She went into the hall, put on her coat and left, not forgetting to take the lion's head umbrella with her.

CHAPTER SEVEN

Zoë did not follow the route which might have been calculated to catch up with Ralph Horniman. She, instead, took a detour, which led her past a short row of shops, and she went into the last of these.

The following day was her father's birthday. Mr Giddins had an extremely lazy left eye; on those occasions when the family went to see a play in London, he would always carry a pair of opera glasses and remark when he took them from the leather case, "Of course, what I really need is a monocular." And so, Zoë had made up her mind to go into the local camera shop and buy exactly that for him. She knew they sold them because one was displayed in the window. She bought it, put it into her handbag, and only then turned her feet towards the hotel.

The Giddins family had lived in Paunceton for nearly five years, but Zoë had never been inside the Hotel Splendide, though she had walked past it many times. She always wondered why Ralph had never suggested to her that she should visit him there, but it had never occurred to her that it might be because he felt that yet another female presence could only add further complications to his position. Indeed, though it was an open secret among the hotel staff that he was engaged to be married, they all knew it was a topic to be mentioned only in whispers, and only when Horniman was not around.

So it was that Zoë did not reach the hotel until thirty minutes after Ralph's arrival there.

She went over to the reception desk and rang the bell. There was no answer, and, taking a little notepad from her handbag, she began to write a note for Horniman to let him know that she was leaving his umbrella behind the desk. The little clock on the desk merrily struck five o'clock, and on the last chime, Horniman appeared from the little room behind the desk.

For a moment, he was taken aback by seeing Zoë standing there, but he tried not to look startled. Instead, he smiled and guided her into his own comfortable office.

"You left your umbrella, Ralph," said Zoë, passing it to him.

"Did I, how stupid of me," he said as he opened the door, "but you needn't have bothered to come all this way to bring it to me. I could have collected it the next time I visited you. Let me take your coat." They went into the office, and Horniman closed the door and turned on the light.

Zoë sat on the green leather sofa that was positioned almost against the wall opposite Horniman's imposing desk. Horniman laid her coat over the arm of the sofa, went to the window where he drew the curtains, and then perched on the edge of his desk.

He looked down at her, and she smiled up at him. However, he found himself looking not at her pretty face, but at the pearl necklace that rested just below her collarbone.

Outside, the clouds gathered themselves into charcoal-like pillows; the sky had become dark, and an oppressive atmosphere developed into a lowering gloom. The electric light flickered off and on for no apparent reason. Horniman reached behind himself and turned his desk light on. Oddly enough, this seemed to make things worse. The hard light it gave forth collected itself in a pool onto the leather desktop and made the ornamental inkstand appear to be almost in silhouette, except where it was lit in the one place that stood within the circle of light. He thought for a moment, turned the light off again and then dragged one open hand over his mouth. He suddenly felt tired and thirsty.

"Aren't you going to say something?" said Zoë.

"Of course, I'm so sorry, would you like something to drink? Shall I order some tea?"

"No, thank you, I really should be getting back, they'll wonder where I've got to."

It was such a good opportunity, and now it seemed that he might miss the chance of getting the necklace back from her, unless he could be more persuasive than he had ever been before.

"Do you know," said Horniman, playing for time while he thought of a plan, "you really do look charming in that dress."

"You're sweet," said Zoë, reaching for her coat.

"I'm not sure that that necklace is quite right for it, though."

"Don't you think so? Mother thinks it's lovely."

"And so it is. I'm just not sure that it goes with that particular dress. May I see it for a moment?"

"Now Ralph, really, don't think I'm not wise to your little plan."

"What do you mean?" Horniman was taken by surprise by this last remark, supposing she really did know.

But he was relieved when she said archly, "You just want me to stay here so that you can flirt with me and... well, who knows what!"

"Well, yes, but... just let me see the necklace for a moment." He reached his arms out towards her and took a step forward.

"Really, Ralph, I don't think that... what are you doing? Stop... I'll scream!"

But Horniman put a hand over her mouth and clasped her strongly with his other arm.

She struggled, and then they both fell over onto the large rug by the door, he on top of her. Horniman suddenly felt ashamed, he released his grip and looked at her.

"I'm sorry," he said as he got to his feet. He held out a hand to help her up. Zoë was silent; she lay there very still. There were some wet blood stains on the door stop which lay next to her head.

CHAPTER EIGHT

Earlier that afternoon, Alice, Mary and Andrew met on the hotel roof. It was the first opportunity that Mary and Andrew had to take time away from work. A wall surrounded the roof, and in the centre of their place of assignation stood a high domed tower which had no function except to be ornamental. It was as if the architect, whoever he was, had tried to make an imposing statement: HERE I AM, to attract more wealthy guests by showing the importance and superiority of this hotel above all others in the town.

Andrew leaned against the tower with one foot raised and the shoe that should have been worn by that foot in one hand. He shook the shoe and then felt inside. "I thought there was something in here," he said, "but there's a nail poking through, I'll have to get it mended." He put the shoe back on, walked to the area behind the tower and looked out over the parts of the building that lay at the back. The town stretched out towards a tree-covered hill to the right of which could be glimpsed one edge of the ruins of Paunceton Castle. Behind the castle and out of sight lay the market town of Paunceton Muffet. The day was windy and quite bracing.

"Have you been to the castle, Mrs Winsome?" he called, looking round as he spoke.

"Not yet," said Alice, "I only arrived yesterday."

"It's really worth seeing," said Mary, "there's a sort of stone cupboard where someone is supposed to have been tortured hundreds of years ago—a monk, I think."

"It was a fortified monastery originally," said Andrew, "there's a story about lost treasure buried underneath it."

"And what's that?" asked Alice. She was looking out over the front of the roof. The sea looked choppy, and the tide was in. Andrew walked over to her. Mary, who was already by Alice's side turned to see what it was that Alice meant. A grey mist was rising over the water, but through it could be seen a dense outline.

"That's Muffet Island," replied Andrew, "not much to see there, and it's practically impossible to get onto it even with a boat."

"There's a mystery about the island," said Mary. "Apparently someone's living in an old building there, but no one knows who."

"Except that it's a woman," said Andrew.

All this time, none of them had mentioned the one thing that was uppermost in all their minds. It was Alice who broke this deadlock.

"Necklace!" she said baldly.

"What shall we do with it?" said Mary. "Andy and I were going to dispose of whatever we finished up with, but I'm not sure that this is really quite what we had in mind."

"We were after cash," remarked Andrew.

Alice had been thinking about the pearls all night long.

"We can't put it back where we found it," she said. "Mrs Garthwaite's back in her room. Hopefully she won't notice it's gone for a while, though."

"Is it worth anything?" said Mary.

"I don't think so," said Andrew, "not much, anyway."

"So, it really wasn't worth all the effort," Alice said. "Any ideas?" They all paced round the roof for some minutes.

"Gosh!" exclaimed Mary suddenly, "we should've been back in our lifts ten minutes ago." She and Andrew began to hurry away.

"I have an idea," said Alice, "leave it to me, I think I know just what to do."

Mary and Andrew were gone a moment later. Alice was inexperienced, but she was not a fool. An idea had occurred to her. It seemed that another hiding place must be found for the pearl necklace. Why not put it in the most obvious place of all? If Mrs Garthwaite should notice it was gone, the first person she would turn to would naturally be the hotel manager who would then undoubtedly telephone the police. But suppose she managed to put the necklace inside Mr Horniman's own office. Then, when its rightful owner went to report it missing, it would be found as if it were simply lost property. Mr Horniman might be puzzled by its appearance there, though.

"Why not just take it to him and tell him that I found it?" she thought. But the more she dwelled on that possibility, the less she liked the idea of associating herself with the necklace's disappearance. Alice made her way down to her room and retrieved the bag with the necklace from behind the radiator.

It was Saturday, and the hotel was very busy that afternoon. Alice went to the reception desk and asked Angela, who had been standing in as receptionist all day, much to Ben's disgust, where Mr Horniman was.

"He's out, Mrs Winsome," said Angela, "probably won't be back till late afternoon." Alice felt relieved. She sat in an armchair with a view of Horniman's office door and waited. There seemed to be a never-ending stream of people: new arrivals wanting to be taken to their rooms and a postman with a late delivery. The postman was a distinct annoyance to Alice, as he arrived just at the moment when the foyer seemed to be empty, and he kept Angela talking with irrelevant chitchat for what seemed like an age. Ben, Mary and Andrew were busy taking people up and down in their lifts; Alice could hear them from time to time, but the lifts were out of sight from where she sat waiting for her moment.

At half-past-four, Horniman arrived back at the hotel. He sent Angela back to her lift duties, dallied at the desk for twenty or so more minutes, and then entered the little room behind Reception. For a moment, all was quiet.

Alice had, of course, noticed Horniman's arrival, and tutted with frustration. At five-to-five, she decided that it was either now or never. She walked to Horniman's own office and entered. The room was dim, but she did not turn on the light. She went straight to the big desk that stood near the window, walked round to where the chair stood with its back to the window and tried the desk drawers, intending to put the necklace in one of them. But then she had another idea. On the desk was a wooden cigar box. She picked it up and opened it. The lid made a soft creaking sound as she did so, and the strong but familiar aroma of unsmoked Havana cigars filled her nostrils. The odour reminded her of her mother, but she did not have time to reminisce, so she put the pearl necklace into the box between two fat cigars and shut the lid. Then she walked to the office door.

At that moment she heard a voice from outside—someone was coming in! Alice turned and ducked down behind the green sofa onto her hands and knees, trying not to let her breathing be heard.

CHAPTER NINE

Horniman's first instinct was to panic. "I've killed her," he thought. Then he knelt by Zoë's side and tried to revive her by calling her name, but Zoë did not respond to exhortations. At this point, he went into the small private toilet, which was accessible only from within his office, and took some paper towels, which he moistened at the sink and then returned to Zoë and began to caress her forehead with one of them in the hope that this operation might waken her, as well as wipe away the blood. Zoë's head had hit the antique flatiron which Horniman kept as a doorstop. The iron lay there innocently; it seemed to mock him.

"You fool!" he muttered to himself, "you stupid, stupid fool. Gone and made things much worse now." But there was still no response from her. He went to the desk, lifted the telephone receiver, and began to dial, but then stopped. "They'll think I did it on purpose. Everything will come out. It'll be the ruin of me. Prison. The noose." He clapped his hand over his mouth to stop the panic from overwhelming him again. "Think, idiot, think!" he whispered out loud. He went once more to look at Zoë. Then, lifting two corners of the rug on which Zoë was lying, he dragged her to the small, tiled toilet. Once the body and rug were inside, he stepped over them and shut the door. Horniman took a deep breath though his nose but did not exhale for some moments. When he did so, it came out as a great sigh. There was a sudden knock at the office door.

"Yes," said Horniman in a voice which sounded nothing like his own.

"There's a gentleman here to see you," said Ben's voice.

"I'll be there in a moment," said Horniman. Outside, it was dark. He looked at himself in a mirror on the wall. After straightening his tie and smoothing his hair, he opened the office door and was on the point of leaving, when he was suddenly struck by a thought. He closed the door again, bent down, picked up the flatiron, wiped it with another paper towel, and then took all the paper towels back to the toilet, which he gingerly entered so as not to look at what was there, and flushed them away. Then he shut the toilet door, went back to the office door and left the room, locking it behind him, to see who it was that needed him at such an inopportune moment.

As soon as he had gone, Alice emerged from behind the sofa. Her face was flushed, and she did not know what to do— or what to think. She had heard everything, and this was certainly something that she had not planned on getting herself mixed up in. There had been a few scares too. She had been sure that Horniman would put the body behind the sofa— and then he had not done so. Then, while Horniman had started to use the telephone, she had adjusted her position as she was extremely uncomfortable, and the sofa had moved, but he had not seen this. Then she had sneezed while he was in the toilet, but it seemed that he had not heard. Finally, just as he was leaving the office, Alice had begun to get up from her place behind the sofa but had had to dive down again quickly when he had changed his mind.

There was no doubt that she was in an awkward spot. The door was locked, and there was no way out without alerting everyone to the fact that she had been there. She went to the office window, but the windows were all securely fastened, and, in any case, there were security bars immediately beyond them.

And so, there was only one place left. She was not happy about it, but she knew the moment would have to be faced. She held her head in an upright position, pursed her lips and opened the toilet door.

Ralph Horniman guided his visitor not to his office (which was just as well as far as Alice was concerned), but to a small meeting room, which lay beyond the hotel restaurant. The last place he would have taken him at that moment would have been his office.

When he had seen who was waiting for him, he had gulped in surprise before advancing with hand outstretched. Something about Horniman must have struck this new arrival as strange because the first thing he said was,

"Everything all right, Ralph? You look white as a sheet."

Horniman muttered something about being fine as the two of them proceeded along the corridor. His extreme nervousness will be understood once the identity of the man is revealed. He was one of Ralph Horniman's friends, Jack Jackson was his name, and a more ordinary individual than Jack would be hard to imagine. He was of usual height, and when he took his hat off, one could see that he had brown hair that was thinning on top; he might go unnoticed in a crowd. Jack Jackson wore plain clothes and a sad moustache. Although unnecessary to this tale, it might be added that he was married to a pleasant lady, and they had two teenaged children, a boy and a girl. All very nice. The simple dullness of 'Jack' Llewelyn Jackson did not exactly make him an unwelcome visitor on those occasions when he called round to see his friend, though his conversation could hardly be described as scintillating. However, on this occasion, the visit of Detective Inspector Jack Llywelyn Jackson had most certainly not come at the most convenient time. And Jack did like to talk, though he never seemed to have anything to say. Conversations with him were hard work.

"So, Jack," said Ralph once they were seated in the meeting room with some small libations poured from a bottle kept in a cupboard on the wall to which only Horniman had the key, "what's news?"

"Nothing much," said Jack Jackson.

"Oh, I see. How's the family?"

"Doing well, thanks, Liz is decorating, and the kids are helping, you know."

There was a pause. This part of the conversation had come to an end, and Jack was, as usual, waiting for Ralph to start the next topic.

"I'm thinking of having the hotel redecorated, you know," he said, falling easily into the same vocal cadences used by his friend.

"Is that so?"

Horniman started to talk at length about his projected plans for this fictional project. He finished by asking Jack about the decorating plans for his house, and Jack began to tell him in great detail about his wife's colour schemes for each room one by one. Ralph had two internal reactions to this, firstly, the inconvenient timing of his friend's visit was causing an inexorable tide of anxiety to rise within him. The other was what a bore this all was. And all this, while he was longing to be back in his office. Once or twice he almost brought himself to the point of interrupting Jack, who was in full flow describing this particular green or that particular yellow, interrupting him so that he could lay this latest disaster before this most ordinary of men, but one who would certainly know what to do.

Alice, on seeing Zoë lying on the rug, was completely at a loss. She had never before seen a dead body. She tried to think quickly. Should she raise the alarm, or might that put her in a difficult position? Perhaps she could phone the police, anonymously of course, but that seemed an unattractive option too.

There was a window at the back of this little room, just above the sink, and Alice stepped over Zoë's body to see if it would open. It did open, and she climbed up onto the sink to open it far enough for her to squeeze through. At that moment, there was a most unexpected noise. Only a little sound, but enough to make Alice turn to look behind.

Zoë moved. She groaned softly and moved again. Alice was by her side in an instant. Zoë began to cry, and Alice helped her to sit up. Zoë put her hand against her head where it hurt; she could feel a large bump there.

"Listen," said Alice, "we don't have much time. He may come back at any moment, and the door's locked. We need to get out, and quickly." Zoë allowed herself to be helped to her feet, and the two walked to the office door. "It's locked," Alice repeated.

"Maybe there's another key," said Zoë.

Alice could have kicked herself for not having thought of that before. She began to look round the room and soon found a small cupboard on the wall with a number of keys inside, each one hanging on a hook and labelled. In no time, the door was unlocked, and the two walked out into the now deserted foyer. Alice relocked the door and spoke in a low voice. "You'd better come with me to my room; I think you need to lie down somewhere safe."

"I've been lying down," said Zoë, but her mild protest was unheeded.

Alice summoned a lift,

"Try to look happy," she said to Zoë, we don't want anyone to think there's been anything wrong."

"We should call the police," breathed Zoë. "He attacked me!"

"Call the police, but let's talk about it first," said Alice, who did not want to be involved with the constabulary and was trying to think of an excuse not to call them.

Andrew's lift arrived, and Andrew, looking quizzically at Alice, stood aside to allow them in. Alice affected not to notice Andrew's look and shook her head when he tried to attract her attention again. Once on the third floor, she helped Zoë along the corridor, and both were soon safely inside Alice's room.

Once there, Alice rang for room service and ordered two cups of tea to be brought up. Then she got Zoë to lie down on the bed. Zoë thanked Alice and, as she did so, put her hands to her throat to adjust the pearl necklace, which had moved into an uncomfortable position at the back of her neck.

Thus, it can be seen that, in his anxiety to deal with this latest disaster, one of his own making, Horniman had forgotten to pocket the pearls.

Meanwhile, Ralph Horniman had finally managed to rid himself of his unwelcome guest. They shook hands at the main entrance, and he promised to visit Jack at his home at the next possible opportunity. Then he walked as calmly as he could, under the circumstances, to his office door, unlocked it, and went inside. A few people were milling around the foyer, and Horniman felt as if they were watching him. Their large, coarse faces seemed to loom before his eyes, magnified into ominous and shadowy demons. A loud, high cackle assaulted his ears as he entered, and it was with relief that he shut the door, and then locked it from the inside. He stood still for a moment, before turning on the light and heading to his desk. Under normal circumstances, a feeling of comfort and power would have suffused him as he sat there, but instead now he stared numbly into space, hardly daring to think of the huge difficulty he had yet to overcome. He switched on the angle-poise desk lamp, and then reached for the cigar box, but withdrew his hand at the last moment.

"First thing's first," he muttered. Then, getting to his feet, he marched to the toilet door, which he opened cautiously.

"Damn!" he exclaimed out loud when he saw that Zoë's body was not there. The rug she had been lying on had been pushed to one side, and at the end of the room, the window above the sink was open. The explanation, as far as he could see, was obvious. Zoë was not dead (relief), but she had recovered and had climbed out of the window (mixed feelings), and she would by now be recounting her experiences either to her parents or to the police, or both (horror!). Horniman began working out excuses and explanations in his mind. What could he say? What could he do? On top of that, he knew there was something that he had forgotten about, but he couldn't for the life of him remember what it was.

He shut the toilet door and returned to his desk. At that moment, there was a knock from outside. Upon unlocking and opening the door, he saw, with some irritation, Angela standing there.

"Will I be seeing you later?" she asked with a suggestiveness which irritated Horniman still more.

"Erm, no, I don't think so. Is that all?" he said dismissively.

Angela stared at him feeling somewhat slighted by this reply. She turned on her heels without another word and walked away. Perhaps she expected him to call after her, but if she did, she was disappointed. She went to find Ben, regretting at that moment that she had ever thought of looking elsewhere, even though she now found him dull.

Horniman relocked the door and went to his desk feeling very much in need of a smoke. As he opened the cigar box, he remembered exactly what he had been striving to recollect, for there, in the box, was a pearl necklace. He lifted it from the box with his little finger and dallied with it, in a puzzled fashion, listening to the gentle clacking noise it made as he ran it through his fat fingers and watching how the pearls reflected the light from the angle-poise.

"Did I put it there? I must have done." Once more he had jumped to a wrong conclusion; it did not occur to him that the necklace which he now held in his hands actually belonged to Mrs Garthwaite.

The lifts continued to travel up and down, dispensing their various passengers to their chosen floors. Angela was thinking that Ben was not so bad a catch after all. Ben was wondering why Angela suddenly seemed to be more affectionate towards him. Andrew was trying to find a moment to tell his sister about the recent puzzling events, and Mary was trying to find a moment to listen. In one of the hotel lounges someone had turned the radio on, and a small number of people were listening to the Last Night Promenade Concert of the season relayed from the Queen's Hall; the Ride of the Valkyries could be heard clearly by those in the foyer. Others milled around waiting for taxis or arriving for supper. The hotel had suddenly burst into 'Saturday evening' life.

At the same moment that Horniman was removing the pearl necklace from the cigar box, Mrs Garthwaite was lying on the bed in her room, but was contemplating getting up. She had been ruminating upon a plan that was uppermost in her mind. Her late husband had died a number of years before, and she had decided to remarry. She considered that, although she was now of more mature years, she was still attractive enough to find someone with whom she could share a happy life, provided that the gentleman in question was of a compliant nature. And so it was that her thoughts had travelled towards Ralph Horniman as the most likely candidate. Horniman was not unaware of Mrs Garthwaite's intentions towards him, though he would have been very surprised had he known quite how advanced she was in her planning of their joint future. She, on the other hand, was certain that the attractions she might supply in the way of financial stability and respectability would be enough to sway the heart of even the most recalcitrant of potential suitors—in other words, that by devious means she would be able to persuade Horniman to abandon ideas of marrying a young inexperienced person and propose of his own volition to her, Euphemia Garthwaite. She, knowing of Horniman's engagement to Zoë, had spent some time and money investigating his personal life, and had even managed to meet the girl, just by chance, of course, in order to size up the opposition. Though, despite the reports of a private detective watching his movements, she had not managed to discover the blatant way in which he had been defrauding her by syphoning off hotel funds to pay for both his gambling debts and the pearl necklace he had given to Zoë.

Feeling that she had been in her room for long enough, and also that the time had come for supper, Mrs Garthwaite dressed herself in a smart outfit, looked at herself in the mirror, approved of what she saw, and went to the safe in her wardrobe to collect that which she felt would give the finishing touches to her preparations, for there was no doubt in her mind that this was the evening to begin her campaign to attract Ralph Horniman into her gossamer web. But her pearl necklace was gone!

CHAPTER TEN

Mrs Garthwaite, after dressing, took a pink stole from her wardrobe, wrapped it round her shoulders, and began to make her way elegantly down to the ground floor. As she did so, she counted the floor numbers. Past the third floor, where Alice and Zoë were; past the second floor where, had she looked just round a nearby corner, she might have seen Angela and Ben engaged in frenetic, whispered conversation; past the first floor, where she saw a waiter delivering a supper meal on a trolley to the bridal suite; down, down she went past the mezzanine floor, taking her time, imagining the opening words she would speak to Ralph Horniman. Firstly, she had to report her necklace missing. She was, naturally, upset by the invasion of her privacy, but not worried unduly by the loss in financial terms, because the pearls were not expensive but a very good imitation of the real thing. Perhaps, she mused, after making her report, she could then be gracious towards him, for Horniman would doubtless be devastated to hear what had happened and most apologetic. Perhaps that would be the time to invite him to partner her at the dance due to take place the following weekend. How could he refuse? Was she not a lady of means, maturely attractive in the best possible sense?

As Mrs Garthwaite began the final descent from mezzanine to ground floor, Horniman was cramming the pearl necklace he had found in the cigar box into his coat pocket, after which he put on his coat and hat and whisked himself out of his office, forgetting to lock the door after himself. And so it was that Mrs Garthwaite just missed him, for by the time she had reached his door, he was ensconced in a taxicab, en route to a place kept by an acquaintance of his.

Mrs Garthwaite knocked at the office door and, receiving no answer, opened it and went in. The light was still on, and she could see that all was not as ship-shape inside as was usually the case. Chairs were not in their usual positions, the rug was not on the floor, and papers were scattered untidily on the desk. She walked to the desk and idly tidied the papers on it. They were largely of an inconsequential nature, though there was one envelope addressed to Horniman and marked "Urgent", and since it had been opened already, she put her hand inside and drew out the letter, keeping an eye on the office door as she did so, just in case Horniman should suddenly return.

The letter was stamped inside with the words in red "For your urgent attention".

Below this was the letter heading, and then the letter itself. It was handwritten, dated October 1st, and read,

Sir, with regard to the monies outstanding on your account, early settlement would be gratefully received. We regret that if we have not heard from you by Fri. 2nd inst., we will have no option but to place the matter in the hands of our agents.

The letter was signed with the single letter S.

That today was the evening of the 3rd did not escape Mrs Garthwaite. Something was not right. Horniman evidently owed money to this S, but she could not think who S might be. There was no clue from the other documents on the desk, but upon opening the desk drawers, she found a locked cashbox. Taking a pin from her hair, she fumbled with the lock and succeeded in unlocking it. Inside were a number of invoices, some for hundreds of pounds, and one for more than a thousand. All were addressed to Horniman, and some were stamped in blue with the word "Paid".

"How can he possibly afford to pay all these bills?" she thought. "I don't pay him this kind of money." Then she realised that there was much still owing, and that a number of the bills had not been paid. Mrs Garthwaite felt suspicious, if not a little nauseous at the thought that he may have had been draining hotel funds. She went to the safe that stood by the side of the toilet door. It was set with a combination lock, one which only she and Mr Horniman knew. But when she tried to open it, the combination would not work. Feeling very worried, she put her hand to her head, but then remembered the letter from S. The sender's address was at the top.

Mrs Garthwaite was not of a particularly brave disposition, nevertheless, she decided that she would visit S at that address. There was no time like the present, late though it was. And so it was that twenty minutes or so after Horniman's departure, she climbed into a taxi.

Alice and Zoë took an instant liking to each other, and they sat in Alice's room discussing recent events.

"I don't know what came over him," said Zoë. She was puzzled by her own reaction, feeling that she ought to have been far more upset, but was surprised to find herself suddenly empowered, elevated to a new awareness of herself.

"What are you going to do about it?" asked Alice.

Zoë was unsure.

"Perhaps it would be best to go home and just call the engagement off," she murmured.

But Alice wouldn't hear of such a pusillanimous course of action.

"I've a much better idea," she said. "The room next to this one is empty, and no one will book in now, it's much too late. Why don't you stay there tonight?"

"My parents don't know I'm here," said Zoë.

"I'll deal with that," said Alice. "We'll give that so-and-so a real fright. We'll tell the police your necklace has been stolen and get him into real hot water."

Zoë agreed with Alice's plan, and so it was that about twenty minutes after Mrs Garthwaite had left in her taxi to follow Horniman, Zoë went into the room next to Alice's through the interconnecting door, which had accidentally been left unlocked by a chambermaid. She had been persuaded, with some reluctance, to lend Alice the pearl necklace she had around her neck—the one Horniman had given her, and Alice, armed with this in her handbag, left her room and began to make her way to the ground floor. Just as Mrs Garthwaite had done earlier, she chose to use the stairs, first passing the second floor, then the first where Angela and Ben were still arguing. They had been interrupted from time to time by the necessity to convey people to various floors in their respective lifts but had managed to keep their conversation going, reconvening wherever convenient. Alice sneaked past them without looking to see who was arguing, but as she disappeared round the bend in the staircase, Angela looked up and saw the back of her head.

"That's Mrs Winsome," she said to Ben, "I wonder where she's off to."

"That's not the point," said Ben. "What I want to know is—are we engaged or are we not? Because if not I think you should tell me."

"Not, then!" declared Angela, suddenly feeling relieved. And she left Ben and walked slowly down after Alice, keeping her distance.

Ben was taken aback by Angela's reply. He returned to his lift, and went down to the mezzanine floor, and then over to the bar where he ordered a double whiskey (Irish).

Alice had by now reached the ground floor. She walked over to reception, trying to appear nonchalant. Angela, from a position near the foot of the stairs, watched her out of the corner of her eye, trying not to look as if she was doing so. The reception area was fairly busy at that moment, and the new receptionist was dealing with a portly gentleman in front of him while speaking on the phone to a very demanding lady. Alice moved slowly to Horniman's office door, which was still unlocked, and when she judged the moment was right, went in. Angela, not knowing that Horniman was out, was surprised that Alice had not knocked on the door, and was on the verge of feeling jealous, though she couldn't for the life of her think why, when the door opened, and Alice came out again. Angela quickly ran back up the stairs to the first floor where her lift was waiting for her and tried to look as if she had been busily working the whole time.

On the ground floor, a group of people had collected by the lift doors and were impatiently pressing the buttons to summon the lifts. Alice walked over to the reception desk, wrote a quick note which she passed to the receptionist, who was now free, exchanged a quick word with him, and then walked over to the crowd by the lifts and stood with them as if she had been there all the time. Angela's lift arrived soon after. Ben was still drowning his sorrows on the mezzanine in a spot hidden away from the hotel guests. Mary and Andrew were nowhere to be seen; they were on the roof, smoking cigarettes and discussing plans for the future.

"We need to find somewhere else," said Mary, leaning out over the road below.

"Agreed," said Andrew, stubbing his cigarette out on the parapet.

Mary and Andrew, abandoning their lifts, strolled down the stairs all the way to the ground floor, past the people who were still queueing for the only lift operating, and walked out of the hotel in brother-and-sister-like fashion.

While in Horniman's office for the second time, Alice had gone straight over to the desk, opened the cigar box, noticed that Mrs Garthwaite's necklace had gone, and put Zoë's inside where the other had been before. The note she had passed to the receptionist after leaving the office was to be a telegram addressed to Zoë's parents advising them of their daughter's whereabouts, though Alice, inexperienced in the ways of the Post Office, was unaware that the telegram could not possibly be sent until Monday morning. After she had done everything, instead of taking the lift to the third floor, she made her way to the bar on the mezzanine and ordered a glass of white wine. She sat at a table in a corner for an entire hour, feeling a sense of great relief. She wondered if she should be brave and order a cocktail—they sounded so romantic, but decided that it was probably better to go to bed.

HOTEL SPLENDIDE

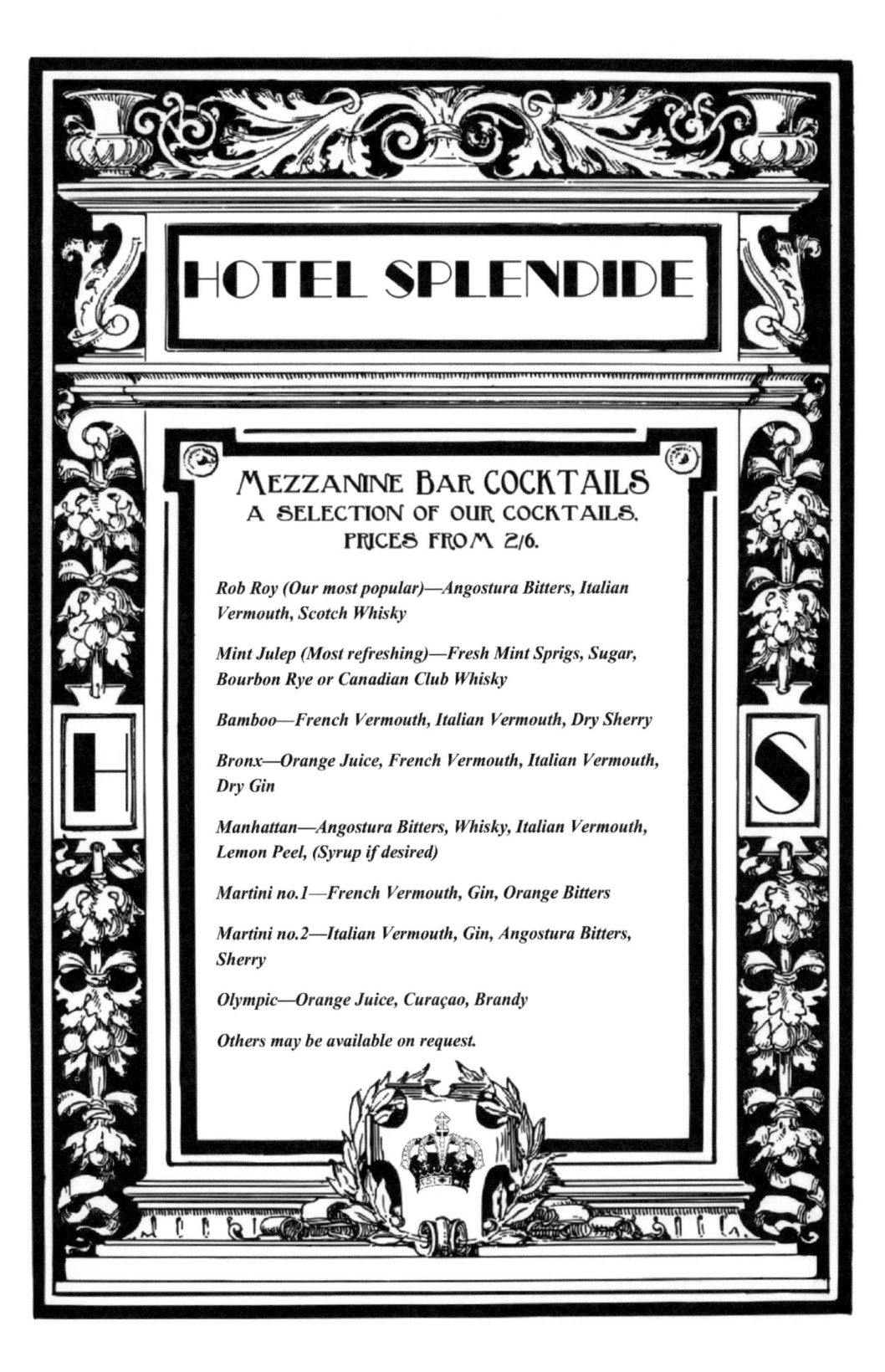

Mezzanine Bar COCKTAILS
A SELECTION OF OUR COCKTAILS.
PRICES FROM 2/6.

Rob Roy (Our most popular)—Angostura Bitters, Italian Vermouth, Scotch Whisky

Mint Julep (Most refreshing)—Fresh Mint Sprigs, Sugar, Bourbon Rye or Canadian Club Whisky

Bamboo—French Vermouth, Italian Vermouth, Dry Sherry

Bronx—Orange Juice, French Vermouth, Italian Vermouth, Dry Gin

Manhattan—Angostura Bitters, Whisky, Italian Vermouth, Lemon Peel, (Syrup if desired)

Martini no.1—French Vermouth, Gin, Orange Bitters

Martini no.2—Italian Vermouth, Gin, Angostura Bitters, Sherry

Olympic—Orange Juice, Curaçao, Brandy

Others may be available on request.

HOTEL SPLENDIDE

Mezzanine Bar Cocktails
A SELECTION OF OUR COCKTAILS.
PRICES FROM 2/6.

Old Fashioned—Sugar lump, Angostura Bitters, Whisky

Orange Blossom—Orange Juice, Gin

Polo—Lemon or Lime Juice, Italian Vermouth, French Vermouth, Dry Gin

Pooh-Bah (Savoy recipe)—Bacardi Rum, Apricot Brandy, Swedish Punch, Dry Gin

Planters—Lemon Juice, Syrup, Jamaica Rum

Quarter Deck—Lime Juice, Sherry, Rum

Rose—Lemon Juice, Grenadine, Apricot Brandy, French Vermouth, Dry Gin

Side Car—Lemon Juice, Cointreau, Brandy

White Lady—Lemon Juice, Cointreau, Dry Gin

Others may be available on request.

CHAPTER ELEVEN

Horniman arrived at S's residence. It was in a seedy part of town in which he did not care to be seen. The street was unlit, though, at one corner, a solitary streetlamp tried vainly to send glorious rays out from beneath dirty glass. He asked the driver to wait for him, and then went to the front door and knocked at it. The door was opened by a cross woman who looked at him with a squint and with her lower lip pressed out by the long upper one.

"Well?" she said abruptly. Horniman mentioned a name.

"Oh, 'im. He's upstairs. You better come in. Go into the front room and I'll get 'im."

We pass over the details of the interview between Horniman and the mysterious S for the moment. Suffice it to say that it was most unsatisfactory to both. Horniman was most distressed to discover, upon offering the pearl necklace to S in part redemption of his debts, that the necklace was not the valuable one he had presented to Zoë, but a vastly inferior item with little intrinsic value. S was not pleased to be offered it and made his displeasure quite plain.

Horniman left the house hurriedly, thrusting his arms into his coat as he went, nearly dropping his hat as he did so. It appeared almost as though he had been pushed out of the door. S watched from an upstairs window as Horniman clambered into the taxi that then drove away. This was also observed by Mrs Garthwaite, who had just arrived in her taxi. She commanded her driver to go back to the hotel, whither, she had no doubt, Horniman would return. She was feeling most exasperated by the whole affair, and this sense of frustration was made worse still when the car she was riding in went over a nail or a rock and sustained a puncture.

"Most inconvenient!" she exclaimed. But there was nothing to do except wait for the driver to change the wheel, for they were not in a part of the town where other transportation might easily be summoned, and they were too far from the hotel for her to walk the distance. For a moment, Mrs Garthwaite considered walking, but she knew it would not be a good idea, for not only was it dark and the streets badly lit, but she was wearing her patent leather high heels. Though the driver was, as far as these things go, very efficient, it was some thirty minutes before they were able to move again.

CHAPTER TWELVE

Ralph Horniman moved like a whirlwind once he arrived back at the hotel. In no time, he took charge of the reception area, sending the new receptionist back home, and then began quickly rifling through every document he could see. It was important to ascertain that no evidence of Zoë's arrival at the hotel could be easily found, as he had just remembered that she had been writing something when she had arrived. However, there was no sign of it, and he was breathing a sigh of relief, when he suddenly remembered the little drawer used for telegrams.

Sometimes other things finished up inside, and being a methodical man, he opened it fully and took out the few notes that were in there. It took a little time for him to find the message Alice had written to be sent to Mr and Mrs Giddins. It had not been stamped with the mark normally used to indicate that the telegram had been sent. Horniman lifted it up with the middle and fourth fingers of his right hand, twiddled it in the air for a moment, and then stuffed it into his waistcoat pocket.

"It can stay there," he said.

The note had puzzled him, though. What on earth had Alice Winsome to do with Zoë Giddins and her parents that she was writing to them with urgency?

"Come at once. Hotel Splendide. Zoë here," it had read. He left reception and hurried over to the lifts. Ben was by his lift door, picking his fingernails, but he stopped immediately when he saw Horniman approach.

"Third floor," said Horniman abruptly, and Ben worked the lift in his usual efficient way, trying hard not to exhale too much in case Horniman detected the smell of alcohol on his breath.

"Wait for me, Ben," said Horniman as he exited the lift. He made his way to Alice's room, determined to have a word with her to find out, if he could, exactly what her relationship with the Giddinses was. There was no answer to his knock, and, taking his pass key, he unlocked the door.(At that precise moment, Alice was in Horniman's office, putting Zoë's necklace into the cigar box.) Horniman walked into Alice's room. The bedside light was on, and he looked around, opening everything in sight, making certain to leave no trace of his activities. Then his eyes turned to the door which connected Alice's room to the next room, the one he supposed was empty but in which Zoë was sleeping. He quietly opened the door. The light from Alice's room was enough to see that someone was lying on the bed. He moved over to it and looked at the sleeping figure. His surprise at seeing Zoë there was only exceeded by the urgency he felt to leave as quickly as he possibly could.

Some little while later, he returned to the ground floor and innocently slid his way to the office, where he removed all traces of his struggle with Zoë before returning to the foyer. This time, he remembered to lock the door, and once back in reception tried his best to look unconcerned. The left side of his face suddenly twitched in anger as he thought of the meddlesome Alice Winsome (who, at that moment, was eating crisps in the mezzanine bar), but as quickly as the anger passed over his face, it vanished, when he saw Mrs Garthwaite walking through the main entrance.

Ralph Horniman had no idea that Mrs Garthwaite had spent some considerable time that evening following him, watching him, or tailing him. Nor did he suspect, for a moment, that she had even the slightest suspicion that he had been playing fast and loose with the hotel funds.

"Good evening, Mrs Garthwaite," he said with the falsest of friendly smiles, for he had no real liking for her.

"Don't you 'good evening' me," she responded, giving him a hard look.

Horniman was nonplussed by this. The twitch returned, though this time not one of anger, but one of concern for himself. "I trust you are feeling better now," he said.

"Not a bit of it. Worse, if anything!"

"Is there something I can do to help?"

"Yes, there is. You can follow me to your office. I want a word with you."

And the usually self-important Ralph Horniman meekly followed his employer. Mrs Garthwaite, upon trying the doorknob impatiently, had to stand back to let him open the door for her. He unlocked it, pushed it open, and she marched past him into the room. He followed and closed the door.

Mrs Garthwaite did not allow him to speak, and in order to prevent him doing so held the palm of her hand towards him in a gesture of denial.

"I have a number of questions for you, and I want you to answer them truthfully."

"Of course, Mrs Garthwaite, how could I do anything else?"

"Very easily, I expect. However, that is of no consequence. Kindly answer me the following. Firstly, what is the name of the young lady to whom, I hear, you are affianced?" A slightly disingenuous question, since she knew very well the answer.

"I must tell you, Mrs Garthwaite, that as of this afternoon that engagement no longer exists."

"I am very pleased to hear it. We cannot place this hotel's management in the hands of a person who is distracted by young ladies, can we?"

"No, indeed, Mrs Garthwaite," replied Horniman, totally at a loss. What had inspired this line of questioning; where might this conversation lead?

"Now then," continued his interlocutor, "it has come to my attention that certain financial matters connected with this hotel, and yourself, may not be in order?"

Horniman flushed a deep puce.

"Really, I don't know what…"

"… Just what are you going to do about it, that's what I want to know?" interrupted Mrs Garthwaite.

Horniman put the index finger of his left hand into his left ear and wiggled it.

"Don't do that," said Mrs Garthwaite, "it makes you look like a country bumpkin."

Horniman was completely lost for words. He tried to begin to make excuses, to say that any small irregularities which might appear in the accounts would easily be made up, but each sentence came to nothing. He felt like a small boy in the presence of a formidable teacher. Indeed, he had not felt like this since he had been a small boy facing a teacher who had puffed up with indignation like a turkey-cock because of some minor infringement of school rules that he had committed.

Mrs Garthwaite looked at him pityingly and decided to put him out of his misery.

"I'll tell you just what you can do about it." She gave him a smile which was intended to be attractively girlish but succeeded only in being crocodilian. "You can become engaged to me."

"Do you mean engaged to be married?"

"Of course," she said with a sudden merriness. "Then all your financial problems would disappear just like that." She attempted to snap her pudgy fingers.

Horniman was quick. He saw immediately the advantage of allowing himself to become engaged to Mrs Garthwaite, even if he had no intention whatsoever of actually marrying her. He began to say something but was interrupted once more.

"Of course," said his soon-to-be affianced, "you will have to ask me nicely to marry you."

Horniman knelt on the rug, the same rug he had used to drag Zoë into the small toilet.

"Euphemia," he said, trying to sound sincere, "Euphemia." He swallowed. "Euphemia…"

"Yes, Ralph," said Euphemia Garthwaite, "only don't take so long."

"Will you marry me," he suddenly blurted out.

"Yes, Ralph," said Euphemia Garthwaite, "there now, that wasn't so bad, was it?"

She tilted her head slightly to one side. Ralph stood, not without some effort on his part, and gave her cheek a peck.

"My, how hungry I am!" said Mrs Garthwaite. "Come on, you can take me to supper."

Horniman nodded his assent to this, but, feeling that he would very soon need to smoke, he strolled over to his desk to take a cigar from the box. Upon opening it, he saw Zoë's pearl necklace staring at him impudently. Several things happened almost simultaneously. Horniman put his hand to his pocket wherein lay Mrs Garthwaite's necklace, the one he had thought was Zoë's; he could feel it was still there. Mrs Garthwaite saw clearly that something unexpected lay in the cigar box and moved over to the desk; Horniman tried to close the box but was prevented from doing so by Mrs Garthwaite's chubby hand.

"My pearl necklace!" she exclaimed, jumping to the wrong conclusion. "What on earth is it doing in your room?" She put her hand into the box, removed the necklace and enclosed it in her fist. Some of the pearls peeped out from between her fingers, appearing to wink cheekily at Horniman as if to taunt him.

Horniman was not slow on the uptake, but he did need time to appreciate fully the situation.

"Have you lost a pearl necklace?" he asked.

"Yes. How did it get here?"

"Lost property," said Horniman. "Handed to me this afternoon."

"But why were my pearls in your cigar box?"

A light seemed to shine through the clouds of confusion, though Horniman could not quite make a connection. He realised that in all probability, the necklace in his pocket was the property of Mrs Garthwaite, and that the necklace in Mrs Garthwaite's hand might very well be the one he had given to Zoë. The problem was how best to effect an exchange without Mrs Garthwaite realising what had happened.

"I put lost items of value in unexpected places so that they won't be stolen," he said lamely.

"Not in the safe, then? I would have thought that a far better place."

"Do you know, you're right," said Horniman, trying to change the topic of conversation into one where he was appearing to accept advice from a wiser head.

Mrs Garthwaite took the bait and felt a sensation of one almost preening her feathers, though it was with some disquiet, for she realised that she had lost track of something important that she had been about to say.

As for Horniman, he had several matters to deal with: how to exchange the necklaces; how to get away from Mrs Garthwaite; how to realise the value of the real pearls so that he could begin to pay off his debts; how to cover all traces of any of his wrongdoing effectively. He grinned in as charming a fashion as he could muster. "What about that supper?" he said. He opened the office door to show Mrs Garthwaite out and, after she had passed him, wiped his handkerchief over his sweaty face.

The meal was an uncomfortable affair, for Horniman at least. When they finally rose from the table, he still had not found a way of exchanging the necklaces, and he was feeling very sorry for himself when his Euphemia coyly waved at him as the lift doors closed on her. She, although she was certain his sorry appearance must be on account of having to take his leave of her, decided to take no chances and, once back in her room on the fourth floor, locked Zoë's pearl necklace in the room safe, smiling a little as she did so.

Horniman, meanwhile, turned his mind to the other problem which had been occupying him: Zoë herself. What could he do about Zoë? He turned to his right and, with a grim look on his face, began to climb the stairs.

CHAPTER THIRTEEN

Alice unlocked the door of her room and went inside. It was almost as if nothing extraordinary had happened at all. Everything was neat and in its place. She kicked off her shoes, sat on her bed and rubbed the top of her left foot where a strap had been digging unpleasantly into the flesh. She looked at the connecting door, which led to the room where, she hoped, Zoë would by now be sleeping.

Now she decided was the time to begin reading Great Expectations. She took from her suitcase the copy she had recently bought and began to read the first chapter.

The dramatic scene on page 2 and the line:

"O! Don't cut my throat, sir," I pleaded in terror. *"Pray don't do it, sir."* recalled to her some of her own writing, and she pulled out the manuscript of her play and started to make annotations and amendments. But after a while, she suddenly realised how tired she was. She yawned and decided that it was time for bed.

A muffled thud from the next room gave her a sudden jolt. She knocked at the connecting door, but there was no answer, and after knocking a second time but still receiving no response, she opened the door and went into Zoë's room.

The dim light from her own room showed a dark shape on the bed, and she stood still for a moment, expecting to hear the sound of her new friend breathing as she slept. But there was no sound. Alice moved softly forward and then suddenly cried out in pain, for she had stepped on something hard. She sat down on the carpet and rubbed her foot again. There was still no sound from Zoë, and this surprised and alarmed Alice who went over to the bed, loudly whispering Zoë's name. Once by the bed, she bent down over it, fumbled for the switch on the bedside lamp and turned it on.

She now saw that some of the bedclothes had been tossed onto the floor by the window, and various items lay scattered on the floor. The bed was empty except for the pillows which lay on it in such a way as to make her believe Zoë had been there. Zoë herself was nowhere to be seen.

"I wonder what I stepped on," she thought. On turning towards the door and looking down, she saw a large brass coat button on the carpet. This provided the answer to her question, but not to the real puzzle, which was the whereabouts of Zoë.

Alice was not innately a brave person, but she had been thought particularly bright when she was at school. Her mind was now working like clockwork, and she found, to her own amazement, a desire to fight. She decided to go back to her room, put her shoes on, and then start investigating. She did so, and then ventured out into the corridor.

With all that had been going on, Alice had completely lost track of the time, and the corridor was too dimly lit to make it out from her wristwatch. Logic might have sent her back into her room to look at her watch by the light there, but she was not thinking logically at that moment, and instead, she turned her arm this way and that in an attempt to catch the light. She was eventually rewarded by finding that it was nearly ten minutes past one.

All was silent. Where had whoever-it-was taken Zoë? That was the question. Alice forced her mind to work. Might they have used the lift? No, for that would need a lift operator. Down the stairs? No, for that meant the abductor might have met other people. Into another nearby room? No, for the other rooms on the floor were all occupied, as far as she knew. Up to the floor above, or to the roof? Perhaps. Alice decided to explore the third floor first. Her room was near the end of a corridor, so she began to walk past Zoë's door and towards the lifts. She continued on, following the corridor as it turned round a corner, and then another, and another still. All was quiet, all was dim. A little gust of cool air blew in from an open window high up on one wall where the corridor made yet another turn. The way then forked into two; Alice kept to the left. By now she was thoroughly disorientated. She had been counting the room numbers, but they no longer seemed to make sense.

"This place is simply enormous," she thought. From inside one of the rooms she passed, she could hear sounds of deep snoring. "At least someone's having a good time," she muttered out loud.

A small door with the word "CLEANER" painted onto it was at the end of this left corridor. Alice tried to open it, but it was locked. She turned and retraced her steps till she came to the place where the corridor had forked and decided to explore the right-hand passage. This led, most unexpectedly, down a slight incline, then down some steps to a brown door with a glass panel. Beyond the door was a large reception room in a state of some disrepair. Not a sound could be heard. It was as if she was deep within the heart of the hotel, inside a muffled space with a strange atmosphere in which time itself seemed to stand still. She found a light switch and flicked it down. Two unshaded light bulbs began to glow in the ceiling high above. She looked at her watch; it was half past one.

On the floor at the far end was a large chandelier, not very well covered with a sheet.

The room was thickly carpeted with a patterned carpet with a snake-like motif that almost reminded her of something, but she couldn't remember what. She walked to the other end of the room and to another door at the far end. As she moved silently over the dusty deep-pile carpet, she turned her head to the left and noticed in the orangey light a large, ornamental, marble fireplace with a hearth surrounded by padded leather benches. Above the mantlepiece was a large portrait in oils of a bald-headed man with an impressive beard and moustache. It was a fleeting glance, and there was no time to stop and examine the painting, but something about it troubled her, though she could not think what it was.

Once through the door at the end of the room, she found herself in a part of the hotel that was evidently not often visited. That it was dirty could be seen by the dim lights she had turned on in the room behind her. But she could also see that the dusty wooden floor, which stretched for a few feet ahead before another carpet began, had signs of someone passing along it. Heart in mouth, she began to make her way along this corridor.

Alice had always dreamed of romantic, Gothic adventure, but now that she seemed to be caught up in a real one, she felt a great amount of trepidation as she left the great hall and trod silently along the dusty corridor that lay beyond. She turned momentarily to look behind her. Had there been a small sound, as though someone or something had scuttled away into a dark corner? Should she retrace her steps and head back to safety? But what safety was there in going back if, as was entirely plausible, some danger lurked behind?

By this time, in any case, she felt as if she was lost—deep in a maze of corridors, with no certainty that she would be able to find her way back. An old wooden chair lay in pieces where the corridor became carpeted again. She bent down and picked up one of the legs, and then, holding it in her right hand, brandishing it before her like a truncheon, she continued on her path. It was impossible to predict where this might end, though she felt sure there was a great mystery ready to be solved, a mystery that involved Zoë's disappearance. She thought of all the great heroes and heroines in the books she had read, but her mind kept wandering back to the play she herself was writing. Suppose there was some dastardly villain waiting to seize her, to carry her off, too. It was too frightening to think of, and yet, think of it she did. And poor Zoë! What had become of her?

There were doors lining both sides of the corridor; Alice tried several of them, but all were locked. The passage then turned to the right and, after a few feet, came to an abrupt dead end. A large ottoman had been placed against the end wall. Alice bent down to open it but was disappointed to find it empty. "Pity," she thought, "just the place to hide a body!" And then she realised that she fully expected to find that Zoë really had been murdered this time. She wheeled round, for there was a distinct tapping sound behind her—but there was nothing to be seen. Gingerly, she began to retrace her steps and had not gone very far, when she noticed that to the right was an opening in the wall about two feet wide, and that some stairs led upwards. Once she had walked up four stairs, she found that it curved round and then began a spiral ascent to higher regions, though ever gloomier as she climbed.

When she finally reached the top, she discovered that she was at one end of a high gantry that stretched over an open space that lay beneath her to her left. A soft green light seemed to emanate from somewhere. As she moved forward, she held onto the iron rail that ran alongside. When she had nearly reached the far side, a draft of warm air swelled from the space below, giving her a sudden surge of adrenaline and a sharp ache in the pit of her stomach. The shock made her drop the chair leg which she had been holding. It fell onto the gantry floor, and then rolled over the edge into the void, landing on the floor beneath with a sharp report. She steeled herself to look out and down, and she saw that below her lay a large auditorium with raked seating covered in dust sheets.

"What is this place?" she thought.

At that moment, the gantry juddered. This time there was no mistake. Someone was following her. In an instant, she was through the door at the far end and making a descent of the spiral staircase beyond. Her shoes clattered as she went, but she did not care, or rather, was glad of the noise, hoping that someone below might be roused and come to investigate. She could hear someone above stepping onto the stairs and beginning to come down them. Below her, at last, was a closed door. If only it was not locked!

It wasn't. In an instant, she was through, then she closed it and, on seeing a key in the lock, turned it to keep her pursuer shut in. Her heart pounded with panic, but she was too out of breath to move straight away. Suddenly, the door handle rattled. Then, just as suddenly, the noise stopped. Alice could hear footsteps on the other side of the door retreating back up the spiral staircase. She turned away from the door and, with face set hard, began the next stage of her exploration of this strangest of hotels.

CHAPTER FOURTEEN

Sunday.

The morning found Mr and Mrs Giddins in a state of great anxiety. Zoë's absence from the house had not been noticed till very late on Saturday evening. Frantic telephone calls to friends had proved fruitless, and a phone call to the police had proved most unsatisfactory. Therefore, they did not know whether to be pleased or worried when, at ten o'clock, Detective Inspector Jack Jackson was shown into the breakfast room.

It was, however, a social call, for Jack Jackson had no knowledge of recent events and had called round to see his old friend, for Mr Giddins and he had been at school together. He saw the worried look on the faces before him and was quickly apprised of the situation.

"Now," he stated in the reassuring voice he had schooled himself to use in these circumstances, "you had both better stay here in case she comes back. Just leave everything to me, and I'll soon find out what has happened. Chances are it's all a misunderstanding, and she's round at a friend's house. Spent the night there, no doubt. It's amazing how thoughtless some young people can be. Gallivanting off somewhere without leaving a word for their nearest and dearest. I see it all the time."

And Jack Jackson, who had really wanted to ask his friend for some financial advice, left the house and rode off on his bicycle, heading to the police station. It was a hard ride uphill, and under normal circumstances, he would have phoned from the Giddins house and called a car out, but something about the story he had been told worried him, and he had not wanted to convey that worry to his friends unnecessarily.

"Suppose I'm wrong," he thought, "I wouldn't like to make things worse, and yet..."

And just what was it that troubled him? It was this: the previous afternoon he had seen Zoë leaving the camera shop, and then walk in the direction that would take her past the bandstand on the sea front near the Hotel Splendide. He braked as this fact penetrated further into his brain, and he decided that he would ride straight over to the bandstand and see if he could find anything out of the ordinary there. Changing direction, therefore, he began to ride downhill.

The morning of Sunday the 4th of October was very windy, and chilly gusts swept around corners, blowing hats from heads, while above, the lowering sky grew steadily darker. Jack Jackson clutched at his trilby and tucked it under his left arm, riding with his elbow pressed tightly to his side so that he would not drop it. "Should've worn something warmer," he thought.

Rain started to fall, not heavy rain, but sharp, needle-like drops that stung the face. With red ears and cheeks, he pedalled on. By the time he was passing the hotel, the heavens had really opened and it was bucketing down. His eyes were half-closed as he rode, and the streets were all but deserted. A young couple holding one small umbrella between them hurried by.

"It's no use, I'll have to stop."

Jack Jackson thrust the bicycle against a hedge and ran into the hotel, dripping water all over the carpet as he entered. He wiped the water from his face and head with the palms of both hands, dropping his hat on the floor as he did so. The doorman who usually stood outside, but who had now stationed himself by the reception desk, bent down and picked it up for him.

All was quiet in the foyer; an air of Sunday morning calm pervaded the place, and the clattering of the rain outside could not be heard. As he walked further into the hotel, the warm air gave Jack Jackson a feeling of great comfort, as if a blanket had been wrapped around him.

A large jardiniere with a beautiful gardenia tree stood against the wall opposite the hotel manager's office, and he stopped by it for a moment, enjoying the scent and exquisite beauty of the white flowers. All thoughts of his mission were, for the moment, wiped from his mind; he closed his eyes and rocked back on his heels wishing that he were in the south of France, soaking up some warm sunshine with a glass of wine at his elbow.

On opening his eyes, he found that Ralph Horniman was standing in front of him, looking at him in a rather quizzical fashion.

"Hello, Jack, what brings you here today?"

"I came in to get out of the rain, actually, and it's freezing out there," replied Jack.

"Come on," said Horniman with a smile, "we can get some tea sent to us in the lounge." He murmured something to a page, who had just appeared with an armful of newspapers, and guided his friend into a private lounge which was not often used, except by those wanting to borrow one of the tatty books on the shelves.

The two men sat opposite each other. Jack knew that he must say something that would come as a shock to Ralph, and he knew that he must say it quickly.

"Your fiancée," he began, "I'm afraid she's disappeared."

Horniman looked shocked.

"Zoë? Why, what could have happened?"

"Actually, that's why I'm out and about this morning, though I was on my way to look around the front, since that's where I think she may have been going. Unless... look here, Ralph, you didn't see her yesterday afternoon, did you? I mean she didn't come here, did she?"

At that moment, a waiter arrived with a pot of tea and a plate of langues de chat biscuits. The two men stopped speaking, and Horniman did not answer until the waiter had left the room.

"I had lunch at her house, but I haven't seen her since then," said Horniman in as convincing a manner as he could manage. "Besides," he continued, "I'm not sure if I should mention this yet as her parents may not know this, but we called our engagement off yesterday."

"Oh! I'm sorry. Any particular reason?"

Horniman's hand wandered to his jacket pocket; the tips of his fingers stroked the necklace that lay inside. He wished that it was Zoë's that lay there, but he knew that it was, of course, Mrs Garthwaite's. Something else was nagging at his mind, though, but he couldn't quite grasp the thought. He knew he was getting himself into a deep tangle of lies, but his recent proposal to Mrs

Garthwaite, however forced that had been, made it necessary to distance himself from Zoë as effectively as possible. His explanation of his rift with her was vague and unconvincing, but Jack Jackson was not one to show confusion about matters of this sort. Years of questioning witnesses and suspects had allowed him to develop an unshakable poker face, while, at the same time, storing all the minutiae of what he had been told in the various compartments of his brain. Indeed, he envisaged his mind as if it were a chest with an infinite number of drawers, all interconnected and cross-referenced.

Something was not right, but he could not yet put his finger on exactly what it was. "But I'll find out," he thought to himself, as, with a smile beneath his sad, wispy moustache, he took a biscuit from the plate before him.

Horniman stood.

"If you'll excuse me for a moment, I just need to make a quick visit." And he left the room. Jack continued to drink tea while he waited for his friend to return.

And this is how things now stand with our assortment of people.

—Jack Llywelyn Jackson is having tea in the hotel's private lounge, while Horniman, with Mrs Garthwaite's necklace in his pocket, has just left the room.

—Euphemia Garthwaite, though not entirely convinced that she has done the right thing, is attending a church service and congratulating herself on having hooked her Ralph. She is now wearing Zoë's necklace believing that it is her own.

—Mary and Andrew, brother and sister (remember them?), have left the hotel for fresh fields.

—Angela and Ben are still operating their lifts (only two are now functioning), but they have fallen out with each other and are no longer engaged. Moreover, Angela is now very disappointed with the pipe dream she had created for herself—a castle in the air with Horniman as King and herself as Goddess Queen of Hearts. Really, she should have known better!

—Lord and Lady Tongue will not receive Alice's letter till tomorrow, and we shall see what their reaction to that missive will be. Will it, indeed, create a reaction in their cranky old hearts worthy of note and enough to affect the telling of this tale?

—Sir Arthur Winsome seems to have disappeared from the scene, though, no doubt, he will try to claim Alice's fortune, for that was a condition of his marrying her.

—We last saw Alice exploring the maze-like passages of the hotel in search of Zoë and discovering that she was being pursued by someone unknown.

—Mr and Mrs Giddins are currently sitting in their lounge on high-backed armchairs. They are staring into space; not a word has passed between them for some time, and, at times, Mrs Giddins cries into her handkerchief. Mr Giddins has wiped away a tear or two when his wife was not looking, but he feels he must stay strong for her. Both are thinking only of their missing daughter.

—And Zoë, what has become of her? Ah! that is the mystery which cannot be told, for no one knows, not yet at least. Well, perhaps someone does, but that person is saying nothing.

CHAPTER FIFTEEN

The weather in October was mild to begin with, but then the nights became bitterly cold. Alice had been wandering the depths of the hotel corridors for some hours and was desperately tired. The upper floors had been well heated; some had been stiflingly hot. For an hour or so, she had seated herself on a cushioned sofa. Tatty and grimy though it had been, she had leant back her head and slipped into an uncomfortable doze. She was awakened by the sound of a door closing somewhere close by. In an instant, she was up and running through long, twisting corridors with doors sometimes on one side, sometimes on the other, all lit by the same flickering electric lights fixed high on the walls, casting shadows of herself that moved eerily before her as she went. There were no windows anywhere; they would have shown her that it was already dawn, and she might have felt reassured had she been able to look out to see where she was. Alice slowed her pace, for up ahead she could see a balustrade, beyond which lay a staircase that led down to floors below. Looking over the top, she saw that there were several flights. Access to each floor was shut off by heavy locked doors. She tried each one as she went; tears of frustration blurred her eyes when she found that none would yield to any attempt to open them.

Eventually, she found her way to a low-ceilinged basement where none of the radiators gave out any heat. It was unbearably cold, and it was only with great determination that she stopped her teeth from chattering. "If only I had pockets," she thought. In the gloomy light she could see the clouds of mist made by her breath. She cupped her hands over her mouth, trying to get some warmth into them.

From behind her came another sound: a jangling noise. Her heart jumped, and with pulse racing and head throbbing, she began to run again. Behind her, the noise seemed to be getting closer. Now it was a kind of clip-clop which echoed her own steps. She turned a corner and hid herself in the dark shadows of a doorway. The sound stopped abruptly. All she could hear was the pounding of her heart thumping painfully away in her chest.

Behind her was a large door, and though every door she had tried in the last few hours had been locked, and though she felt the illogicality of her actions, she turned the doorknob and pushed.

Miraculously, the door opened, and Alice entered a long, carpeted room. She shut the door as quietly as she could behind her. At the far end was a dirty window covered by an equally dirty net curtain with a small area beyond, and a brick wall just visible outside. A ghostly light filtered through the glass. Alice leaned back against the door as she looked around. On one side of the room was another door. Calmer now, and feeling curious, she walked over to it, opened it and entered the next room. It was in darkness, but she felt braver, and she took another step forward.

Suddenly, the room was flooded by a glaring electric light. Immediately, Alice saw something that gave her the shock of her life. Then a great darkness descended as, with one movement, a sack was thrust over her head while she was pushed forward onto the floor.

CHAPTER SIXTEEN

Arthur Winsome rubbed his head. It ached as it had never done before.

"When will I ever learn?" he said to his small companion ruefully.

The other man shook his head.

"You said that already a number of times. Change the tune, why don't you?"

The previous night, the sixth of the honeymoon, after Alice was asleep, Arthur had dressed and left the lodging house. He was in need of a strong drink, and since it was well after closing time, he had driven off to find somewhere such a thing could be found. It was at about ten minutes after midnight, and in a village some distance from Upper Murford, that he parked by a small, dimly lit pub. The front door was shut fast, but the sound of voices from outside of the building encouraged him, and he walked round to a side door where he found two men, one a police constable, each with a pint of beer. They stepped aside to let him enter.

He had no recollection of events after that, merely that he awoke just after noon on Friday to find himself shut in a small police station cell with a loud fellow who wouldn't stop banging on the cell door.

Some time later, the door was opened and unlocked. The doorway was filled with the large body of Sergeant Thomsett, who gazed down at the two reprobates.

"Feeling sorry for yourselves, I suppose, eh?"

"Yes, sir," replied Arthur. His mouth was as dry as leather.

"Drunk and disorderly—it's disgusting! Now, you take my advice, and go home and apologise to your wives. Take a small present, that's what I'd do, anyway."

"My wife!" said Arthur, "good heavens! I'd forgotten."

"Been on a blinder and forgotten your own wife?" chuckled the small man, "that's something I could never do, however hard I tried."

"Something like that," replied Arthur.

The two men were ushered out of the cell. There was some paperwork to complete, some items needed to be returned to each man, and then each went their separate ways. It was raining. Arthur found his car; fortunately, the roof was up so the seats were dry, and he began the return journey to Upper Murford where he had left Alice. He was relieved that he had been able to leave the gaol and his odoriferous cellmate, and now that his head was clearer, the awful fact that Alice had no idea where he was suddenly struck him. The journey took about an hour; there was little traffic, but the way was badly signposted.

Once at Upper Murford, he parked a little way from the B&B and then walked towards the house. The rain had stopped, and the day looked as if it would be fine, though cold and windy.

The landlady was standing on the doorstep talking to her next-door neighbour.

"Such a shame, and she such a polite lady. He upped and left without a word, that's what he did."

"And what did she do?"

"Well, they had already paid for the week, so she..."

At that moment she saw Arthur approaching, or, at least, his head moving above the hedge which separated her front garden from the street.

"Well, young feller, and what have you been getting up to? That's him," she confided to her neighbour, "that's the chap what left his wife to find him gone."

"Don't talk to him, Ada," said her friend, "he doesn't warrant your kind attention."

"Where's my wife, Mrs erm...?" said Arthur, who, by that time, was standing close by on the garden path.

"She's gone, that's where she is, and a good thing too."

"You tell him, Ada," said the neighbour, "that'll teach him a lesson."

"And another thing, sir," said the landlady with heavy sarcasm, "there's payment due for the week. I suppose you haven't the money."

"Why, Ada," said the neighbour in surprise, "you told me..."

"Quiet," said Ada significantly.

Arthur, forgetting that he had already paid, took a ten-shilling note from his wallet and passed it to Ada Stubbings, who, after examining it carefully, tucked it into her sleeve where it took up a nodding acquaintance with the hankie that already lodged there. She winked at her neighbour, who took the hint and remained tight-lipped.

"Your things are in the shed," said Mrs Stubbings, "you can get them yourself, it's just beyond the gate to the back garden."

Arthur turned on his heel and walked away.

"Come inside for some tea, Amaryllis, we can share the profit between us."

"That's very good of you, Ada."

Arthur heard these remarks as he walked through the gate and the ladies walked into the house, but he chose to ignore them, though he understood their meaning.

There was only one possibility, Alice must have gone back to her parents. It was embarrassing, of that there was no possible doubt whatever, but that must be the answer. It did mean that some difficult explanations would be due to the whole family, and not just to Alice, and it was important to keep in the good books of Lord and Lady Tongue in order to be certain that he might be able to obtain control of Alice's money.

The journey back to Mandible Hall was unbearable. There were many interruptions, and Arthur cursed out loud if he needed to slow to a crawl while waiting for a hay wagon to turn aside, or when he made a wrong turn and found himself reversing back up a narrow, winding track through slippery mud, or when the carriageway was blocked by a fallen tree, or a level crossing with a never-ending long, slow train passing before him.

He drove through the night, and it was not until Saturday morning that he finally reached his destination. After ringing the doorbell, he felt the blood rise as he was kept waiting by the ponderous and decrepit Groves. When the front door finally opened, that individual stared down at him from above and peered over his nose. Arthur was almost inclined to forget his troubles and laugh, for a long fringe over Groves' forehead indicated that his wig was on backwards.

"Can I help you, sir?" he said with a sniff. And then, noticing for the first time the dishevelled state of the visitor, added, "The tradesmen's entrance is at the back of the house. I'm sure that something will be left over from breakfast once it is finished if you need some food."

Arthur was hungry, but he was not too pleased at being mistaken for a beggar, and spoke quite sharply, tired though he was. "It's me, Groves, you idiot! Let me in." And he pushed past the servant, who tottered back and sat down suddenly on the wooden settle that had its back to the wall behind the door.

Lord and Lady Tongue were sitting in the breakfast room eating thinly buttered toast and drinking strong black coffee. Arthur suddenly burst in, upsetting the coffeepot onto the tablecloth as he did so, and surprising the cat by almost treading on its tail. The cat left the room in disgust after throwing a reproachful look towards Lord Tongue who did not notice.

"I say, Groves," said the Marquess, "what do you mean by bursting in like that?"

"It's not Groves," said Lady Tongue putting the coffeepot back onto the table mat, "it's Arthur. Good heavens, Arthur, what are you doing here? We thought you were on your honeymoon. And where is Alice?"

This question rather stumped Arthur, as it was exactly the one he was going to ask. Instead of answering immediately, he sat down, pulled the toast rack towards himself and began cramming a slice of toast into his mouth, while speaking and choking at the same time.

At that moment, Groves entered with the post. Lady Tongue took the letters from him and shuffled though them quickly.

"Invitation from the Mayoress, bill, bill...Groves, you know better than to give me bills when I'm having breakfast. Oh! Here's one from Alice!"

Lord Tongue, meanwhile, had put on his glasses and was staring at Arthur.

"Take it easy," he said, "you'll do yourself a mischief."

"Henry, where did you learn that expression," said Lady Tongue. "Do yourself a mischief? Sounds as if you've been talking to Cook. I hope you haven't been indulging yourself in the kitchen!"

"Well, really, Tilda, I can't think what you mean by..."

Arthur interrupted, blowing toast crumbs from his mouth as he spoke.

"What does she say in her letter?"

"Well, let's see, shall we," said Lady Tongue. And she opened the letter and read it out loud.

HOTEL SPLENDIDE
Paunceton-Sur-La-Mer

2nd October

Dear Mother and Father

I hope you are both well and that Father's gout is a little less troublesome. I have some news to you. The simple fact of the matter is that I have gone to the south coast—to Paunceton, in fact. Do you remember those wonderful holidays there? I do.

Anyway, I should say that Arthur is not with me, and I do not expect to see him again. Things have not been quite as I expected, and so I have decided that this would be best. I will write again soon.

Your loving daughter,

Alice

Naturally, her parents had lots of questions for Sir Arthur Winsome.

"Just a misunderstanding, that's all," was the gist of his replies.

Shortly after, Groves was summoned. Lord Tongue rose from his seat and looked at the elderly retainer while polishing his spectacles with a napkin.

"Groves," he said solemnly, "prepare the Sizaire Berwick, we are going on a journey to the south coast."

Groves inclined himself slightly and, with an audible creak, left to attend to Lord Tongue's order. Lady Tongue summoned Clara and told her to pack some things for the journey.

"You know, Arthur," said Lord Tongue, "I was going to suggest your first job when I saw you, but we'll have to put that on hold till we've sorted this out."

Thirty minutes later, the Sizaire Berwick was brought up to the front door. Groves sat in the driver's seat; the rear doors were opened by Clara. Lord and Lady Tongue climbed inside and sat on the old leather seats at the back. The car was shiny and black with a 20hp engine. It had been made in 1913, and the exterior had been kept in pristine condition. Lord Tongue was very proud of it, but Groves had not driven for quite some time, and his attempts at double-declutching always something of a trial, would probably add considerably to their journey time. Clara loaded luggage into the car, and then they were off. Arthur went ahead in his Aston Martin.

Arthur, tired though he was, drove at speed in a southerly direction. He had taken a large apple from a fruit bowl near the front door of Mandible Hall, kept there primarily so that Groves could throw apples at those naughty or insolent local children who had a habit of ringing the doorbell and then running away. Consequently, the apples were not of the best quality. Arthur was hungry. He bit into the apple as he drove and found it unexpectedly hard and sour, but he ate it anyway, and decided to stop at the first or second pub he saw (or at least the third) and have a proper lunch with a glass of cider to wash it down.

The afternoon went somewhat better for him, though the roads were bumpy and sometimes covered in wet mud. But he knew he could not possibly arrive at Paunceton till the following day, and it was with some relief that at about seven o'clock he found himself approaching a small hotel in a village about halfway to his destination. It was fairly dark, so he stopped and booked himself in for the night, continuing his journey after breakfast on Sunday morning. And so it was that he finally arrived at the Hotel Splendide at about half-past-seven on Sunday evening, pulled up outside, sprung out of the Aston Martin, and hurried into the foyer.

Lord and Lady Tongue's journey south was not without incident. In the first place, though the Sizaire Berwick was beautifully clean, it was an elderly vehicle and not without its own personality. It might remind one of a large black coffin on wheels, and perhaps it might have been better had it been consigned to the grave. However much Groves depressed the gas pedal, and despite the size of the engine, the car would not do much more than twenty miles per hour. This particular model had once been famous for its suspension and comfort, but the shock absorbers were now in a dreadful state, and even the slightest bump in the road caused the car to bounce up and down or rock from side to side in a most disconcerting manner.

"Careful, Groves," Lady Tongue called as the car made a loud grinding noise as its driver attempted to change gear. But Groves could not hear her, as not only did the partition between the front seats and rear compartment muffle the sound of her voice, but the noise of the engine was suddenly magnified as Groves tried once more to double-declutch.

Groves brought the car to a standstill by the side of the road, got out and went to look at the engine. They were, to put it bluntly, in the middle of nowhere. He opened one side of the bonnet, removed his cap and scratched his head with the side of his hand. After replacing his cap, he bent over the engine with a determined scowl on his face.

"Well, I dunno," he muttered to himself, "car needs a good old kick if you ask me."

"What are you doing, Groves?" called Lady Tongue, leaning out of her window.

"Fixin' it, y'r Laideeship" he replied hoarsely, reverting unthinkingly to his native Cockney.

Lady Tongue sat back. Groves made a threatening gesture to the engine with his fist, closed the bonnet and clambered back into the car. Surprisingly, it started and began to run smoothly. Lord Tongue awoke from the nap he had been taking all this while.

"Are we there yet?" he asked.

THE SPHERE

AN ILLUSTRATED NEWSPAPER

Price sixpence　　　　　　　　　　　　　　　　November 1st, 1913

SIZAIRE BERWICK STAND 118 The SENSATION of the PARIS SALON

Unanimous Admiration

vide Press:

Motor says:—"We have rarely met with a car possessing such a wealth of detail refinement and showing such care in workmanship and choice of materials." Autocar says:—"In this chassis, original and thoughtful consideration is found at the first glance."

The Standard says:—"It is well thought out, and the dash is a model for the way in which its half-dozen tell-tales and indicators are disposed on it."

The Westminster Gazette says:—"Ultra Smart and imposing appearance."

The Daily mail says:—"One of the best finished chassis in the Show—by this I do not mean polish, but real beautiful finish—there are several instances of clever designing in the chassis."
F.W. Berwick & Co., LTD. 18, Berkeley Street, PICCADILLY, LONDON, W.

CHAPTER SEVENTEEN

The air inside the sack was unbearably close and warm, and Alice felt stifled almost at once through lack of oxygen. She struggled as she felt a rope being wrapped around her, pinning her arms and the sack to her side. In great panic, she tried to scream but could make no sound. The heat was unbearable. Her struggles became weaker as she lost consciousness.

Then, the soft sound above her head of material being roughly torn brought back some level of awareness, and moments later, her face was uncovered enough for her to take some gasping breaths. Someone was staring down at her, but Alice was so intent on recovering her breath that initially she could not see who it was.

A voice spoke:

"The knots are too tight, relax, I'll try to undo them." All was confusion. Alice was desperately impatient to be free from her bonds, but it was half an hour before she was able to feel anything like herself. By then, she had realised who her rescuer was, for it was Zoë.

Zoë too, was herself a prisoner. She had been chained by her left ankle to a large radiator, and a padlock secured the chain.

"What's been going on?" asked Alice. "I saw a body!"

"It was Ralph," gasped Zoë, "he's dead, he's been shot."

"Ralph?"

"Ralph Horniman, my fiancé, well he was, but we broke it off. Everyone will think I did it!"

"And who did?"

"I don't know. I only saw his back. He was wearing one of the hotel uniforms, like lift attendants wear. I think he would have shot me too, but he didn't see me."

"So, who..." said Alice, trying to work things out, though her head still had an unpleasant fuzzy feeling inside, "who brought you here and tied you up?"

"That was Ralph, too." And Zoë began to cry. "He was very angry with me because I wouldn't give him my necklace, and then he wasn't angry about that anymore, and then he found me in the room next to yours and was angry that I was there, and then he made me follow him because he didn't want me to tell my mum and dad what had happened, and he kept lecturing me on and on, and we walked all the way here, there's a hidden passage, I don't know how you got here; it's very complicated, and then he stopped talking and made me walk quietly because he thought we were being followed, and he locked me up here with this chain, and then he went away for ages, and I couldn't get free, then he came back and had only just opened the door when he was shot, and I saw it happen, so I kept very quiet and didn't even scream, and the man with the gun hid somewhere, and then you came in, and just as I was about to warn you, that man put the sack over you, and I stayed in the shadows and hid till he went away."

Zoe's ability to speak at such a fast pace without drawing breath made Alice's head spin, but Zoë was now calmer now.

"Where is the body?" said Alice.

"Over there," said Zoë with a shudder, as she pointed to a shadowy area behind a large chest of drawers. "We need to get away before he comes back, but I can't break this chain."

Alice was nothing if not practical, and from deep within herself she suddenly found that she also had nerves of steel. This was unexpected, and after debating with herself for a moment whether she should look first at Horniman's body, or try to release Zoë, she opted for the latter, and began pulling at the chain.

"It's no use," she said, "I need to find something to use as a lever, then I might be able to pull the radiator away from the wall."

"Ralph has the key in his pocket," said Zoë.

"Well, why didn't you say so?" Alice pursed her lips and then walked over to the chest.

"There's nothing here!" she exclaimed. "He's gone. The body's not here!"

"That's impossible," said Zoë.

"Calm down," said Alice, seeing that Zoë was becoming flustered again, "let's see if we can pull the radiator away from the wall.

It was at that moment that both of them became aware of approaching footsteps.

"We must hide," said Zoë.

But it was too late. The door was pushed open.

"So here you are, Zoë" said Jack Jackson as he looked at the two women standing by the radiator. "I've been looking for you everywhere." He was staring at the chain as he spoke.

"What on earth's been going on? Come on, we'll soon have you out of that."

Brute force was needed, and the three of them struggled for some time before the pipework was damaged enough to separate the chain from the radiator. Zoë was desperate to leave, but Jackson would not agree to leave the scene of the crime until he had examined the room. Alice, of course, had never seen him before, but to Zoë he was an old family friend, and after introducing him to Alice, she started a long, complicated explanation of all that had happened to her. Alice remained silent for the most part, only speaking when Zoë wanted her to confirm a detail or two. Jack Jackson appeared not to be taking too much notice, though in actual fact, as always, he was listening.

"Where did you say the body was?"

"Over there," said Zoë, indicating with her hand.

"And whose body was it?" he asked, though he had already been told.

"It was Ralph," whispered Zoë.

"And did *you* see the body?"

"Yes," said Alice. "Briefly, but I didn't see who it was."

"He was shot, you say. Who shot him?"

"I already told you," said Zoë. "He was wearing a hotel uniform; I didn't see his face."

Alice looked puzzled. Jackson noticed this and sucked at one end of his moustache. "Something troubling you, Miss...er..."

"Winsome," said Alice, "Mrs Winsome." The surname sounded strange to her as she spoke it. She hadn't thought about her husband for some time, and she suddenly wondered where he was and what he might be doing. Quickly dismissing that thought from her mind, she returned to the matter in hand.

"There is someone in the hotel whose behaviour seems a little suspicious."

Jackson stopped examining the room and looked at her.

"And that would be…?"

"Well, I shouldn't like to jump to any conclusions, but one of the lift operators may not be honest, and I happen to know that he had a reason to dislike Mr Horniman."

"Because…?"

"Because he was demoted. His name's Andrew, and his sister Mary was working here too. But I can't think that he would do something like this."

"You'd be surprised," said Jackson. "You would be surprised." And he ushered them from the room. "Once we get back to the foyer, I'll get proper statements from both of you. Then I'll have to interview everyone in the hotel."

CHAPTER EIGHTEEN

How was it that Jack Jackson had appeared at the moment he did? He was last noticed drinking tea in the lounge while awaiting Ralph Horniman's return. He had waited for some minutes before he began to worry. Horniman had not returned, and an irritating, nebulous thought which had been troubling him for days now began to crystallise. Things between Zoë and his friend Ralph were just not right. As a friend of Zoë's parents as well as Ralph Horniman, he had felt himself to be in something of an invidious position when told of the engagement some weeks before. He could not find the words to mention his opinion to the Giddinses, but to Ralph he had voiced some doubts, and had even gone so far as to mention the age difference as a reason to abandon thoughts of marriage.

He liked Ralph, he had known him for nearly eight years, but there was always the air of a wideboy about him, something of the conman. Very likeable and with the gift of the gab, but someone one might not trust to look after his wallet if it was full.

Jackson had left his tea and walked to Ralph's office. The door was unlocked, and upon going inside and turning on the light, he saw at first little to arouse suspicion. The door to the little toilet was ajar, and the window beyond was open. Suddenly feeling the urge, he walked in, relieved himself and was in the process of washing his hands at the small sink, when, looking at his reflection in a small mirror on the wall, he noticed the reflection of a cupboard door just behind him. He turned, hands still wet, and opened the cupboard. Why did he do so? Because there was no towel by the sink to dry his hands, and he thought there might be one in the cupboard. He expected to see some cleaning things inside it, or perhaps office equipment. But he was most surprised to discover that it was not a cupboard at all, but a concealed entrance to a short passage with a spiral staircase leading downwards at the end of it. Curiosity aroused, he felt compelled to see where the stairs led, and so he entered the "cupboard" and began to explore.

And so it was that he had found Alice and Zoë.

Once back in Ralph Horniman's office, Jackson wasted no time but instantly went to the telephone. His first call was to Mr and Mrs Giddins to tell them that he had found their daughter, that they should not worry, and that he would bring her back himself. Immediately afterwards, he called the police station.

"Well," he said when he had finished the call, "I'll take statements from both of you, and then, once assistance has arrived, I'll organise a search of the premises."

They were all hungry, so he walked out into the foyer and ordered some sandwiches.

Upon returning, he went to the desk and began to write in his notebook. He looked up and smiled in what he hoped was a comforting avuncular fashion.

"You first, Mrs Winsome," he said. "Just take your time."

It was now Sunday evening; the moment that Zoë had finished giving her statement there was a knock on the door, and two policemen entered. Detective Inspector Jackson began to give them instructions. Alice stood, distractedly gazing through the office door towards the hotel's main entrance. Jackson noticed this.

"Perhaps," he said, "it would be best if you take Zoë, Miss Giddins, that is," correcting himself since the two constables were present, "somewhere else…" His voice tailed off as he saw that Alice was not listening.

"Is something the matter?" he asked—perhaps not the best question to ask the victim of a violent assault.

Alice was staring with a most startled surprised expression.

"Andrew and Mary," she replied. "They've just walked into the hotel. I thought they would have gone, particularly Andrew, if he shot Mr Horniman."

Jackson motioned to his men.

"Get those two in here now, I want a word with them."

CHAPTER NINETEEN

About an hour after leaving the hotel, Andrew and Mary realised that their departure had been premature. They had walked to the railway station and had bought two tickets to London. But once on the train, they realised that neither of them had come away with the wages owed to them.

"Damn!" said Andrew, "we'll have to go back to that wretched place now."

"Never mind," said Mary, who, if truth be told, was feeling angry with her brother, but even angrier with herself.

"Perhaps we should forget about it," said Andrew.

"Well, I've left all my clothes there and I want to pack. It's all your fault, dragging me away like that without a thought."

"We'll get out the next time the train stops and go back," said Andrew.

But when they got out, they found that there were no more trains back to Paunceton-sur-la-Mer till the following morning, and they had to stay all night lying on wooden benches in a draughty waiting room.

And so it was, on the evening of Sunday 4th October that the twins entered the hotel, only to be faced by a burly policeman who demanded their attendance in Horniman's office.

Inside they found Detective Inspector Jack Jackson, another constable, Alice, and Zoë. A moment later, Mrs Garthwaite arrived. She was wearing Zoë's pearl necklace in the belief that it was her own. Mrs Garthwaite's necklace was in

Mr Horniman's pocket, but Horniman himself was apparently dead, and no one knew where his body was, or how it had disappeared.

Inspector Jackson had been about to say something as Mrs Garthwaite entered the room, but before he could utter a word he was interrupted.

"Just what has been going on in my hotel?" demanded Mrs Garthwaite in rotund tones. "Where is Ralph?"

"It seems that Ralph has been shot," said Jackson. Mrs Garthwaite looked shocked. "Is he hurt?"

"Possibly, but at the moment we don't know where he is."

"Rubbish!" declared Mrs Garthwaite, recovering a little, "he'll be in his bedroom, or, or, or…"

At that moment, she caught sight of Zoë. She was not pleased to see her there.

"What are you doing here, child?" she said in a wheedling voice.

Zoë may have been young, but she was not one to stand for any nonsense from older ladies, however formidable they appeared to be.

"I'm not sure that is any of your concern," she replied pointedly. And the two ladies glared at each other.

"I think you should show some respect," said Mrs Garthwaite.

"Because of your age, you mean?" said Zoë.

Mrs Garthwaite began to redden and puff up with indignation. The others looked on, stifling any amusement they may have felt; the situation was, after all, not funny.

Jack Jackson decided to take control. He looked at Andrew and said in a clear voice: "Now then, young man, it seems that there was an incident in the hotel last night, and you have been implicated. What have you got to say for yourself, eh?"

Andrew immediately thought that Jackson must be referring to the theft of Mrs Garthwaite's pearl necklace. But he felt puzzled, because she seemed to be wearing it.

"I, I, I…"

"I, I, I, doesn't cut it with me," said Jackson.

"Well, if you want to know about the pearls…"

"Quiet, fool," hissed Mary, "he doesn't mean that."

"What is she doing wearing my pearl necklace?" said Zoë suddenly, looking hard at Mrs Garthwaite.

"Your pearls?" said Mrs Garthwaite, "These are mine. I've had them for years." And she reached round behind her neck to undo the clasp. "I know them well, because they have a special… ohh!" And the sentence was left unfinished, because as Mrs Garthwaite looked at the necklace, she realised that it wasn't hers at all.

"I don't understand," she whispered. "What does it mean?" and she sat down on the sofa. Alice, who had remained silent all this time, sat down next to Mrs Garthwaite and put an arm comfortingly round her shoulders.

"All right, young fellow," said Jackson to Andrew, "where's Ralph Horniman?"

"How the devil should I know," said Andrew, "I haven't seen him for hours."

"You have been identified as the person who shot him a few hours ago," asserted Jackson.

"Well, I saw someone in a hotel uniform," said Zoë.

"And I said it might be Andrew," said Alice looking up from where she was seated.

"It's ridiculous," said Mary. "We've been out for hours and hours."

"And who are you?" said Jackson.

"His sister."

Mrs Garthwaite looked up.

"Siblings are not allowed to work in this hotel," she said. "You're both sacked!"

"But why?" asked Alice.

Mrs Garthwaite started a confused explanation of company policy, but Mary interrupted her.

"It makes no difference; we were leaving anyway."

"Oh, yes?" said Jackson, "and just why were you leaving all of a sudden?"

"Wait a moment," said Alice. "I've just had a thought. I think I may have jumped to a wrong conclusion." She looked at Zoë. "You said that someone in a lift uniform shot Ralph Horniman."

"Yes," said Zoë. She pointed at Andrew, "and he took us up in a lift yesterday evening."

"It must have been Ben," said Mary.

"Get him in here," said Jackson to the two constables. "On second thoughts, I'll come with you." And the three policemen left the room.

"We need our wages," said Andrew to Mrs Garthwaite. "We're both owed for at least two weeks' worth."

"You were working under false pretences," said Mrs Garthwaite. "You'll get nothing from me."

Andrew slid his hand into an inside pocket.

"Perhaps this might persuade you otherwise." He took out a small booklet. "Recognise this?"

It was Mrs Garthwaite's journal, the one Andrew had stolen from her room.

"Give that back at once," said Mrs Garthwaite, "that's private."

"Of course, at once," said Andrew handing it to her. "It doesn't matter, because I read it earlier, and I have a very retentive memory. You have been writing some interesting things."

"Yes, well that doesn't matter now, I have it again."

"Let me see," said Andrew, "Thoughts of a Lady on How to Catch a Man."

"And what is that to you?"

"Nothing at all, but you wouldn't want to be made a laughing stock, would you?"

"Young man, I've been a source of merriment for years, don't think I don't know it, but never mind that now, I was a little hasty, I admit. I'll see that you both get paid."

"And I'll take my pearl necklace, if you don't mind," said Zoë.

Mrs Garthwaite handed it to her sorrowfully.

"Where are my pearls, then?" she said.

At that moment, Jackson and the constables returned with Ben in tow.

Jack Jackson was known by his superiors to be unconventional in his methods but was given a certain amount of latitude as he usually got results. His colleagues and juniors regarded him as eccentric. He was known for his lugubriousness and for having no sense of humour.

This would have surprised him had he known of it, but he did not. He kept himself to himself, and never discussed his home life while at work. It would not have surprised his friends to discover that his mind was methodical as well as sharp, though he spoke slowly, as if everything was considered twice before being said. He enjoyed reading and kept his books carefully, after he had finished them, in strict alphabetical order by author, never lending them or giving them away. But despite all this, he did have a penchant for the dramatic; he liked everyone to see him in action, and, therefore, it was with a certain sense of pride that he arrived back in Horniman's office with Ben. He would not usually have quizzed him there and then in front of the others, but in this case, he wanted to see how matters would play out between everyone. He had already drawn certain conclusions from the recent arguments he had just witnessed: Mrs Garthwaite, for example, had more common sense than one might at first sight have credited. She evidently knew a thing or two about his friend Ralph, and he realised that there must be more to 'The Case of the Pearl Necklaces' than he had at first thought.

Ben stood before him. All was silent. Jackson looked at Ben while Ben did his best not to make eye contact.

"Before I ask you what you know about this," said Jack Jackson, "is there anything you would like to say?"

"I don't know what you mean," answered Ben nervously. "You haven't told me yet what all this is about."

"Your employer, Mr Horniman," said Jackson carefully, "just where would you say one might find him, that is, if one wanted to find him?"

"How the blazes should I know?" said Ben.

"Now, now, don't let's be getting in a frazzle. It has been suggested that you might have been the last person to see him..." Jackson paused for a moment, and then added, "alive!"

Mrs Garthwaite gasped; this was the first time she had heard that Ralph might be dead.

"Why did you do it, Ben," she said, "was it out of jealousy over me?

"I didn't do anything," said Ben with a note of desperation.

"Come on," said Jackson, "you know what this is about. You were seen with a gun aimed at him, and the gun went off, and he fell. Now, it wasn't self-defence, so that seems to leave only one possibility."

Ben looked around the room at the others. Perhaps he hoped for encouragement, but none was forthcoming.

"I want to see Angela," he said weakly.

Angela was at that moment outside the office, with her head pressed up against the door, trying to hear everything that was said. Her natural curiosity had caused her to follow Ben as he had been led away. Although she had now disengaged herself from him, she did somehow feel responsible for his behaviour, so she opened the door and went in.

"It's all right, I'm here," she said.

Ben looked at her mistily. She walked over to Jackson,

"I expect it was all my fault really. He thought there was something between Mr H and me, but there wasn't really, not much," she lied.

"You two," said Jackson to the constables, "stand outside the door and see that no one else is loitering with intent to eavesdrop."

The men left.

"Out with it," said Jackson to Ben.

Then came the strangest confession that Jackson had ever heard. Ben spoke in a hollow voice,

"I don't know really if I've done anything wrong or not. It all started yesterday evening when Mr Horniman came to me with a very strange request. He wanted me to act out a little scene for him. He said he would pay me a hundred pounds. I was to take his gun and follow him and then, when he gave the signal, I was to shoot him. It was quite a long way round the back of the hotel through the passages that lead up to the old monastery. After a while, we stopped, then he walked on a few paces and gave the signal to shoot, so I did, and he fell."

"Oh..." said everyone else.

Alice, meanwhile, was wondering if she should mention that Ben had nearly smothered her with a sack, but just as she started to speak, she was interrupted.

"Now I'm arresting you..." began Detective Inspector Jack Jackson.

"It's all right," said Ben, "really it is. He's still alive. I didn't point the gun at him, I only fired it once. Look, here it is." And he took a gun out of his pocket and held it out.

Everyone except Jackson cowered away.

"It's not loaded," said Ben.

Jackson took the gun from Ben using a handkerchief so as to avoid touching it. Then he checked that it was not loaded, wrapped it up and put it into his own pocket.

"Where, then, is Ralph Horniman?" he demanded.

"I really don't know," said Ben. "My instructions were to leave him and go back to the lifts. But he must be somewhere in the hotel."

And so, a search for Ralph Horniman was instigated while Ben remained in the custody of the constables, just in case it should prove that the hotel manager was actually dead.

CHAPTER TWENTY

It was just as the search was about to start that Sir Arthur Winsome entered the hotel.

The first person he saw was Alice, who emerged from Horniman's office with the others. Her first thought was to go to the reception desk to find out if there had been any messages for her from her parents. She pulled up abruptly when she saw her husband, and the two of them faced each other, both momentarily lost for words.

Alice drew herself up to her full height, which was not particularly tall, but which made her seem impressively confident. Arthur swallowed; this was not exactly how he had envisioned finding Alice. He had imagined a scenario in which he might be seen as the gallant rescuer coming to the aid of a tearful and repentant young woman. Instead, he was faced with a hard stare and a challenge. Just as he was about to say something, Alice spoke. Her cheeks began to glow as her voice assumed an unaccustomed depth.

"What are you doing here? How did you find me? And what *are* you doing here?"

"Hello, old thing," he said in reply, trying his best to ignore Alice's manner, "been looking for you all over the place. Tracked you down to this spot, came straight away. Jolly good thing too, I should think. How did you finish up in a dingy hole like this?"

The last remark was hardly true, as the Hotel Splendide, though slightly decaying, was still an impressive-looking place, although perhaps he was referring to the whole town rather than the hotel. Also, and this point did not escape Alice, bearing in mind the wretched accommodation he had booked for their honeymoon, he was hardly qualified to criticise.

In any case, Alice was not to be mollified. By now, though, there were a number of hotel guests in the foyer, and she was not one to make a scene in public.

"I really don't know how you have the nerve to face me," she whispered loudly through gritted teeth. "I know exactly why you came here, it was for your own selfish sake, not mine."

"Quiet down a bit," said Arthur, suddenly serious, leading her to the far side of the aspidistra by the reception desk. "You knew that the arrangement was purely financial. I could've had my pick."

"Then why didn't you?"

Arthur saw his opportunity slipping away from him. His mind worked quickly; if there should be a divorce, how much money would come his way? He needed money, and he needed it now! Why, oh why had he let those Tongues persuade him that this was a good idea. He had no intention of following Lord Tongue's suggestion that he become a burglar in order to give amusement, but he did need money, at that precise moment, as his most recent scheme, which involved swindling a casino in Monte, had failed miserably, leaving him in debt to a couple of hard-nosed characters who expected payment. In this respect, he was not unlike Ralph Horniman.

Arthur did not answer Alice immediately, instead he tried to formulate the most effective reply. Alice, on the other hand, was developing a steely personality not unlike that of her mother. She glared at Arthur, and then said in with a voice laden with contempt,

"I don't want anything to do with you. As far as I'm concerned, it's over between us."

Arthur lost his composure for a moment.

"Going back to mother?" he scoffed.

That finished it. Any hope he had of effecting a reconciliation was over. Alice turned on her heel and walked away from Arthur without glancing back until she reached the staircase beyond the lifts. He followed part of the way, and then stood still as she turned.

"Go away, Arthur!" she said. And she walked up the stairs.

Arthur knew when he was beaten; now was not the time to chase after her. He left the hotel and drove away.

CHAPTER TWENTY-ONE

Mrs Garthwaite suddenly came into her own. She took a pass key from the office, and then assembled a small team of hotel employees in the mezzanine bar, and, making certain that no services would be interrupted, directed them to search every available room for Ralph Horniman.

Alice arrived there just in time to see them disperse to follow their instructions. She went over to Mrs Garthwaite.

"Where did Zoë go?" she asked.

"She went home, of course, nothing else for her to do. That detective man is taking her. I expect he'll be back soon. Ben's still being guarded in the office by the policemen."

"Where do you think Mr Horniman's gone? Perhaps he left the hotel."

"I doubt it," said Mrs Garthwaite, "he'll be holed up here somewhere, there are plenty of places to hide; you've seen some of them. I've sent people to look everywhere they can. We should search his room, though. I left that joy for myself. That's the one place he won't be. It's on the 5th floor, a kind of penthouse suite."

They were walking up the stairs as they spoke. Alice really felt in need of a wash and change of clothes.

"Do you think we could stop off at my room for a few minutes? I really need to change into something else."

"I suppose so, dear, as long as you don't take too long."

While Alice had a shower, Mrs Garthwaite sat on an armchair by the bed. On the dressing table close by was Alice's copy of *Great Expectations*.

"Hmph, Dickens!" she thought, "never had any time for him."

She picked the book up and flicked through the pages for a few seconds, and then noticed another book on the table. She put *Great Expectations* down and picked up what appeared to be a diary. From the bathroom she could hear the shower cascading water into the bathtub. Of course, there were no diary entries in the book, for it was the text of Alice's play, *Mandeville's Mind*. Alice's handwriting was beautiful, a pleasure to read.

Mrs Garthwaite was still reading when Alice emerged from the bathroom wearing a bathrobe.

"I'll be dressed in a jiffy," said Alice. "What are you reading?"

"Did you write this?" said Mrs Garthwaite. "It's very good. An excellent part for the heroine."

Alice put her glasses on so that she could see more clearly what Mrs Garthwaite was looking at. She felt no resentment at invaded privacy, feeling rather flattered instead.

"Yes, I've been writing for a while. It's nearly finished. I don't really know why I wrote it. Just for myself—to pass the time really."

"I've been looking for a play like this," said Mrs Garthwaite, "let's talk more about it later."

Alice nodded. Mrs Garthwaite put the book into her own handbag, and Alice dressed quickly. They then left the room and walked up to the 5th floor.

Both ladies felt rather nervous as Mrs Garthwaite took the pass key and opened the door to Horniman's penthouse suite. Beyond, all lay in darkness; the curtains were closed. Mrs Garthwaite felt around the wall just inside the door till she found the light switch and flicked it on. The interior of the suite had a most unusual appearance.

"This is not what I expected to see," remarked Mrs Garthwaite.

"How unusual," said Alice.

On the walls of the room hung a number of beautiful works of art.

Several questions popped into Mrs Garthwaite's head. Alice, of course, not knowing Horniman, had no idea what to expect, though it did strike her as odd that the paintings should be there.

Alice was the first to speak,

"Are these all originals, do you think? They're splendid."

"Question is," replied Mrs Garthwaite, "what are these doing here? And also," she continued, "if Ralph was in financial difficulties, and I have every reason to think that he was, why didn't he sell these?"

"Dishonestly acquired?" said Alice.

"Come on," said Mrs Garthwaite, "let's look around."

Horniman certainly had exquisite taste. Everything was immaculate. Aside from the paintings on the wall, there were some beautiful porcelain vases in a glass cabinet, and a shelf of beautiful leather-bound books. A coffee table stood on a silken Turkish rug, and upon it, a large volume had been left open at a page with colour illustrations of birds.

Alice went to the large curtain at one side of the room and drew it back to reveal a picture window with a view of the sea and Muffet Island. The rain had stopped some hours before, and all looked calm in the light of a half-moon.

"I stood on the roof above this position," she said. "It's a lovely view."

To one side of the window was a large telescope on a tripod. Mrs Garthwaite stood behind and looked through it towards the island.

"Strange," she observed, "there's a boat out there. Someone's trying to get onto the island. They'll find it hard, it's practically impossible to land there, even though the sea is comparatively calm at the moment."

"You don't suppose Mr Horniman could be on it, do you?"

"I can't tell who's on board; it's too far out. But if he is it's too late to worry about that. Let's carry on looking around."

Alice was looking at the paintings again.

"Some of these are beautiful. This is a Constable and that one looks like Turner."

"There's certainly more to this than meets the eye," said Mrs Garthwaite. "Come on, let's see what else we can find." And they continued examining the room.

A bureau of magnificent proportions was empty.

"How on earth did he get this up here?" said Alice.

"Without being seen, you mean?"

"Yes, that, but also, I don't know how they got it through the door."

"Oh, removals men are wonderful," said Mrs Garthwaite.

The bathroom had marble floor and walls but little else to offer. They moved to the bedroom. This was more plainly laid out, though there was another landscape on the wall opposite the bed. A pair of large oak double wardrobes looked promising. The first contained several suits of the best quality.

"All unworn," said Mrs Garthwaite, "what a waste!"

CHAPTER TWENTY-TWO

Alice opened the second wardrobe.
There, at the bottom, under a blanket, was...

CHAPTER TWENTY-THREE

...Ralph Horniman!

CHAPTER TWENTY-FOUR

Horniman peered up at Alice. Mrs Garthwaite's face appeared over Alice's shoulder.

"Ralph!" she exclaimed. "What on earth are you doing there? Hiding, no doubt, like a silly schoolboy. It's disgraceful."

"Help me up out of this," gasped Horniman in a restricted-sounding voice. "I'm stuck!"

With some heaving, he was finally released from his uncomfortable position. He stood before Mrs Garthwaite and Alice with hanging head.

"Ow!" he said, "Pins and needles!" And he began to rub his left arm, which tingled painfully. He was in his shirt sleeves and trouserless, and this humiliating appearance did nothing to appease Mrs Garthwaite.

However, he pulled himself together quickly and tried to look authoritative.

"You're sacked!" said Mrs Garthwaite, "I expect you to be gone by the end of the day."

And she turned on her heel and walked out of the room. Alice followed her, turning to look over her shoulder at Horniman when she reached the door.

Horniman shrugged and smiled wanly.

"I think she likes you," said Alice.

Once on the ground floor and with Jack Jackson, Mrs Garthwaite and Alice explained what and whom they had found in the penthouse apartment.

"All those magnificent paintings," said Alice, "do you think they're stolen?"

Jackson opened his mouth to answer, but at that moment, Horniman himself appeared at the top of the stairs leading to the foyer.

"At least we can let that fellow go since Ralph is obviously not dead," said Jackson aside to Alice as he began to walk towards Ralph.

Horniman had reached the foot of the stairs.

"Hello, Jack," he said. "Nice to see you..." His voice trailed off when he saw Mrs Garthwaite approaching with Alice.

"Paintings, Ralph," said Mrs Garthwaite. "What were you thinking of?"

"You like those? Rather embarrassing, really."

"Yes, but how did they get there?" said Alice.

Jackson felt the need to be leading the questioning, and before anyone could say anything else, he spoke.

"I'm sure there's a reasonable explanation," he said, looking hard at his friend while raising an eyebrow.

"Yes," said Horniman, "I suppose I'm rather glad that it's out in the open now. You see, I hate criticism. I would keep them hidden away, but I rather like looking at them—a bit proud of them really. No one else was supposed to see..."

"What do you mean?" said Mrs Garthwaite. "Who do they belong to?"

"I think I understand," said Alice.

Mrs Garthwaite and Jack Jackson looked at her.

"You painted them yourself, didn't you?"

"They're really nothing special," said Horniman.

"Ralph, how marvellous!" said Mrs Garthwaite. "I've misjudged you... though, there's still the matter of all those bills..."

Jackson interrupted,

"Well, I'll just let you get on with it shall I? Better see to the release of that chap in the office." And he left them to continue their conversation. Shortly after, Ben appeared, a little flustered, but much happier. He walked back to his lift and began operating it as before. Angela smiled at him from her own lift, but he chose to ignore her.

The search for Horniman had come to an end. All returned to their usual occupations. Mrs Garthwaite and Horniman walked together into the office and shut the door. Alice turned towards the main entrance feeling that all must be right with the world. Would that all was as easy as that, but this was by no means the end of the matter.

At that moment, Lord and Lady Tongue arrived, followed by Groves who was carrying Lady Tongue's suitcase. The meeting was affectionate; Alice was delighted to see them. They could see that something had happened to change her, for she was no longer the shy but sulky person she had been before, but a confident and charming young woman.

Over tea in the lounge, she told them about her separation from Arthur.

"I'm not a bit surprised," said Lady Tongue, "he seemed most unreliable."

"Pity," drawled Lord Tongue, "I was hoping for some rare adventures."

"Nonsense, Reginald, the child's happiness is far more important."

In Horniman's office, Mrs Garthwaite and Ralph Horniman were arriving at an understanding. Ralph was not particularly happy about it, but he hid his true feelings with a smile. It had been agreed that his debts would be paid, that money missing from the accounts would be forgotten, and all his misdemeanours forgiven. Mrs Garthwaite had seemingly dismissed from her mind thoughts of the condition that ex-receptionist Philippa was in, or perhaps she had forgotten about it. After all, if she had remembered, Ralph might not have been so easily forgiven.

However, all this came at a price. And that price was Marriage... with a capital M.

"I think it would be best," said Mrs Garthwaite, "if I took over management of my hotel myself, don't you?"

Ralph was about to argue, but she silenced him by placing her index finger over his mouth.

"Naughty boy," she said kittenishly, "you can paint your daubs freely now, and we can hang them in every room. That will make a nice change from those dismal prints of old London, won't it?"

Lord Tongue sipped pink lemonade from a tall glass.

"Insipid stuff, this," he said, pulling a face.

"Nothing stronger for you, Doctor's orders," replied his wife as she raised a small brandy to her lips.

"Really, m'dear, there's no need to be so literal, after all, we're on holiday."

Alice smiled at them. Supper finished; they had seated themselves in one of the hotel's comfortable lounges. Lord Tongue had asked for a suite of rooms to be prepared for them on the second floor. He intended, now that they had arrived, to take it easy for a few days. Alice's things were transferred to the suite so that all three of them could spend their time together. And Alice felt more comfortable in her mind. She settled back in an armchair with a glass of Adam's ale on the low table between her and her parents.

"You could try some of this, father. It's very good for you."

"Ah, yes, your favourite—'A spring, that never yet grew stale—Such virtue lies in—Adam's Ale!' not for me, Alice, not for me. I like my waters strong."

Lady Tongue tutted and was about to venture some remark about her husband's propensity to quote forgotten poets, when Mrs Garthwaite walked into the lounge and waved shyly at Alice who signalled that she was welcome. Mrs Garthwaite walked daintily over the thick pile carpet to where the three were sitting. Lord Tongue rose slightly and indicated an armchair. Mrs Garthwaite sat in as genteel a fashion as she could, though the seat of the chair was lower than she would have liked.

"Good evening, all," she said. "I trust you have settled in nicely. I just wanted a quick word with your daughter regarding her play."

"Oh, yes," said Alice turning a little pink, "did it make you smile?"

"I thought it was very enjoyable, and I wondered..."

"I noticed a sort of auditorium in the hotel," said Alice.

"Yes," said Mrs Garthwaite. "It would be perfect. Unused for some time, I'm afraid, but I've always wanted to dip my toe, so to speak, in theatricals. I have thought of a perfect way to cast your main characters."

Mrs Garthwaite naturally intended that the lead role of Julia, the heroine, should be assumed by herself. Alice, of course, had other ideas, having always imagined the part as a young ingenue. She herself, despite her inner cravings to play the part, had no actual desire to appear on stage in front of people. When Mrs Garthwaite began to mention how her casting would work, Alice, being quite intuitive, realised what she was intending before she actually uttered the words. Before they could be spoken, therefore, Alice interrupted.

"Of course," she said, "the role of Julia needs to be played by someone in her late teens, or early twenties at the oldest."

"You think so, dear," said Mrs Garthwaite, trying to hide her disappointment. "Well, perhaps you're right. We should discuss this more another time, perhaps tomorrow morning."

Alice agreed to this, and Mrs Garthwaite left.

All this while, Lord and Lady Tongue had remained silent.

"I had no idea you were writing such a thing," said Lady Tongue.

"Reminds me of that time when I wrote a little trifle for you to appear in, Matilda," said Lord Tongue.

"Yes, well, let's not bring that farrago up now," said his wife. "Anyway, I think it's time to climb the wooden hill."

"Except that it's carpeted," said Lord Tongue.

"Except that we can use the lift," said Alice.

And the three of them retired to their suite.

CHAPTER TWENTY-FIVE

Tuesday. The Giddinses were at home, all four of them: Mr and Mrs Giddins, Zoë, and Zoë's elder brother, Stephen. We met Stephen once before, perhaps you remember, it was way, way back in Chapter Six, when he and Ralph Horniman grunted at each other as they passed on the Giddins's doorstep.

Stephen Giddins did not live with his parents. He had his own place, a townhouse on the far side of the town, and an apartment in London from where he conducted his business. Thirty years old, always sharply dressed, he had been given a start in life by his father who had loaned him a considerable sum of money—a sum which he had paid back quickly. Stephen had a keen eye for a good business deal. His method, as he told everyone: import cheap, sell dear. Although he could be charming when he wanted to be, to his business associates he was a hard man with a ruthless streak that would have surprised his parents and sister.

That morning, he had popped round for breakfast with the "folks", leaving his house in time to arrive shortly before 8 am.

Breakfast commenced.

"My man's calling for me at about 9," said Stephen, waving a fork with a piece of sausage on it. "Got a difficult matter to clear up, nothing too serious, but I like to be on top of these things, you know." And he put the sausage into his mouth.

"Everything going well, Stephen?" asked his mother.

"Oh, yes," came the reply through a mouthful of sausage, "you know me."

"Zoë's broken her engagement with Ralph," said Mr Giddins.

"Has she though?" said Stephen with a rather odd smile, "good for you, Zoë, I never did like him."

Zoe did not quite know how to answer this. She had just made up her mind to say something disagreeable to her brother when there was a knock at the door.

"That'll be for me," said Stephen, and he left to deal with his 'difficult matter'.

"Always so busy!" said his mother once he had gone.

CHAPTER TWENTY-SIX

Andrew and Mary were back at their usual positions, operating lifts. Ben and Angela likewise. Angela would have liked to reconcile with Ben, but Ben had no intention of forgiving her for treating him so badly.

Tuesday morning was a busy one. Nevertheless, at nine-thirty, all four were summoned into the Hotel Management Office—no longer deemed to be Horniman's since Mrs Garthwaite had taken charge. While they were absent from their posts, only one lift was in operation, and that by the hotel doorman, who had huffed and puffed resentfully when he was told what was expected of him.

"I dunno," he told his friend, the publican at his favourite watering hole, that evening. "The comings and goings at that hotel—it's enough to drive one barmy!"

Alice was in the office when the four lift operators arrived and so was Mr Horniman, though not in his usual place behind the desk, but in the background near the window. Mrs Garthwaite was seated at the desk, playing idly with her pearl necklace, recently recovered from her Ralphie.

"Ladies and gentlemen," began Mrs Garthwaite in a condescending manner intended to be friendly, "we have a task to perform, namely this." And she waved Alice's play in her left hand. "It's a wonderful play written by Mrs Winsome. We are having copies made, they will be ready by the evening, and then we shall perform it at the end of the week, and I expect all of you to take part." She looked at Mary. "I have a delightful task for you, Mary. You are to play the young lady, the leading role!"

Mary, having last appeared on stage playing her namesake in a school nativity play at the age of five, was slightly alarmed by this information, though she did feel rather excited.

Ben, however, was not flattered to be told that his part would be that of the elderly retainer, Harewood Ruskin. Andrew was to play the Reverend Anthony Goodpoint, which he thought strange since it meant playing opposite his sister, but this point was waived aside by Mrs Garthwaite, "If the Astaires can do it, so can you." Angela was to play a parlour maid, and the role of Sir Robert Mandeville would be played by Ralph Horniman.

They received their instructions with varying degrees of enthusiasm. Horniman had heard about the arrangements a few times and was now feeling rather bored. He had been given a chance to read the play before it had been sent off to be typed up, and he regarded it as pretty poor, old-fashioned, sentimental stuff. The kind of thing his grandmother might have gone to see, not his kind of thing at all.

"I think I'll just step out for a breath of fresh air," he said.

Mrs Garthwaite looked at him with a toothy smile.

"Yes," she said, "you may do that, but don't be too long."

Horniman left, and the others continued the meeting. Alice was happy to think that something she had created was about to be presented before the public. Her parents had been most encouraging over breakfast.

At eleven, the meeting was finished. Mrs Garthwaite looked perplexed once alone.

"Where did that naughty man go to?" she said, and she left the room to find out. But there was no sign of Ralph Horniman anywhere.

Horniman strolled eastward along the sea front in a direction away from the town with his hands in his pockets, kicking idly at pebbles that lay in his path.

"What to do, what to do," he thought. There were all sorts of possibilities, but none seemed particularly attractive to him. His desire for life, and for good living at that, was as strong as ever. Perhaps it was his experiences in the trenches during the Great War that had made his determination so powerful; he had seen things that many saw, but which no one should have to see. But now he felt deflated. All his energy seemed to have been sapped away. He looked out over the sea, which was grey and nasty. Everything was grey. The sky was grey, his life was grey, even the suit he was wearing was grey; everything about him was grey except for the flower in his buttonhole, a pink anemone. Euphemia had given it to him that morning and pinned it on with an air of great significance.

"I suppose I should think of her as Euphemia, now," he said to himself. "Bit of a mouthful, isn't it? I wonder what's short for Euphemia. It's all Greek to me!" He laughed ruefully at the little joke he had made, for the name Euphemia is Greek in origin, and he knew that, because Mrs Garthwaite, Euphie... no, wait, that can't be right, erm, Phemia, no! Anyway, she had told him it was.

"Pink for love", she had said. What was that all about? He didn't love her, he felt trapped, but his fate seemed unavoidable. He almost preferred Philippa, though her nagging had led him to break all ties, especially when she told him that she was pregnant. (He was not to know that it had been a lie, a ruse to try to get him to marry her.) Anyway, that was all done with, and Philippa had left the town (for good, he hoped).

By now he had walked the best part of a mile out of the town and onto the coastal path that led towards the top of the chalk cliff. A solitary bench seemed an ideal resting point, and he sat on it, not far from the road, facing the sea and Muffet Island. The air was cool, but not unpleasant, the sort of day that happens once after it has stopped raining: a soft day.

Somewhere in the background came the sound of a motor car door being closed. A few moments more passed, then...

"Hello, Ralph," said a voice from behind him, "I've been looking for you." It was a voice he recognised, and not with pleasure!

Ralph Horniman swivelled round on the bench and then stood. It was not pleasant to be brought face to face with the one person he hoped not to have seen again. It was the individual who signed himself "S" at the end of threatening letters.

"You owe me rather a lot of money, Ralph," said S, "and I want to know what you are going to do about it."

"How did you know I was here?"

"I didn't. Just good luck, I suppose."

"You've had someone spy on me."

"Perhaps."

"Anyway, it's done with, everything I owe will be paid later today." Ralph suddenly realised the advantages of an alliance with Mrs Garthwaite, even to the point of marriage.

"Not so fast," said S. There's more than money involved in this, or do you want me to tell your little secret to the police?"

"Blackmail!"

"That's an ugly word. Let's just call it a gentleman's agreement, shall we?"

"I could kill you with my bare hands!" said Horniman, stepping forward.

S raised a hand, and a large man got out of the car parked on the verge.

"Now, now, keep your temper. It sounds as if you have come into some money. Good. That will keep me happy for a while."

Horniman bit his lip; S smiled.

"A good thing you broke off your engagement with my sister," he said.

For S was, perhaps you guessed it, Stephen Giddins.

And only now do we come to the truth of the matter that Ralph Horniman would have liked to keep secret at any cost: the great matter, which he had buried away for over twelve years; the fact that he was not Ralph Horniman at all.

PART 2
THE FLIGHT OF THE TABLOID

CHAPTER ONE

Finding a way onto Muffet Island was extremely problematic. Mrs Garthwaite had noticed a motorboat approaching it, and this was unusual. There were two people on board: an elderly man and a young woman.

They rounded the island to the far side, for there was a spot there at which a landing might occasionally be made.

"Are you all right, miss?" said the man.

"Yes, thank you," came the reply.

A huge wave buffeted the boat at that moment, and it was swept sideways.

"Should've avoided that one, miss."

"Do you think we'll be able to get in?"

"Maybe, maybe not."

But they were close enough to the rugged edge of the island to see that it would be impossible for a safe landing to be made.

"Oh, for goodness' sake!" said the young woman, "I really need to get on the island this evening."

"Watch yourself," said the man as another wave nearly rocked the boat. But this time, he had steered in order to go straight through it.

"It's getting a bit choppy now."

"Just a bit. Look," said the young woman, "there's a way in.

"Too dangerous to chance it," shouted the man through the noise of the motor and the wind, which was now whipping up.

"No, really, look."

And, just briefly, the sight of a pebbly flat place, hardly a beach, could be seen.

"Through that channel there!"

The boat headed in and just made it through without hitting any of the rocks either side.

"I need to be heading back, miss, you're sure you'll be all right?"

"Yes, of course."

"I'll be back the day after tomorrow."

"That's fine, Joe. I've got everything I need."

And the young woman clambered out of the boat, rucksack on her back, and stood in the icy water up to her shins while Joe turned the boat and headed back out.

The wind grew stronger, but after climbing onto the grass meadow at the top of a steep incline, she could see, in the moonlight, that Joe was already well on his way back round the west side of the island from where he would be able to set his course back to the mainland.

Elspeth MacGregor loved Muffet Island. She spent as much time there as she could, sleeping, when she was there, in a rustic stone cottage on the south side of the island. The island itself was a haven for wildlife, and she spent hours lying hidden in long grass looking through binoculars and sketching birds. Thirty years old, independent, comfortable, but often bored, it was her way of escaping from a world of lawyers who were always trying to advise her and who always wanted to know what she was doing.

The following morning, after a breakfast cooked over a fire, in Girl Guide fashion, she assembled everything she needed and walked the short distance to the north side of the island, put a waterproof groundsheet onto the grass, lay down on it, and looked out over the sea toward town through her binoculars. A stiff breeze made her shiver, but she was warmly dressed and ready to spend a few hours relaxing. After all, this would probably be the last opportunity she would have to visit the island until the spring.

An hour or so passed. She took out her sketchbook and opened it. It was only when she sat up that she became aware that she was not alone on the island. She heard the sound of angry voices approaching. Elspeth rolled into the shade of a clump of high bushes to one side of her, hoping that she would not be seen.

Three men appeared over the brow of a mound about fifteen yards away from where she lay. They did not see Elspeth as she lay in the shadows.

The three men could be clearly heard. Elspeth was still holding her sketchbook, and, taking a pencil from her coat pocket, she began to draw them, and also to note down as much as she could of what they were saying.

A large, middle-aged man with a moustache was gesticulating wildly.

"If you want me to give you the stuff, I can't exactly do it while I'm here, can I?"

"We've got something else to do first," said another of the men. "I think you may need a bit of encouragement to give us your full cooperation."

The third man, powerfully built, said nothing for the moment, but looked on meaningfully.

"Look here," began the middle-aged man.

"Do you want a bunch of fives?" said the third man, clenching his fist.

"Not at all, but we're reasonable men."

"Reasonable?" said the second man, "I think the time for reason has passed."

Elspeth became very worried. Something bad was about to happen, and she was powerless to do anything about it. She looked around to think of a solution, but the only thing she could think of was to try a distraction technique.

So, she stood and cleared her throat loudly.

All three men stopped and looked in her direction. For a brief instant they did not see her standing there. She was still in shadow, her clothes were dark, and her dark skin gave further camouflage.

"Who's there?" said the second man. Elspeth stepped forward.

"It's a woman," said the third man.

"Yes, well don't let that bother you," said Elspeth bravely. "I've studied jujutsu, so I can take care of myself."

The second man took a pistol out of his pocket and pointed it at her. "Come here," he said.

And Elspeth, feeling that her desire for solitude was perhaps ill-conceived, walked towards him.

CHAPTER TWO

It was in mid-1917 that Ernest Sallow found it no longer possible to avoid conscription into the army. That he had done so thus far was in no small measure down to a remarkable talent to feign illness. He had managed to defer entry twice, but the third time, all efforts to demonstrate his lack of fitness for active service proved to be in vain.

This was of no little annoyance, for he had been on the verge of a business deal, which was worth a considerable amount of money, and which would have to be abandoned. In all his thirty-three years of life he had never owed so much money, and this would not only have wiped the slate clean but would also have left him with a tidy surplus to invest in another scheme.

On the other hand, his creditors would hardly be able to follow him once he was in the army, so there were compensations—just as long as he could make it obvious that he would best be suited to a nice desk-job in England, and not be sent abroad, for he had no desire to fight.

This wish was not unreasonable, for he was not unintelligent, and he was a quick learner. Furthermore, he knew how to do accounts well (oh, yes, indeed, very well— particularly if figures needed moving around a bit) and could type at speed, though not as fast as his sister.

However, his preference for sitting out the war in a quiet army base, somewhere in Wiltshire perhaps, with plenty of opportunities to meet pretty girls, drink beer and—who knows—to continue business operations, was quickly scuppered. He was disabused in short order, as soon as he arrived for training, by a fearsome sergeant major who put the fear of God into the men.

And so it was that in November, he found himself in the trenches at Cambrai fighting for his very existence. This was not, he reflected at quiet moments (and there were some), how he had planned his life—or his death. In fact, in his mind, he had planned his death. It was to be at an advanced age, in bed, surrounded by loved ones who would mourn for him greatly.

When the battle raged, he kept his head down; when tea was served, he made sure to be ready. Everyone was scared, but some were foolhardy while others were more cautious. At last came the moment when the British Army sent tanks out. The men showed strength, and a great success was achieved with huge rejoicing, only to be followed by the German Army reviving itself and making a tremendous counterattack.

Private Ernest Sallow of the 3rd Corps found himself cut off from his company. He lay hidden behind a tree, watching for a moment when he could rejoin his comrades, but they were moving away, and he knew that soon he would no longer be able to make any attempt to get away.

In desperation he ran and, by some miracle, was not hit by a bullet, though several were shot at him. After an hour, he was completely lost. Over to his right, he could hear the battle raging, but he was disinclined to rejoin it.

"I'll say that I didn't know where they were if they ask," and he continued his flight.

His flight did not last for long. Two days later he was picked up by a platoon from another regiment and returned to the 3rd Corps and thence to a place to be court-martialled for desertion. Being shot was not a fate he was prepared to risk. He and another private, also about to be tried for the same offence, plotted an escape, and in a moment of confusion, escape they did, but at the expense of the life of a soldier set to guard them.

Even Ernest was shocked at the behaviour of his comrade. He had no desire to take a life, but their escape was discovered, and before the alarm could be raised, the soldier was dead. Ernest Sallow was a nasty piece of work; he was lazy, he was a coward, he was a swindler, and now he would be wanted for murder. He muffled up his anger and cursed inwardly at his own folly, though he could not trace its origin: he had been a bad lot for so long. The two men made their escape but went their own ways, hoping nevermore to lay eyes upon each other.

Two years later, he was back in England, though a wanted man. He had reinvented himself, grown a moustache and put on a little weight. He now called himself Ralph Horniman and assumed a mantle of respectability. All would have been fine had this matter not come to the attention, albeit in a rather garbled fashion, of Stephen Giddins.

His wanderings took him to a town in North England where he was unknown, and where he found a job in a hotel. He was lucky; promotion came his way quickly, and he began to save money and to establish an identity. But old habits die hard, and there is no doubt that he began to tire of earning not much more than £2 per week (plus bed and board). This was no life. When working on the reception desk, he found ways to increase his personal takings by taking money that was not his. Dangerous work, and he was nearly found out on three separate occasions. But he knew that if he wanted to prosper, he must change location, and so he forged a reference for himself on the hotel's headed paper and handed in his notice. He had worked there for two years of dullness, talking to dull people about dull things, but he had saved enough to allow himself time to find another position in another town, and so he moved elsewhere.

Ralph Horniman began working at the Hotel Splendide, Paunceton-sur-la-Mer as Assistant Manager in 1923, using a forged reference to gain the position. He was not honest in his dealings, and he acquired a fair amount of money by stealing from the safe in the back office when the manager was not there. He gambled on horses, won, and replaced the money—a procedure he repeated a number of times. At that time, the hotel was managed by its owner, Mr Garthwaite, a man in his mid-sixties with a jovial character but a tendency to gout, which sometimes laid him up for days on end. A year after Ralph Horniman arrived, Mr Garthwaite died while playing a round of golf, and his widow promoted Ralph, trusty Ralph, to the position of manager in his place.

Ralph was a stout fellow. He looked the very picture of health, and with the combination to the hotel safe officially known to him, he had access to as much money as he needed—at least for the moment. Ralph had big ideas; he was teeming with ambition.

Actually, it was a surprise to him, when he thought of it, that he was still working there in 1931. But when he analysed the matter in his mind, he realised that he had become satisfied where he was: a captain in charge of a ship. He took up painting, something for which, in his youth, he had had a real talent, and he amused himself by creating copies of famous works of art, which he hung upon his walls. It was the one thing that he really enjoyed, the one thing for which he might have made a modest name as well as a little money, but it was the one thing that embarrassed him, for as a boy, his schoolfellows had mocked him, calling him Remby or Vermy because he was interested in art and not in football or cricket.

For a time, all went well for Ralph Horniman. He had friends, the Giddinses and Jack Jackson; he had enough money to be able to dream of a comfortable retirement, not to say marriage, and, who knows, offspring; and he was a respected member of the community. He became pompous and overweight, but still imagined himself to be a fine fellow.

Then he began to get a little overambitious with his betting on horses. He found himself owing uncomfortably large amounts of money, more than he could afford. Outwardly, no trace of worry was allowed to darken his brow. Inwardly, he groaned each time he abstracted something from the safe, for he knew that sooner or later the deficit would show.

And then, something dreadful happened. Truly awful. A monstrous calamity.

He owed rather a large sum to Stephen Giddins. Young Stephen had been all smiles when he started to lend Ralph money. That soon changed when repayments were sometimes not forthcoming. Ralph was no longer the confident swindler he once had been. He craved too much for the maintenance of his respectability. One day, in the spring of 1931, Ralph met Stephen in the park, and the following conversation took place.

"I say, Ralph, payment's overdue now by two weeks." Stephen grinned the fairest and pleasantest of grins as he spoke, partly for the benefit of a young family who were passing just at that moment. Then his face grew darker. "You'll have to get it somehow, I don't care how, whatever you did last time works for me." This was said with a knowing look, for that previous time had been one of the occasions when Ralph's repayment was made with money dishonestly got, and Stephen knew it.

"I'll see what I can do," said Horniman, swallowing slightly.

"Well, see that you do. Oh, by the way, a business associate of mine is coming here tomorrow. He can't stay at my place, and I certainly don't want him mixing with the folks, so he can't stay there either. I told him you would put him up at the Splendide, you won't mind, will you? I expect there'll be no charge, or you can put it towards your account if you like. It'll only be the tip of the iceberg though, won't it?"

Horniman agreed to this, and the following afternoon, Stephen Giddins' business associate arrived at the hotel. Philippa was at the reception desk while he registered: George Burville, Ivanhoe Court, Kensington, London. Ralph Horniman was standing not far off while this took place, and it was then that it happened. Philippa went into the little room behind reception while, at the same moment, Mr Burville looked up and saw Ralph.

"I know you, don't I?" said Burville. "Now, now, don't tell me," he continued before Horniman could answer, "I never forget a face, though, it must have been a long time ago. I daresay you may have put on a little weight, weight, weight, wait, wait. Wait a bit, I've got it! France 1917. But aren't you the chap that...?"

Horniman turned a sickly green. "Not at all," he began, "I wasn't in France in 1917, I was in..."

"No, it's you all right, I'd know that piggy nose anywhere."

"I don't know what you're talking about," said Horniman.

"Well, I'm not staying here now. You can tell that young lady I changed my mind. I expect the police would be interested in your doings."

And Burville picked up his suitcase and walked out of the hotel.

Horniman was puzzled, for he had no recollection of ever having met Mr Burville.

Had he done so, he would have known him to be a loutish, mean-spirited man who, when on active army service, had been caught cheating at cards and ostracised by the other men in his platoon. But there was no doubt that things were becoming rather difficult for him, so Ralph Horniman went to his own rooms, and began to pack in case he might need to make a quick getaway.

But things seemed to calm down, and Burville did not return with the police. To tell the truth, Horniman was as surprised as he was relieved. As far as he was concerned, that was the end of the matter.

Later that week, he met Stephen Giddins in the park and gave him some money.

"Not enough, Ralph, not enough. You better get me some more, a lot more, I'll tell you how much and when."

"Look here…"

"Don't start getting uppity with me. Guess what little piece of information has just dropped into my lap!"

"What are you talking about?'

"Oh, yes," said Giddins, "I've been told all about you. Wanted for murder, it seems.

What a turn-up, eh?"

CHAPTER THREE

Ralph Horniman had been taken to Muffet Island by Giddins and Burville. Once inside the stone cottage, Stephen Giddins indicated to Horniman and Elspeth that they were to sit at the dining room table and say nothing. Burville entered a little while later.

"I've made sure the boat won't be seen if anyone should come snooping."

For a moment, Elspeth felt a glimmer of hope, for Joe was due back at the island the next day to collect her. But then she realised that Joe would be no match for these men, two of whom she knew by sight though not by name. She had recognised Ralph Horniman from the hotel where she sometimes went for tea or supper, though she did not know his function there, and she recognised Stephen Giddins from having seen him about town a couple of times. The third man was completely unknown to her.

George Burville was a powerfully built man in his early forties with florid features and a habit of opening his eyes wide and staring with a fixed gaze when he wanted to make an important point. "There had better not be anybody else snooping around here," he said significantly. He looked hard at Elspeth.

"What are you here for?" he demanded.

Elspeth was reluctant to say anything at all just then, and Burville repeated his question. Stephen Giddins shushed him and, looking directly at Elspeth said, "The question is 'what should we do with *you*?'"

Horniman looked glum, but his natural tendency to pompous verbosity, which he had cultivated for the last few years, suddenly got the better of him.

"The question really is 'now that you have got us here, what are you going to do with *us*?' Or, to put it another way," he said, clasping his hands together with his elbows on the table and speaking with an air of confident command, "If I'm not back soon, they will start looking for me."

"Thing is, Ralphie—Ernie!" said Stephen Giddins, "they won't know where to look, will they? I'm fed up with you not giving me what's owed, and Burville here is even more fed up than me."

Horniman wrinkled his forehead in a perplexed manner. Burville gave an ugly leer and looked at his own fists, which to Elspeth seemed to be as large as London buses. "All right," he said, "I'll change the question." He looked at Elspeth again. "How did you get here and, more to the point, just how were you intending to leave?"

"Georgie-boy, you make an excellent point," said Stephen Giddins. "You must be expecting someone to come for you."

"Look here, Giddins," said Horniman, "leave that young lady alone, she's got nothing to do with this."

The conversation continued for some time, but without resolution. Elspeth, whose mind was quick and analytical, began to think of plans to get away, dismissing in turn each idea as it occurred to her. Finally, Giddins and Burville went outside to confer privately.

"I think I know how to get away," Elspeth whispered to Horniman. "Follow me."

Their captors were too self-confident to have secured their prisoners, and Elspeth led Horniman into the kitchen. The window over the sink was soon opened, and Elspeth climbed out, followed, but with far less elegance, by Ralph Horniman.

Ralph felt almost like a schoolboy and, if it had not been for the fact that they were in such imminent danger, might almost have enjoyed himself.

"There's nowhere to hide on the island," said Elspeth. We'll make our way down below, find their boat, and leave."

This was easier said than done, for Giddins and Burville were facing the only path that led down to the rocky shore where the boat must be. Elspeth and Horniman stayed out of sight. Eventually, the others turned back to the cottage.

"Now!" hissed Elspeth, and they slid their way down to the shore where the boat had not been well-hidden. "We haven't much time, they'll be here any moment."

Horniman said nothing; he was unfit and very out of breath, but he clambered into the boat, barking his shins on the side, followed by Elspeth who started the motor. It spluttered and roared, and as it did so, Giddins and Burville appeared at the top of the path, shouting commands to stop.

The boat was out of their reach, and Elspeth gritted her teeth as she bravely fought to keep a steady course out through the channel into the open sea. Their captors were dancing on the shore with rage on their faces, but they were stranded.

"I'll go to the police when we get back," said Elspeth over the sound of the motor.

"No," said Horniman, "don't do that, let me think first." For an interview with the police was the last thing he wanted.

CHAPTER FOUR

At 7 pm that Tuesday the 6th of October, Ralph Horniman and Elspeth McGregor, both looking very much the worse for wear, entered the Hotel Splendide. Mrs Garthwaite looked furious when she saw them. Though her anger was mostly directed towards Ralph, who had been absent for the last few hours, she did spend a few moments staring at Elspeth who stood next to him in what Mrs Garthwaite imagined was a quite shameless fashion. Elspeth, though, had no self-consciousness. She was perfectly pleased with what she had done, deeming it to be quite a satisfactory adventure.

After a dressing down in what had been his own office (his own office!) Ralph went to his quarters to have a bath. Mrs Garthwaite looked at Elspeth, and Elspeth looked back at her.

"We've had quite a time of it in the last few hours."

"I'm quite sure of that," said Mrs Garthwaite.

"No, really. Goodness, I must get a message to Joe that I'm here so that he doesn't go to the island tomorrow. And we need to call the police." For despite Horniman's request, Elspeth had decided that the two ruffians must be dealt with.

Mrs Garthwaite lifted the telephone receiver and asked to be connected to the police station.

There was a knock at the door, and Alice appeared there.

"Sorry," she said, "I didn't know you were busy."

"Come in, come in," said Mrs Garthwaite.

"This is... I'm sorry, I don't know your name."

"Elspeth," said Elspeth, "MacGregor."

"Alice Winsome, pleased to meet you." They shook hands.

"While we're waiting for the police, I'll order some tea," said Mrs Garthwaite.

Ralph Horniman did not have a bath. He had a hurried wash instead, changed into some fresh clothes, and checked to see that his suitcase was properly packed. It was now far too dangerous for him to stay in Paunceton; Giddins and his associate were making life too complicated, and he felt threatened.

"Discretion," he murmured, "...the better part of valour."

In one of the lounges, Angela, Ben, Mary and Andrew were rehearsing their lines.

"This is hopeless," said Andrew, "nearly every scene involves Mandeville, and we can't do them without Horniman."

"I'll read it in," said Angela, "My character doesn't have many lines."

"And we can try our scene," said Mary, "he's not in that."

Ben was in a corner studying his role.

"Have you seen this? How am I supposed to obey orders from the Baronet, and be on your side too?"

"It's in the part," said Andrew.

"Yes, but what's my motivation?"

"Oh, really, Ben," said Angela, "what does it matter? Just do it. If you want motivation, just remember that you're being paid, that should be enough."

"I'll never learn this speech in time," said Mary, "it's so-o-o long. That Mrs Winsome's very nice, but really...!"

"Just be grateful that it is a speech," said Ben. "She was going to write music for it all, and we'd be singing the lot."

While all this was happening, the doorman was operating a lift again—in full expectation of a nice bonus.

In the hotel office, Mrs Garthwaite, Alice and Elspeth were drinking tea, though it was really past the hour for that, while waiting for the imminent arrival of Inspector Jack Jackson, who had been called at his home and had left before eating his supper.

On Muffet Island, Stephen Giddins and George Burville were making the best of it for the night, hoping to be rescued from the island the following day.

Lord and Lady Tongue were dining in the hotel restaurant, a little surprised that Alice was not there with them—and yet not surprised, since they knew her well!

Meanwhile, Ralph Horniman slipped down the back stairs, suitcase in hand, and left the hotel.

Jack Jackson, when he was shown into the office, greeted the ladies, and was introduced to Elspeth. She made a great contrast to the others, for Mrs Garthwaite was stout and had a pale complexion; Alice, though she too had fair skin, was slender. Elspeth had a loveliness that lit up further still when she showed her pearly teeth, and a gentle voice that charmed the ear. Her quick mind and intelligence allowed her to explain everything in very few words.

Jackson looked at her thoughtfully.

"And you have no idea what these men wanted with Ralph Horniman?"

"None whatsoever, I only met him today."

"You would recognize these other men again?"

"Yes."

"It's too late to get them now," said Jackson. "Impossible to land on the island in the dark." (Elspeth smiled at this.) "I'll arrange for them to be picked up as soon as it's light."

So, it was early on Wednesday morning that Stephen Giddins and George Burville were arrested. The Giddins family were shocked, of course, when they heard of Stephen's arrest. Stephen Giddins began to tell his story in a way that would redound best to his own name, not wishing to reveal himself as a blackmailer, but only as someone who had the general good of the nation at heart. Burville, on the other hand, stumbled and fumbled over his statement.

Jack Jackson gave the order for Ralph Horniman to be brought in. But, not for the first time, Ralph Horniman was nowhere to be found.

CHAPTER FIVE

Some days passed, and Alice's parents returned to Mandible Hall in the Sizaire Berwick driven, as before, by Groves. They had suggested that Alice return with them, but she disliked the old car with its coffin-like appearance. The idea of a play-reading had been abandoned, much to the disappointment of both Alice and Mrs Garthwaite, though other members of the company seemed to take the news with equanimity.

In the absence of Ralph Horniman, the investigation into the affairs of Stephen Giddins and George Burville was halted. Burville disappeared into the hole from which he had emerged, and Stephen Giddins went up to London avoiding his parents and his sister. Mr and Mrs Giddins took Zoë to the south of France for an extended holiday.

Alice decided to stay in the hotel for another couple of weeks and invited Elspeth to share the suite she was occupying; there was plenty of room now that Lord and Lady Tongue had left. Elspeth was delighted to accept, and the two of them were often seen during that time strolling about the town and taking trips to explore the nearby villages.

The hotel doorman had returned to his usual position and grumbled as much as ever about his lot. The four lift operators were once more conveying guests to their various destinations and talking to each other in between.

All seemed to have returned pretty much to normality, except that Horniman was gone, and

Mrs Garthwaite occupied the office. And one more thing, of course, Ben and Angela were still not on speaking terms.

And then, on Saturday 17th October, Mrs Garthwaite was made aware of an incident that had happened some eighty or so miles away. Jack Jackson called to see her.

"I think you should take a look at this," he said, and he handed her a copy of the Thanet Evening Echo of the previous day, already folded to show page 8, which carried the following report:

MIDNIGHT MYSTERY

UNKNOWN MAN DROWNED AT MARGATE

Mystery surrounds the identity of a man six feet in height and well-built, whose body was recovered from the sea under remarkable circumstances at Westbrook, Margate, shortly after midnight on Saturday 10th October.

The body was first seen floating in the sea at high tide about twenty yards from the shore by two youths engaged in a ratting expedition and was only recovered after hazardous rescue work.

Two young Margate lads, Robert Teall, aged 17 of 35, Eaton-road, and Alfred Norman Eastland, aged 18 of 43, Ramsgate-road, were rat hunting on the waste dump at Westbrook, where the promenade is being extended.

A GROAN FROM THE SEA.

A few minutes after midnight the pair succeeded in killing a rat; upon going towards the edge of the promenade in order to throw it into the sea, they heard a groan.

After throwing the rat into the sea, the lads saw what appeared to be an overcoat floating about twenty yards from the shore. A closer observation, however, revealed the fact that it was not an overcoat, but a body floating in the water. The tide was high at the time and reached the promenade.

One of the lads ran along the promenade for assistance, and, meeting P.C. Galer, informed him of their discovery. The lad went on for other assistance, and P.S. Woodward and P.C. Taylor reached the spot a few minutes later.

In the meantime, P.C. Galer plunged into the water from the promenade in an endeavour to bring the body ashore but was quickly seized with cramp and was compelled to return. The constable obtained a lifebelt from the side of the bathing huts on the promenade and, divesting himself of his clothing, again plunged into the water.

UNAVAILING RESCUE

Mr Ernest James Morris, of Princes-crescent, Margate, in the employ of the Margate Gas Company, also went into the water to the constable's assistance, and, between them, P.C. Galer and Mr Morris succeeded in bringing the man ashore.

The police officers commenced artificial respiration, which was maintained until the arrival of the police surgeon, Dr Brocklehurst, who, on examining the body, pronounced life extinct.

An overcoat, neatly folded, was later discovered on the slipway opposite Barnes-avenue, on top of which was placed a black bowler hat.

The deceased man is described as being between 50 and 60 years of age, 6 ft. in height and well-built. He had dark hair—greying—and going bald on the crown of the head, and a moustache. The man was dressed in a dark blue suit, black socks, black shoes, black and white shirt with Selfridge's marked on the tab. He wore a white linen collar, size 16½, and on the collar was found a laundry mark in red cotton. A similar laundry mark was found on a blue bordered handkerchief found in one of the man's pockets. The overcoat was dark, and the initials R.H. were inscribed in gilt letters in the inside of the bowler hat, made by Harman and Sons, Ltd., hatters, of 87, New Bond-street, London. The bowler hat was size 7.

The deceased man had a prominent upper lip and high forehead.

In his pockets were found some cigarettes, a Venus pencil, a petrol lighter, over £1 in money and a set of lower false teeth.

The pockets contained no wallet or papers from which the name of the drowned man could be definitely established, and the police are appealing to anyone who can lift the shroud of mystery which surrounds his identity.

VENEFICIA PUBLICATIONS
OWNED BY
DIANE NARRAWAY AND MARISHA KIDDLE
PUBLISHERS OF
FICTION, DARK FICTION, NON-FICTION, JOURNALS, POETRY, FANTASY/SCI-FI, AS WELL AS MAGICKAL, PAGAN, HEATHEN AND OCCULT WORKS.
veneficiapublications.com
veneficiapublications@gmail.com
FOR WHOLESALE APPLICATIONS PLEASE EMAIL ABOVE ADDRESS FOR DETAILS
FIND US ON
VENEFICIA PUBLICATIONS
the power behind the written word

Mrs Garthwaite gave a cry when she read of the initials in the bowler hat and began to shake when she read the description of the man, for surely, it had to be none other than Ralph Horniman.

"Before you say anything," said Jackson, "I've just sent word to Margate to get further details. It may not be Ralph, but the description does match."

"It does," said Mrs Garthwaite tearfully, "even down to the lower false teeth."

And so it seemed, that, after all, Ralph Horniman had finally met his maker by taking his own life, perhaps unable to bear the shame of all he had done.

CHAPTER SIX

"How long have you lived here?" said Alice. I hope you don't mind my asking, but I've never met anyone before who was…"

"Black?" said Elspeth.

"Mm."

"No, not at all." Elspeth smiled and put down her teacup. "All my life. My family has lived in England for generations. There are all sorts of stories about how we got here—family traditions, you know."

Alice smiled back at her and leaned forward. "Do you find people are…"

"Prejudiced? Sometimes, but not too often, fortunately. It's rather upsetting when it happens, but I keep myself to myself, and that way I avoid any risk of confrontation."

"How sad not to have friends."

"Yes, well, you're my friend."

"Yes, I am," said Alice. "I never had many friends either. So, tell me about your family."

"Well," said Elspeth, "I had an ancestor who came to England with the crusaders."

"How interesting!" Alice wrinkled her forehead and thought for a few moments.

Elspeth regarded her with a feeling of slight amusement.

"I'm the last of the line," she said, "too much money and nothing to do with it, that's what my solicitor says."

"So, what do you do?"

"I support worthy causes, mostly anonymously, and I enjoy myself. And I collect old machines and repair them. And... I invent things."

"How wonderful!"

"When you come to visit me, I'll show you."

And so, it was arranged that Alice would leave Paunceton-sur-la-Mer with Elspeth and spend a few weeks at Elspeth's home.

Mrs Garthwaite continued managing the Hotel Splendide until the end of November. But she had lost her interest in it. "After all," she said to her sister Millicent during a long telephone conversation, "I have enough money to live on, so I really don't need to keep it on. I think I'll just sell the place."

News of the sale came as no surprise to the hotel staff; it seemed inevitable. One morning, Mary and Andrew were on the roof discussing their own future plans with each other. It was a very cold day, and they were both warmly dressed.

"Time to go, Sis," said Andrew. "This is too boring. I thought Horniman made life difficult, but at least we had fun dodging him."

"Mrs Garthwaite's quite demanding," said Mary. "She told me that it's all about productivity. How can you be productive in a lift?"

"I really don't know why they need four lifts anyway," said Andrew. "There aren't enough guests staying to justify it."

Angela appeared on the roof. She overheard the last remark and said, as if in reply,

"There won't be four lifts operating from next month. Apparently, the new owners only want two."

"Did Mrs G tell you that?" said Andrew.

"No, Ben told me."

"Is Ben talking to you now?" asked Mary.

"Barely, but I think he's gradually coming round."

"How does Ben know?"

"He always seems to know everything that goes on here. His beady little eyes are everywhere, and he never seems to let me out of his sight for long. Apparently Mrs Garthwaite is going to Capri."

"For a holiday?"

"No, to live—she's loaded."

"I don't believe it."

"Well, that's what Ben said, though he may be wrong."

Ben was, at that moment, looking for Angela who had escaped his "beady little eyes" as she put it. But he did not have to search long, finding her on the roof with Mary and Andrew.

"Anyone operating a lift at the moment?" asked Angela when she saw Ben approach. Frantic buzzing could be heard, and all four of them hurried back inside.

CHAPTER SEVEN

Elspeth MacGregor lived in a tall house, which, from the outside, appeared to be a tumbledown, ramshackle building. However, the inside was a wonder to behold. It stood in the middle of a large field, set back from the road halfway up a Welsh mountain between Newtown and Machynlleth, in such a way that passersby would not know it was there, unless they already knew about it.

"I love coming to this place," said Elspeth when she opened the door. She walked in, followed by Alice. "I don't lock the door or windows when I'm away—if someone wanted to break in and steal something, I'd rather they did minimum damage. Anyway, the place is practically inaccessible, not even a telephone. Come on, let's have some tea."

In the kitchen was a cooking range.

"It's the latest thing," said Elspeth. "The farmer who used to own this place built a new farmhouse in the next field, and his wife gets the range going and brings in supplies when she knows I'm coming. How about some toast as well? I just put the bread straight onto the hotplate, it's a bit unorthodox, but it works for me."

Alice and Elspeth were cold and tired, but the range was warm, and there was a log fire in the sitting room, which was soon crackling away merrily. It was November and the sky was already fairly dark though it was not yet four o'clock. After sitting for a short time by candlelight, they went outside to bring in the things they had left on the porch.

"I'll show you everything properly tomorrow. Gosh, I hope you like what you see."

"I'm sure I shall," said Alice.

"I have a collection of crystal radio sets in the next room. Some are better than others, but we can pick up broadcasts here sometimes, though it's a bit intermittent. Best done with headphones."

"Do you have electricity, then?"

"Oh, yes. There's a generator at the back of the house. I'll get it going tomorrow, that will make things much easier."

The following day was a revelation to Alice as Elspeth gave her a tour of her house. Gadgets, mostly unfinished inventions, lay in various stages of completion in different rooms.

"I find it hard to settle to any one thing," said Elspeth. "I keep getting new ideas. Mind you, I don't think any of these are very much good, but one day I'll come up with a good idea. Come outside, the best is yet to come."

The house stood in a large grassy field, which was almost level, though it sloped down on one side and up towards the mountain on the other. The driveway, which curved around towards the road and away from the mountain, was long, but it forked at one point. One branch curved round to the house, the other ran straight for some distance and ended at a long and wide shed with large double doors.

"It's in here," said Elspeth with a feeling of pride as they approached the shed. "Mind you, I didn't invent it, I'm just restoring it to its former glory."

Alice could not imagine what Elspeth was talking about, but the shed doors were opened one by one, and she saw revealed before her a long, canvas-covered object.

"Isn't she gorgeous?" said Elspeth. "It's a Sopwith Tabloid. One nearly like this won the Schneider Trophy in 1914, but that one could land on water. This one's a year older. It's the original prototype, a two-seater with seats side by side."

"It's beautiful," said Alice. "Have you flown it?"

"Well, no, not yet. The wings need reattaching and they're at the airfield. I'm just working on the fuselage. Once I've completed work on that, I'll get her transported back to the airfield and finish the job properly. They all think I'm mad there, but they're quite helpful. I'm a bit nervous about flying her to tell the truth, even though I have a licence. Perhaps I'll take you flying one day. Then we can really go up in the world!"

The Belfast News-Letter

Saturday, April 25, 1914 — Price 1d

AERO AND MOTOR NOTES
British Waterplane Triumph

The victory of Mr Howard Pixton with the Sopwith "tabloid" biplane in the Schneider Cup waterplane race at Monaco on Monday marks a new era in the British aviation movement, for this is the first occasion on which an international event of any importance has been won by a British machine. Five nations had entered—viz. France, Switzerland, Germany, America, and Great Britain. The German machines, however, having previously been damaged, were unable to start, whilst the two American pilots, Weymann and Thaw, were so impressed by the performances of the Sopwith machine during practice that they decided that their own craft stood not a ghost of a chance, and so withdrew... Mr Pixton's Sopwith biplane was of the small, single-seater type that had recently impressed the military authorities so favourably... Unhappily, it was not equipped with a British engine, but with a 100 hp Gnome Monosoupape, though there may be some consolation in the knowledge that the make is shortly to be manufactured in England...

Sopwith Tabloid 1913
Length: 23 feet
Span: 25 feet 6 inches
Height: 10 feet
Wing area: 241 square feet
Weight: 1,120 lbs
Capacity (prototype):
One pilot and one passenger side by side
Engine (prototype): 80 hp Gnome Lambda rotary piston
Range: 315 miles
Maximum speed: 92 miles per hour
Build: Open-air cockpit, rectangular fuselage with aluminium wire and wood frame, canvas covered. Two-bladed wooden propeller.
First flight: 27 November 1913

CHAPTER EIGHT

Artillery Street, Horselydown, Bermondsey was not the most salubrious of addresses. In point of fact, like much of that part of London, it had its fair share of squalid dwellings, and a room on the second floor of one of them was home to a man of less than prepossessing appearance. He only left the house when absolutely necessary, but he paid his landlord promptly when the rent was due, though he seemed to do no work and had no income.

The remainder of the house was divided thus: on the ground floor lived Mr and Mrs Jones and their two children—Mr Jones was a hairbrush manufacturer—on the first floor lived Mr and Mrs Hopkins, a retired couple who didn't like noise— unfortunate, bearing in mind the young children living on the floor below. And on the second floor, aside from our subject, lived a middle-aged woman, Miss Smyth, in rather straitened circumstances.

Charles Johnson had been living in his room on the second floor for only a short time when he realised that Miss Smyth was more than usually interested in him. Miss Smyth had introduced herself to him on the stairs as they were passing each other one morning, she on the way down, he on the way up.

"...yes," she said, "a very old family, Smyth spelled S M Y T H, but pronounced Smith not Sm*y*th. I don't know why people insist on changing the pronunciation. Simple affectation, that's what it is. I never let any of my pupils pronounce it wrongly. That is," she added wistfully, "when I used to teach. I don't anymore."

Charles Johnson could not wait to get away from her.

It was October 1932. Oswald Mosley had just founded the British Union of Fascists, and the Fascist anthem was already being heard chanted tonelessly by his followers. It irritated Johnson when Miss Smyth insisted on singing Mosley's praises, for Johnson found him objectionable, but it was worse still when she tried to teach the anthem to everyone in the house. The children who lived on the ground floor, innocents that they were, found that the tune was easily learned and sang and whistled it all day long. The Hopkinses also objected, though not to fascism, but to the caterwauling of the little brats.

Miss Smyth had placed a card in the window of a local shop, advertising her services as a private teacher for children. This was fortunate for Mr Johnson, as it meant that she began to teach once more, and was sometimes out, but unfortunate for the children she taught, as she was a poor teacher. She would, of course, never disclose the fact that she had been dismissed from her last teaching post for incompetence and being unable to control her class. Instead, she might on occasion drop the name of some well-known person implying, as she did so, that his or her children had been among her pupils. An avid reader of newspapers, she scoured the pages for any item which might back up her arguments and her political views, which were extreme.

And so it was that, despite all her endeavours, she realised that she could neither interest nor attract Mr Johnson into her lair, for she was rather like a spider weaving a web for an unfortunate fly. (In this case rather a large fly for such a small spider.) So it befell, as writers of the past might have written, that her untold passion for Mr Johnson turned into hatred. He, unprepossessing though he was, and rather toad-like in appearance, if truth be known, was grateful when she began to ignore him, turning her nose up if he came near.

Charles Johnson kept in his room an old briefcase which he guarded jealously, never leaving it for an instant, always taking it with him if he went out. This was not unnoticed by Miss Smyth, and a curiosity burned deep within her to find out just exactly what was contained inside it. When the opportunity finally presented itself, she was not slow to take advantage, and it was to the undoing of them both.

It happened like this: one Sunday just before noon, Miss Smyth returned from church and climbed the stairs to her room. Mr Johnson emerged from the shared bathroom on the ground floor at that moment. It was a matter of great annoyance and inconvenience to Miss Smyth that she was compelled to share the facilities with others, and Mr Johnson was a particular irritant. The bathroom contained an iron bath, poorly enamelled, and a sink into both of which the water ran tepid and brown (the toilet was outside behind the house). Mr Johnson did not notice his neighbour, but she took full notice of him. He went straight from the bathroom to the front door and left the house. She followed as far as the door and looked after him, watching as he disappeared round a corner. What was particularly noticeable was that he was not carrying his briefcase, and Miss Smyth triumphantly ran up the stairs and, without waiting, opened the door to Mr Johnson's room and went in.

It was only when he was about to pay for a copy of the Sunday Times that Charles Johnson realised that he did not have his briefcase with him. He went hot and cold; a feeling of nausea rose from the pit of his stomach. It was unusual for him to have gone to the bathroom to wash without taking the case with him, even though it was only two flights down from his room. But as he went into the bathroom on that occasion, he suddenly realised that he had not taken the briefcase with him, but he reasoned that he would not be there long, and, knowing that the only people in the house at that moment were the Jones family and himself, he did not imagine there would be any risk. Mr and Mrs Hopkins and Miss Smyth were all at church.

Johnson had lain in bed late that morning—he lay in bed late most mornings and went to bed early, but night-times were difficult as he often found he could not sleep. With nothing to do, he would sit up in bed and read by the light that came into his room from the streetlamp outside his window or, taking his case with him, would pace around the streets of Bermondsey, fearing less about being robbed while out at night than that he might be burgled if he left it behind. Such is the illogicality of the human mind!

While he washed and shaved that Sunday morning, he sang a little tune under his breath to which he put the words, "Go upstairs and fetch my case, go upstairs and fetch my case," over and over again, so it was doubly annoying to him that despite this precaution, he had still forgotten to go upstairs to collect it before leaving. He had walked a few minutes' distance from the house, and now turned to hurry back. Charles Johnson was not physically fit; he was overweight and flabby. Before he was halfway home, he was already wheezing. His heart was pounding, and he was sweating profusely. He decided to sit for a moment on a bench, which was set back from the pavement, opposite a small patch of scrubby grass. One or two passersby looked at him. One of them went so far as to ask if he was all right. He could not answer, but merely nodded slightly and feebly waved his right hand a little. It was very evident that he was not all right. An ambulance was called, and he was taken away to St Olave's Hospital.

This was not as things were meant to be. He lay in a bed in a large ward for two days and two nights: how he cursed!

On Tuesday morning he was discharged, and he made his way back to the house in Artillery Street, his heart in his mouth. Every step was like torture. What might he find?

Would his briefcase still be there? All his money was inside it, the best part of £1,000.

That Sunday, when Miss Smyth had entered his room, was a special red-letter day for her. She hesitated not, for she who hesitates is lost, but went straight over to Mr Johnson's bed and looked underneath it (for where else might one hide anything important?) and dragged out the briefcase. It was locked, but she had no qualms about breaking open the lock with a rusty knife that lay by a plate, on which was the remains of a meat pie. Her eyes opened wide when she saw what lay within, but then it suddenly dawned on her that to remain where she might be caught at any moment in fragrante delicto was not something to be desired. So, she took from the bottom of the case a wad of banknotes, shut it, put it back where it was, hoping that the damage she had done would not be noticed, and hurried back to her own room.

On counting the money, she found that it amounted to £50. This frightened her for a moment, for it had been some time since she had seen that amount of money. It made her wonder if she should move to a different address where she could not be found by Mr Johnson. And then, something occurred to her.

"Where did he get so much money?" For she realised that there was a considerable sum still in the case. Had it been stolen? She was certain it must have been. Was the money she had taken, therefore, safe to keep? She had no doubt that if used prudently it would be so. Might there be a reward for the capture of a desperate criminal who had stolen hundreds and hundreds of pounds? Surely there must be. So, Miss Smyth left the house, after first hiding the £50 under a loose floorboard, and went to find a policeman, to whom she explained that Mr Johnson had asked her to clean his room, and that, quite by chance, she had come across something unusual.

And so it came to pass that when Charles Johnson reached the second-floor landing of the house in Artillery Street, after having climbed the two flights of stairs with great effort, he found himself faced by two gentlemen in police uniform.

"Good morning, sir," said one, "Are you Charles Johnson?" Johnson nodded.

"I have a warrant to search your premises..."

"This is monstrous!"

A search was made despite Johnson's protestations, the briefcase was found, laden with money as they had been told it would be, and then came the following request:

"Would you mind accompanying us to the station, sir?"

"What is this about?"

"Never mind that, sir, all will be revealed. Just come with us, please."

CHAPTER NINE

Charles Johnson was questioned about the money that had been found in his room. It would have been vain to declare that it had been planted there, besides, he declared that it was his own and honestly got.

"And just how did you get it?"

But he refused to say, and after a little discussion, it was decided that he would be detained pending inquiries, just in case something should turn out not to be not quite right. But the notes did not bear any numbers that would suggest they were stolen, and so, after two hours or more, it seemed that Charles Johnson would be released.

"I suggest you put this in a bank where it can be kept safe," he was told.

There was a knock at the door.

"Just one moment, sir," said the officer who had been quizzing him.

Another policeman stepped inside.

"Detective Inspector... would you mind?" he said.

The inspector was beckoned into the corridor where he remained in hushed discussion for three or four minutes.

After that, he re-entered the room together with his colleague and sat down opposite Johnson, looking at him across the table. The other stood by the door, watching intently.

Johnson began to get impatient and was about to say something pointed, when the policeman opposite him spoke.

"Are you, by any chance, Ralph Horniman, late, of the Hotel Splendide, Paunceton?" he asked.

Johnson, or should we say, Horniman opened his eyes wide, rolled his upper lip to his nose and nodded.

"Not that it's any business of yours," he said.

"Never mind that, sir, we'll be the ones to decide whose business it is. It may interest you to know that you have caused a certain amount of trouble with regard to your disappearance and apparent death, and the death of an unnamed individual."

"But I had no hand in that. He was dead already, I just rolled him into the water."

"Oh, we know this, sir, we're pretty quick in the force."

"Then I can go?"

"Now, just wait a minute, sir. I have another question to ask you first, and then we'll see." And he made a note in his notebook.

Horniman, for we must now refer to him by that name, was nervous. He wanted desperately to leave, but he felt cornered. His forehead became shiny as beads of sweat appeared there.

"Now then, sir, could you tell me this—are you also, in fact, Ernest Sallow, late Private of the 3rd Corps, last seen some time in 1917?"

Horniman/Johnson/Sallow gulped.

"Ah," continued the detective inspector, "I see I've got you there, that was unexpected, I think."

From outside the room came a sound as if someone was noisily resisting being brought into the police station.

The detective inspector stood. "Charles Johnson, also known as Ralph Horniman, also known as Ernest Sallow, I am arresting you on suspicion of having, in 1917, murdered Lance Corporal William George.

"Do you wish to say anything in answer to the charge? You are not obliged to say anything unless you wish to do so, but whatever you say will be taken down in writing and may be given in evidence."

Sometime later that day Miss Smyth found herself in the very same interview room undergoing a series of questions intended to elucidate another mystery. Her mouth formed a thin line; she had strongly objected to being brought to the police station, but no choice was given her. Tears pricked their way through her eyes.

"I didn't mean it," she whispered, but it was too late. "I can never go back there, I'm so ashamed."

The other residents of the house had watched as she had been escorted away; she knew she would never be able to live it down.

What had happened was that, while the police were busy arresting Johnson/Horniman/Sallow, Mr Hopkins from the first floor had spoken to another policeman waiting outside. He had complained that money was missing from his wife's purse, and that his own watch was missing. Mrs Jones from the ground floor apartment then approached and mentioned some losses of their own. "It wasn't the children, either, because they were with us when the stuff was taken."

Miss Smyth was, by that time, standing by the front door looking as if the end of the world had come. At last, she could bear it no longer and asked the policeman to follow her to her own room, where she confessed to having taken the money herself. She gave him all she had taken, including the £50 that lay under the floorboard. He was very kind but insisted on her accompanying him to the station.

"I should never have gone to the police," she said. "It's because I tried to get Mr Johnson into trouble that I've been punished."

So instead of a reward for catching a criminal, she found herself sentenced to two weeks in prison for theft.

For Sallow/Horniman/Johnson a fate of a different sort seemed more likely.

CHAPTER TEN

The arrest of a dangerous criminal who had been on the run for fifteen years was reported in the national press, and so it should come as no surprise that Mrs Garthwaite should read all about it.

She had been having breakfast with her sister Millicent in Bath with whom she had been staying for a few days, not having gone to live in Capri after all. The sale of the hotel had fallen through too, so she was still working hard. Millicent had brought in the paper and placed it on the dining table to one side, ready to be read once they had finished eating.

Mrs Garthwaite was horrified to see, beneath the front-page headline that announced the arrest of a murderer, a photograph of Ralph Horniman. She choked on her toast, then cleared her throat with a hurried gulp at the teacup and, while wiping her mouth with her napkin, said,

"It's Ralph, but he's dead, it can't be!"

"It can't be, dear," said her sister, "not if he's dead. Let me look." The two sisters looked at the paper.

"It doesn't give the name," said Millicent. "Are you sure it's him? Seems unlikely."

"It looks like him," said Mrs Garthwaite, "except that Ralph had a moustache and was always smiling when he wasn't looking pompous, and that man looks like a real brute."

Millicent looked at her sister in a supportive kind of way.

"Don't worry, Effie," she said. "You're well and truly out of it."

"Suppose they want to ask me questions about him. It's too horrible, I nearly married the man!"

Millicent was wrong, the police did want to speak to her sister, and that very afternoon, Mrs Euphemia Garthwaite gave a formal written statement regarding all she knew about Ralph Horniman. She left nothing out, including all the dubious things of which she suspected him, but she felt guilty afterward, and said as much to Millicent on her return.

"Why should you feel guilty, dear? The man's a brute as you said. If he's guilty, I hope he hangs!"

"Oh, Millie, how could you!" And Mrs Garthwaite ran out of the lounge where they had been sitting, and into the garden where she began to contemplate the grass.

Millicent went to her and, with soothing words, drew her back into the house and poured her a cup of tea.

A year had passed since Alice had first met Elspeth MacGregor, and now she was back in Wales visiting Elspeth again. She had not been home to Mandible Hall for all that time but had instead taken herself on a tour of European capitals, in particular Vienna, where she had admired the huge marble palaces, and Venice, where she had taken rides in gondolas, despite the advice of acquaintances who told her that gondola rides were vastly overpriced. "But after all," she had thought, "why go to Venice if you don't ride in a gondola." Every gondolier showed her the outside of Marco Polo's house. Each one indicated a different house, and she came to realise that probably no one knew where exactly Marco Polo had lived. It had, nonetheless, been marvellous to visit the city where her parents had first met, and she sent them many postcards, which they were delighted to receive.

"I finally managed to get the Tabloid going," said Elspeth. "I've been up in her three times. I keep her at the airfield now. It's not far from Machynlleth."

And Alice nervously agreed to go for a flight with Elspeth the following day. That very next day was the one that the newspapers published details of Horniman's arrest together with his photograph. But newspapers were not delivered to Elspeth's house, so neither she nor Alice had any inkling of this news. So, when the Sopwith Tabloid finally ascended into the heights with them on board, it was a happy and excited pilot and a happy though nauseous passenger who both gazed at the ground below with wonder.

"What do you think?" shouted Elspeth.

"Wonderful!" shouted Alice, but she suddenly felt the need to sit back for a moment and close her eyes.

"It's supposed to be able to do up to 92 miles per hour," shouted Elspeth. But Alice did not answer.

The biplane was beautiful to behold. Down below, people looked up to marvel at the sight as she flew over their heads. Her small dimensions had inspired the name "Tabloid", and she flew as sweetly as she had done on her test flight nearly nineteen years before; Elspeth had done a marvellous job of restoration.

But all good things must come to an end, and it was with regret on Elspeth's part, and relief on Alice's, that they finally landed in the same airfield they had started from. Elspeth helped Alice to climb out, and the two walked towards a hut on one side of the field.

"I bet you're thirsty," said Elspeth. "Hungry too. I am. I could murder a sandwich. They'll give us something to eat in there if we ask nicely."

Over tea and sandwiches, they found plenty to laugh about.

"Gosh, you looked green," said Elspeth, "I thought you were going to throw up."

"So did I," said Alice.

Two local men in deep conversation walked in. "...got him after all this time."

"Yes, he'll come to a sticky end now."

The first man rolled his eyes.

"End of a rope," he said meaningfully.

"What are you two on about, Roger?" said Elspeth.

"Been in all the papers," said Roger. "They caught a chap who deserted during the war and murdered someone too."

"Oh, sounds like a bad lot."

"His picture's on the front page—here." said the other man, passing a newspaper to Elspeth as he spoke.

Elspeth looked at the photograph.

"He looks familiar, but I don't know why, what do you think? Looks like a ruffian to me." She handed the paper to Alice.

"It's Ralph Horniman! He's supposed to be dead!" Alice was truly shocked. "I don't know what to think. Don't you remember him? You were the one who helped him on that island."

"Is it?" said Elspeth. "I suppose it is a bit like him."

"I don't believe it! Ralph Horniman!" Alice read the article beneath the headline, but there were not many details, not even a name.

The days passed pleasantly. One afternoon, Alice took a local bus into Machynlleth. Elspeth remained at home, tinkering with one of her radios. The day was fresh, though away to the south, the sky looked dark and threatening. Alice, once she had stepped off the bus, walked to the second-hand bookshop she knew to be there—just to browse, for she did love bookshops, and she was in need of something new to read.

Behind the counter, a drab looking man perched on a stool was drinking tea from a chipped cup while reading a newspaper. Every so often, he chuckled to himself, and Alice, from her place at the back of the shop, heard him say at least once, "Is that so, well, I never!"

She had found two books that interested her, and was trying to decide which of them she should buy, when the bell over the shop door rang, and the postman walked in.

"Here you are," he said to the man behind the counter. "Only one for you this afternoon, a bill I'm afraid." And the postman left, calling back into the shop as the door shut, "Will we be seeing you later at the rehearsal?"

"Oh, yes, I'll be there."

"Right," said the postman, trilling his r with glee, "See you later, Ralphie-boy!" As he left, the bell jangled.

Alice decided to buy both books, and she went to the counter to pay. Ralphie-boy looked up at her and smiled as he took her money.

"Would you like a bag?" he said.

"No thanks, I have one," said Alice. Having left the shop she found somewhere to have some tea where she could flick through the books she had just bought.

At five-thirty, Elspeth entered at the tearoom where Alice was still sitting.

"There you are," she said, "I've been looking for you. I'm off to a rehearsal, you can come to watch if you like."

"A rehearsal?"

"Yes, the Machynlleth Male Voice Choir. They're rehearsing for a performance of popular pieces. I'm the rehearsal pianist, you see, so I have to be there."

The rehearsal began at half past six. Alice sat at the back of the hall, watching and listening. The singers included both the postman and the bookshop owner. The former evidently enjoyed himself, hugely, though Alice thought he opened his mouth too wide, over- enunciating each word. Since it was all was in Welsh, she understood nothing of the lyrics, but she did notice that the bookshop owner appeared to lose his place a few times and seemed less at home with the language.

The rehearsal finished in rousing style with Calon Lân, after which the singers were dismissed.

"What did you think?" Elspeth asked Alice once they were home. "I think they need more rehearsals," replied Alice.

CHAPTER ELEVEN

Even in his worst nightmare, Ralph Horniman never dreamed that he might one day be on trial for his life. Wherever he was taken, a host of reporters and cameramen seemed to be ready to surround him and his escort.

He slept badly every night, couldn't eat during the day, and looked a shadow of his former self. But he insisted that he had not murdered anyone, that it was all a terrible mistake, and that he had not deserted from the army. He was not believed; the proofs seemed incontrovertible.

Alice was still staying in Elspeth's house; her friend had persuaded her to stay over for Christmas and the New Year, though she was now beginning to feel the time had come to wander away once more, and that a visit to her parents might be in order. Meanwhile, she had arranged for a newspaper to be delivered daily, though they inevitably arrived a day late. She followed the Horniman trial with close attention.

Brecon County Herald

AN ADVERTISER FOR
Breconshire, Monmouthshire, Radnorshire, Glamorgan and Herefordshire

JANUARY 18TH 1933   1D

DESERTER TRIED FOR MURDER

The trial began at the Old Bailey yesterday of Ernest Sallow, one-time private of the 3rd Corps, otherwise known as Charles Johnson, also known as Ralph Horniman (52). Horniman, previously a hotel manager in Paunceton, was indicted before Mr Justice Finlayson, for the murder, in 1917, of Lance Corporal William George of the 3rd Corps who had been guarding him while Sallow was awaiting court-martial for desertion.

      The defendant entered a plea of Not Guilty. Sir Alfred Greene, prosecuting, said that the jury would hear of the despicable behaviour of the defendant, and that he had, with malice aforethought, plotted with a comrade, also a prisoner, to escape their confinement, even at the cost of a life.

The report continued with other trial preliminaries. The Thursday issue, delivered Friday, continued the case with the following details:

Brecon County Herald

AN ADVERTISER FOR
Breconshire, Monmouthshire, Radnorshire, Glamorgan and Herefordshire

January 19th 1933   1D

IDENTIFICATION OF ERNEST SALLOW

The case against Private Sallow continues to interest the public, and the court was full on Wednesday. It was stated that, since he was no longer a serving member of the armed forces, and had not been so for some years, a court-martial was no longer appropriate, and this was the reason for a civil trial. Readers of this paper have written asking about this, so it is good to be able to make this point.

Sir Alfred Greene, prosecuting, stated that since the defendant had denied that he was Ernest Sallow, and therefore denied that he was guilty of the charges, a number of witnesses would be called to identify him before the court.

No fingerprint evidence was available, since in the heat of the Great War, no fingerprints had been taken.

The first witness was ex-Private Arthur Meadows of the 3rd Corps who had served with Private Sallow. He declared that the defendant was undoubtedly Ernest Sallow, and that he "would know him anywhere". Cross-examined by Sir J.F. Muir, defending, he admitted that it was some years since he had seen Sallow, but said that there was a tell-tale birthmark on the defendant's temple that was exactly as he remembered it.

The second witness caused something of a sensation. This was ex-Private James Burnstock who, it seems, was turning King's Evidence, as it had been he who was with Ernest Sallow at the time of the murder of Lance-Corporal George and had himself escaped with Sallow.

Examined by Sir Alfred Greene, he made a clear statement identifying the defendant as Sallow. Sir Alfred stated that he would be recalling Burnstock later in the trial so that the jury would get a clear telling of the events as they had unfolded.

Cross-examined by Sir J.F. Muir, who again made the point that it was some years since this witness had seen Sallow, Burnstock stated that there was no doubt it was Sallow, as not only did he have the birthmark on his temple, he also had two webbed fingers on his left hand.

It was seen that this was indeed the case, and Mr Justice Finlayson instructed that no further witnesses need be called over the matter of identification.

Evidence was then shown to the court regarding the injuries sustained by Lance-Corporal George, and Sir Alfred Greene restated that he would be calling James Burnstock later and that he would describe exactly how those injuries had come about.

On Saturday morning the Friday paper arrived.

Brecon County Herald

AN ADVERTISER FOR
Breconshire, Monmouthshire, Radnorshire, Glamorgan and Herefordshire

January 20th 1933   1D

SALLOW SPEAKS

Private Burnstock described in great detail the death of Lance-Corporal George and pointed the finger squarely at Sallow as having been the one who instigated and actually carried out the killing against his own (Burnstock's) personal inclination. Sir Alfred Greene said that a case against Burnstock on a lesser charge would be heard in due course.

After a break for lunch, Ernest Sallow took the stand to give evidence himself, the case for the prosecution having been completed in a timely and efficient manner by Sir Alfred Greene. Sir J.F. Muir, defending, said that his client would be the only witness he proposed calling, and that he would describe everything truthfully.

The defendant, when questioned by his counsel denied that he was Ernest Sallow, though he admitted to using the names Ralph Horniman and Charles Johnson. He said that he knew no one who could vouch for his identity or for his whereabouts in 1917 but would not give a reason for this. He said that his name at birth was, in fact Charles Johnson and that he had grown up in an orphanage in Canada, now no longer in existence.

Sir J.F. Muir pointed out that although attempts had been made to establish the truth of this matter, there were a number of boys in various orphanages in Canada with the name Charles Johnson during the relevant years. Of those for whom records could be found, two had since died, one was currently a secretary to the current Dominion Prime Minister of Newfoundland, and three could not be traced.

The defendant was cross-examined by Sir Alfred Greene but was unshakeable.

A real mystery, in the opinion of this writer, therefore, exists as to the true identity of the defendant and whether or not he is, in fact, Ernest Sallow.

Mr Justice Finlayson said that he would make a statement about this matter in due course, though it seemed to him that the defendant was prevaricating and that there was little doubt in the matter.

Late on Saturday afternoon, Alice and Elspeth went together to Machynlleth in order to have a meal at one of the local hostelries. They had previously organised a car to take them back at the end of the evening and were looking forward to a pleasant supper.

A raucous crowd could be heard laughing in the saloon next to the private bar in which they were seated. Elspeth smiled when Alice pulled a face.

"Don't mind them," she said, "it's the end of the week; they've probably all been paid today."

A loud boozy tenor voice began singing one of the choir's songs, and others joined in:

Paham Mae dicter, O Myfanwy,
Yn llenwi'th lygaid duon di?
A'th ruddiau tirion, O Myfanwy,
Heb wrido wrth fy ngweled i?

"Dyna ni, Ralph, rhowch y cyfan sydd gennych chi!" called a voice.

"He's telling him to give it all he's got," said Elspeth, laughing. "I've picked up a little Welsh, you have to if you spend much time here."

A waiter came into the private bar with the meals Alice and Elspeth had ordered. "They seem to be having a good time," remarked Alice.

"Yes," said the waiter, "that's the Machynlleth Glee Club, well that's what I call 'em, unofficial-like, you know. They make a bit o' noise, but they spend a lot of money, so that pleases the boss. They don't usually get out of hand. That's Ralph you heard singing at the top of his lungs. His Welsh isn't too bad, considering he's not from round here originally, but he's got a way with the girls, has Ralph. Don't know how, he's nothing to look at, you know. Got a reputation he has for..." and he dropped his voice and leaned over to Elspeth and Alice, "...I shouldn't say this really to two ladies, but he's a bit of a ladies' man, you know. I am too, a bit. Anyway, the girls say he's always a bit horny, if you know what I mean." He stood up straight and laughed out loud. "Bit of an in-joke, you see, him being thought of as horny, because of his name, do you see, 'Horniman'." The waiter left.

Alice looked at Elspeth.

"Quite a coincidence," she said.

Elspeth, whose mouth was full, nodded; Alice looked unhappy.

Later, once sitting by the fire in Elspeth's house, Alice drew up a plan of action, for once her suspicion was aroused, she would not let a subject go till her mind was set at rest.

"There won't be any more news about the trial till Wednesday, I think," said Alice thoughtfully. She continued slowly, "If they start again on Monday, that will be reported in Tuesday's edition, and we won't see it till Wednesday, so that gives me time to do a little digging of my own."

"What are you going to do?"

"I'm going to get to know that other Ralph Horniman; he owns the bookshop in Machynlleth. I just want to make sure..."

Elspeth yawned.

"Even if that Sallow fellow is found guilty, nothing can happen for a few weeks, so there's no immediate urgency. I wonder how long they actually have to wait after a guilty verdict before a death sentence can be carried out."

"What a thing to ask! I don't know, but I expect there's a rule."

Alice was right; of course, there was a rule. Regulations stated that a delay of at least three Sundays was necessary between a sentence of death and an execution. Even if Alice had known this, it would have been of no comfort, for if, as she suspected, or maybe hoped, the authorities were trying the wrong Ralph Horniman, a great injustice might be done. She thought of going to the police, but she knew that she had so little information that she might be laughed at in that awful patronising kind of way that she hated.

Brecon County Herald

AN ADVERTISER FOR
Breconshire, Monmouthshire, Radnorshire, Glamorgan and Herefordshire

January 24th 1933

1D

SENTENCED TO HANG

SALLOW GUILTY— PROTESTS INNOCENCE

Ernest Sallow was, yesterday at the Old Bailey, found guilty of the murder of Lance Corporal William George in France on December 15th, 1917 and sentenced to be hanged.

"I am not guilty," he protested when asked if he had anything to say.

The prisoner heard the sentence quietly and left the dock without assistance.

CHAPTER TWELVE

Alice visited the bookshop a few times and tried to engage the "other" Ralph Horniman in conversation, but with little result. On one occasion, she thought she had achieved something when, on leaving the shop, she had called out to him, "Bye Ernest," and he had lifted his hand and waved in a desultory fashion. She mentioned this to Elspeth who was fairly dismissive, pointing out that this was hardly evidence to show anything of a suspicious nature. Still, Alice was not completely reassured.

January turned to February. Alice was still with Elspeth and had become easier in her mind. After all, she reasoned, one had to have trust in the law, and to understand that those who policed the country and those who decided the fate of a condemned person had only the best interests of all at heart. And did not twelve women and men, people of common-sense, sit on juries? The system was intrinsically fair, of that she was sure, and so, she settled back to a comfortable life. Elspeth agreed with her, though she herself was becoming restless.

The weather in January was mild for the time of year, and February, though cold, looked as if it would continue the trend. But on February 23rd, great gales began to sweep across England and Wales, bringing with them heavy snowstorms and deep snowdrifts. Alice and Elspeth were effectively cut off from the rest of civilisation. But they were snug, for they had plenty of supplies and lots of fuel to keep themselves warm, so they settled down to weather out the days. A huge whiteness covered the land and filled the sky, and they sat talking through the hours, or quietly dreaming in front of the fire. Both had warm hats that they wore most of the time, only removing them when the heat of the fire became too much to bear.

The blizzard lasted four days, and at the end of that time, Alice and Elspeth ventured out to look at the landscape and to stretch their legs. They took shovels with them and heaved away at the snow to clear paths wherever possible.

"I wish we could get to the town," said Alice, "but the bus won't be able to reach us with the roads in this state."

"We'll have to go soon, or there'll be nothing left to eat." Elspeth struggled over to a lean-to shed at the side of the house. "There's a tandem in here, I used to ride it with my father. But we can't ride that either, not through all this." And she swept her arms round in a large circle gesturing to indicate the snow, which lay deeply on the ground.

The days grew warmer, and a thaw began, but it was still another week before the way was clear enough for any vehicles to use the road. Finally, a post van arrived driven by a woman who usually worked at the post office in Machynlleth. She got out and marched as best as she could through the slush and snow, carrying a small basket to the front door, and was immediately invited in.

"We heard you coming, so the kettle's on," said Elspeth.

"Ooh, wonderful. It's freezing out there. I thought I'd bring some supplies with me; I don't suppose you've been able to get much. There's bread and butter and tea, some eggs, and goodness knows what else. I didn't pack it myself you see, my Ifor did that, he's ever so handy with those things, but he's hurt his leg, so I drove here instead of him. I expect you haven't been able to keep up much with the news, so I can tell you about everything I know. I can't stay long, but I brought you a newspaper—it's only the Brecon County Herald, but I expect you're used to that."

Despite her insistence that she couldn't stay long, she stayed for nearly an hour, talking and talking. Elspeth and Alice were very grateful. Not only for all the supplies, but also for the newspaper: it had been impossible to use the radio for days as the signal was so bad. They didn't even mind the chitchat, as it seemed such a relief to both of them to hear another voice.

Later, they divided the newspaper between them and began to read.

Brecon County Herald

AN ADVERTISER FOR
Breconshire, Monmouthshire, Radnorshire, Glamorgan and Herefordshire

March 6th 1933   1D

EXECUTION DATE

MURDERER OF LANCE CORPORAL WILLIAM GEORGE TO BE HANGED THIS FRIDAY

The execution of Ernest Sallow, once known as Ralph Horniman, has been fixed for Friday next at Pentonville Prison.

    Sallow was convicted of murder at the Old Bailey on 23 January. No application for leave to appeal was made to the Court of Appeal.

VENEFICIA PUBLICATIONS

the power behind the written word

The year is 1931. Newly married, Alice Winsome leaves her fortune-seeking husband and travels to a town on the south coast of England to stay at the Hotel Splendide.

But the building is not all it seems to be.

The dark secrets of the hotel staff slowly unravel to reveal a web of mysteries. And while the lifts go up and down, carrying guests from floor to floor, conspiracies and intrigue threaten Alice's peace of mind.

veneficiapublications.com

Alice's heart pounded as she read about the forthcoming execution. Not that she doubted anymore the justice of the sentence, but it had been some days since she had given the matter any thought, and, after all, this was about someone she had met and spoken to, although she had not known him very well.

It gnawed at her! The vision of the hotel manager's face appeared to her in her dreams that night, and the next, and again on Wednesday. Elspeth looked concerned, but though she too had met Ralph Horniman, albeit briefly, she was made of sterner stuff and refused to believe that there was any need for Alice to upset herself. Perhaps a more comforting attitude towards her friend might have helped, but on Thursday night, Alice's dream was worse still.

2 am: A knock at the door; Alice sat up in bed.

"Alice," called Elspeth from outside, "are you all right?"

"Sorry," said Alice, "a nightmare."

She had been dreaming of spectral nuns wandering the corridors behind the Hotel Splendide, carrying lanterns that cast an eerie green light upon the decapitated head of Ralph Horniman, which seemed to float before them, tongue lolling out between his lips and spectacles hanging loosely from one ear. A purple ink stain on his ivory-coloured waistcoat met with a red stain of blood, which glistened as it continued to ooze its irresistible way towards the fob pocket, wherein lay a broken bottle of purple ink, stopperless.

Elspeth opened the door and entered the room.

"Something's not right," said Alice, "suppose they caught the wrong one?" Elspeth looked puzzled,

"I don't understand."

"The wrong Ralph Horniman."

Elspeth looked doubtful,

"He was identified at the trial. We've talked about this before."

"Yes, but he denied everything. What if they're wrong?"

Alice was disturbed enough to get out of bed. "I don't know what we can do," she said, "he'll be hanged in the morning."

"All right," said Elspeth, "if you're really sure you want to do something, there's only one thing to do."

Elspeth had an idea, and only a few minutes later, they were both dressed, seated on the tandem, and pedalling furiously towards Machynlleth and then onwards to the Machynlleth Loop airfield, a further eleven miles to the north.

A night ride on a tandem through the freezing winter is a treacherous thing to attempt. The road was slippery and dark. A light rain fell, but the sky was clear in parts, and a waxing gibbous moon sent occasional beams of silvery light to help show the way. It still took nearly three hours to cover the distance, and they were both exhausted on arrival.

"We'll never get anyone's attention at this time of night," called Alice from her seat behind Elspeth. But Elspeth pedalled on; she had a plan in mind, and on arrival, she went into the hut which served as a base for the airfield. Sure enough, there were two men inside.

"I knew I'd find you here," said Elspeth, "don't you ever leave this place?"

"What on earth..." began one of the men.

"Never mind that. Is the runway clear?"

"Yes, but..."

"I have to get the Tabloid out. Now!"

There was no time, but it took a further hour to prepare for a take-off. Alice was aghast at the audacity of Elspeth's plan. The two men were amazed at the stupidity of it all.

"Why not simply phone?" said one of them.

"Good idea," said Elspeth. "You find a way to make a phone call. We're off on a rescue mission."

And so, with Elspeth and Alice seated side by side in the two-seater Sopwith Tabloid, the race was on. A night flight to London to rescue an innocent man.

CHAPTER THIRTEEN

In 'A' Wing of Pentonville Prison, in the condemned cell closest to 'the drop', Ernest Sallow, also known as Charles Johnson, once known as Ralph Horniman, respected manager of the Hotel Splendide, Paunceton-sur-la-Mer, was seated on a wooden stool eating a sausage. The cell was not cold; sometimes, it was quite stuffy inside. The drab greyness of the walls dulled the senses and made everything seem as if it was happening at a distance, to someone other than himself. It was early Friday morning—the day of the great happening.

The previous day, he had been sized up by the hangman. Not that the condemned man had realised that that was what was happening, finding only that he was being introduced to one of the pleasantest men he had met in a very long time. It was, he felt, one of the friendliest meetings he had ever had, and what a lovely smile his visitor had.

The two men had shaken hands and had a charming conversation, which gave the prisoner a sense of such relief that he almost felt as though he did not mind the inevitable event; he was well past protesting his innocence.

"How are you keeping? Do they give you everything you need?"

"Yes, indeed, though I could wish I was not overlooked by someone all the time."

"Ah, that's the way of it, you see. They have to keep an eye out for your safety. We don't want anything happening to you, do we?" And the visitor smiled with the appearance of an almost brotherly affection.

"Do you have enough to eat, now? Have you ordered your breakfast for tomorrow?"

"Yes, thanks. Nothing special. Sausages and toast and a cup of coffee with sugar."

"Ah, that's nice. One of my favourite breakfasts too. Well, I shan't keep you, I have everything I need."

The visitor looked at one of the prison warders standing nearby. "I'll be off then. Make sure to give him enough sugar." Then he turned back to the prisoner, "Goodbye now, I'll see you again soon." And he was shown out by the warder he had spoken to.

"What a lovely man," said the prisoner to the other warder. "I'll look forward to his next visit."

"Yes, it's often remarked upon. He's very easy to talk to, all his family are, in fact."

The prisoner had no idea, of course, that the gallows itself lay just beyond another door, almost immediately next to his bed. The door was disguised as a sort of closet, and it was through it that he would go when his time came.

Door—Hood—Rope—Drop. That would be it!

But for now, he eats the sausage left over from his early breakfast. A calm contentment steals over him as he drinks the coffee, which remains in the mug he holds in one hand. He leans back against the wall and shuts his eyes, oblivious to the other prison sounds, which echo from corridors both distant and nearby. Clanging, banging, footsteps, shouting—everything fades into the bleak greyness that surrounds him. His time is almost up, as the hangman has entered the prison by the little door under the arch.

The hangman feels a tingle of excitement this morning, for this will be his two-hundredth hanging, quite a milestone. His wife had kissed him on his cheek and wished him luck as he left the house, where, indeed, his breakfast had consisted of toast and a sausage washed down with coffee. He did not eat the bacon this morning as it looked a bit too greasy, sitting on his plate with its waxy stripes. He walks towards 'A Wing' with a happy heart, though he takes his work seriously and never underestimates the gravity of the proceedings.

The prisoner feels a pang of adrenaline like a sharp stab in the pit of his stomach, for thoughts of today have finally entered his brain, though he was trying to ignore them. Beating heart. Thumping in his chest. "Breathe slowly." No good. He just wants it over and done with. The waiting is unbearable.

In his cell, the condemned man thinks of a hidden secret that he knows—something that lies dark and unknown to any but himself—something that might have made his dreams come true. And he thought of what a waste his life had been, and what a waste his death would be. And none would ever know his secret, for he had explored the tunnels that lay behind the hotel, and he knew of a hidden treasure nestled at the heart of the maze of corridors. It was an old legend, but he thought he knew its whereabouts.

"If only I had been given the chance to get it, all my problems would have evaporated, and I would be free." It was a treasure beyond the value of riches, for the stories told of a life-giving power. And still, he dreams on, awaiting his end.

Time moves slowly. Every movement of his head seems slow. But there is no end to time.

CHAPTER FOURTEEN

Alice sat in the Tabloid wrapped in blankets in as low a position as she could, trying her best to keep as warm as possible. Elspeth flew as low as she dared, but it was bitterly cold, though at least the rain had stopped. The moon shone between the clouds as they flew over rivers, ponds and wooded places. Towns nestling in the shadows seemed to hold a promise of warmth whenever, as occasionally happened, a streetlamp remained lit, or where a light could be seen through the window of a house where somebody was still awake, even in the early hours of the morning. Perhaps a mother bringing a cup of warm milk to a child who had been awakened from a bad dream. Alice thought of her own mother and remembered nights like these when she had been enveloped by the comforting smell of warm milk mixed with the burnt tobacco that her mother had been smoking until the early hours of the morning, for she rarely slept. How she wished she was home in Mandible Hall, snuggled up in her own bed.

Elspeth cast occasional glances at her friend as they flew, but for the most part looked only ahead with a grim look on her face, determined to support Alice, even if she felt she might be mistaken in her belief that a great injustice would be done. Both of them were attempting mental arithmetic, unaware that the other was doing the same.

About two hundred miles to travel. Maximum speed of the Tabloid under ideal circumstances: 92mph. Probable maximum speed right now: say... 80mph (on average). Two hundred miles at 80mph equals two-and-a-half hours. We left the house at midnight. Three hours to the Mach Loop, one hour to get airborne equals 4am, two-and-a-half hours, call it three to get to London equals 7am.

"I know where to land," called Elspeth, "Hounslow Heath Aerodrome. It's decommissioned, but there's still a landing strip, and then we can make a rush for it."

The illogicality of the flight never occurred to them, for the hanging would take place at either 8 or 9am, probably the earlier time, and the likelihood of arriving in time to stop it was negligible.

Still, the Tabloid flew on. The noise was indescribable. Elspeth, under normal circumstances, would have been enjoying the flight; Alice loathed every moment of it. The wind sailed past her ears, and she could hardly breathe unless she sat so low in her seat that she might be aware of nothing but the impenetrable drone of the engine. The increasing numbness in her legs and the ache in the centre of her back made her weep in fury at herself, and at last she yelled a great cry of anguish to the passing clouds. No one heard, not even Elspeth who, at that moment, had burrowed down in her cockpit to check a map by the light of an electric torch.

But eventually, Elspeth began to curve around a small area of flat land below.

"I hope those guys at the Mach Loop found a way to get through to Hounslow to let them know we were on the way. I don't fancy landing in the dark."

"What do you mean?" called Alice back to her, shocked. She had not thought about any problems they might have landing; it had seemed so easy when she had flown with Elspeth before.

They needn't have worried; the sky was clear, and the runway was not difficult to see.

Elspeth began the descent.

Once they had landed, Elspeth clambered out and then turned to assist Alice, who was in some difficulty. A man was running over to them waving his arms and shouting.

"You can't land here! What do you think you are doing?"

But Elspeth ignored his indignation.

"Here, you, help my friend to get out, we've been flying for nearly three hours."

"In that thing!"

"Are you going to help us or not?" demanded Elspeth.

Alice was lifted out and assisted to the office on one side of the aerodrome. Both she and Elspeth were in dire straits, but there was no time to lose, and a taxi was summoned. It was now 7am.

"How long will it take to drive to Pentonville Prison," asked Alice. "About one hour and five or ten minutes," said the driver.

"We'll be too late!" said Alice, looking flustered.

"How quickly can you get there if you really step on it?" asked Elspeth.

"I could do it in about forty-five or fifty minutes if the police don't stop me."

"Go as fast as you can," said Elspeth. "It's a matter of life or death."

CHAPTER FIFTEEN

Three things happened within a few moments.

Firstly, the hangman entered 'A' Wing of Pentonville Prison.

Secondly, the prison governor, who was already present, went over to him to have a few words.

Thirdly, the taxi carrying Alice and Elspeth arrived at the entrance to the prison and managed, with some difficulty, to persuade the pleasant gentleman who greeted them there that they were on a mission of some urgency.

Meanwhile the condemned man sat in his cell awaiting his fate.

Somehow a message was conveyed to the governor, who, after telling the hangman to wait where he was, made his ponderous way to the visitors' waiting room.

The governor was somewhat startled by the request made of him by the two ladies who confronted him as soon as he entered the room. "This is not the way these things are done," he said. "This is unprecedented in my experience. But I will put a hold on proceedings and contact the Home Secretary; he is the only person who can make a decision of this nature."

Sir John Gilmour, Home Secretary, was at home. He was not pleased to be disturbed at that precise moment, suffering, as he was just then, with "...an infernal toothache, an' I have t'go to the dentist for an extraction." But he was of the opinion that a halt must be put to the proceedings while an examination into the affair was made.

And so, wheels were put in motion for the prisoner to be granted mercy, though to remain confined at His Majesty's pleasure until the investigation was made.

The hangman was sent away without the satisfaction of receiving the prisoner's suit, as would have been his right, and the governor went to give the good news to Ernest Sallow, a.k.a. Ralph Horniman, a.k.a... etc.

Elspeth and Alice felt that all their trouble was justified; they almost crowed with excitement. They were not, though, permitted to see the man they had saved from the gallows, but, with much to celebrate, they made their way to Piccadilly and treated themselves to breakfast at the Ritz.

A remarkable discovery was about to be made. A lowly clerk in the office of the Home Secretary was sent by his superior, a gentleman who reported to the assistant of the assistant (and so forth) of Sir John Gilmour himself, to Somerset House, to investigate all that could be found pertaining to of the early life of Ernest Sallow—for it was there that records were kept. He waited for some hours to be given all that was needful, having impressed upon the clerk at Somerset House the gravity and importance of his mission. Eventually, he was given a manilla envelope, which upon examination, he found contained two documents. He walked away, reading them as he went. The first was a birth certificate, which confirmed what was already known. The second was more surprising. It was a marriage certificate, and it caused him to pull up short, turn on his heels and go back to make a further inquiry.

"Look here," he said to the clerk who had originally helped him. "This Mrs Dorothy Ann Sallow, née Perkins, is she still alive?"

Some time later he was told that no death certificate could be found, and that, therefore, it must be presumed that the lady was indeed still living.

The matter was escalated, for no mention of a wife had been made, nor had anybody come forward to identify the putative Ralph Horniman as Ernest Sallow who had known Sallow prior to his army service. It was put into the hands of the police who made a search for Dorothy Sallow, but it seemed she had disappeared.

Meanwhile, in Machynlleth, the other Ralph Horniman had also vanished, and since his whereabouts were of some importance, he too was being sought by the police.

The following day was Saturday the 11th of March. Alice went shopping in Knightsbridge, for she needed something nice to wear. She had taken rooms at the Ritz, having decided to stay in London for a week or so. She had never really enjoyed London before but, with her new-found confidence, she had decided to make the most of her time there. Elspeth, on the other hand, decided to return to Wales.

Alice went into Harrods and bought a cashmere coat, as during the flight, her old one had been stained with black oil. She wandered through the Book Department on the 2nd floor and, suddenly, saw someone she knew. She pulled up short and turned away, as it was Arthur Winsome, her husband, and he was with a lady. Alice was not exactly displeased, in fact, she rather hoped that the lady would be a paramour, and therefore offer grounds for divorce. She had not thought about Arthur for weeks, even months, and it occurred to her that the time might have come to give her relationship with him a proper ending. She left Harrods without making eye contact with Arthur and hoped never to have to see him again.

Arthur and his girlfriend continued their perambulation, never dreaming that Alice had been in their vicinity.

CHAPTER SIXTEEN

The Daily Standard

LONDON EDITION   **LONDON Thursday March 16th**   **2D**

DOROTHY SALLOW FOUND

After an investigation of remarkable tenacity, it has been revealed that Mrs Sallow, wife of Ernest Sallow, currently under sentence of death, has been located. Since some doubt as to the true identity of the condemned man has been raised, it was deemed necessary to locate this lady who, it transpires, was married to Sallow in 1911. Surely, she will be able to identify him. The question of course remains as to why she had not been traced earlier, and thus appeared at the trial itself.

However, it has been revealed to this writer that the lady in question had been very ill for a number of years and had been dwelling in a sanatorium.

Since leaving there she has lived at Rye, where she has been living a secluded life, and was unaware of the trial. It is expected that she will see the supposed Sallow tomorrow afternoon, and we will be reporting the result as soon as it is known.

The Daily Standard

LONDON EDITION — LONDON Saturday March 18th — 2D

NOT SALLOW

Yesterday afternoon, Mrs Dorothy Sallow was brought forward to identify the prisoner Ernest Sallow, whose sentence to death for the murder of Lance Corporal George had been temporarily delayed pending identification on her part. It now transpires that the prisoner is not Ernest Sallow at all, and that his name is, in fact, Charles Johnson, sometime known as Ralph Horniman. Matters are now in hand for the arrangement of the pardon and release of the prisoner, Johnson.

The wheels of Justice work slowly, and so, it took some days for the following document, signed by George V, to be produced. And it was on March 28th that the prisoner was released.

George the Fifth *By the Grace of God of the United Kingdom of Great Britain and Northern Ireland and of Our other Realms and Territories King, Head of the Commonwealth, Defender of the Faith, To all whom these Presents shall come Greeting!*

Whereas *Charles Johnson, also known as Ralph Horniman, sometime thought to have been Ernest Sallow, at the Central Criminal Court, London on the twenty-third day of January, 1933, was convicted of the murder of Lance Corporal William George of the 3rd Corps in December, 1917, and was sentenced to a Judgement of Death:*

Now know ye *that We in consideration of some circumstances humbly represented unto Us are Graciously pleased to extend Our Grace and Mercy unto the said Charles Johnson, also known as Ralph Horniman, and to grant him Our Free Pardon in respect of said conviction, thereby pardoning, remitting and releasing unto him all pains, penalties and punishments whatsoever that from the said conviction may ensue; and We do hereby command all Justices and others whom it may concern that they take due notice hereof;*

And for so doing this shall be a sufficient Warrant Given at Our Court at St James's the twenty-seventh day of March, 1933, in the twenty-third year of Our reign.

By His Majesty's Command

Charles Johnson, once Manager of the Hotel Splendide, left Pentonville Prison and disappeared, for the moment, into the sea of people that forms the population of the London metropolis. He looked older than his years and, though still overweight, was not as stout as before. Indeed, he had the appearance of one whose body had sagged, gone to seed, and yellowed with worry.

Mrs Sallow was returned to Rye but was told that there may be a need for her to make a further identification. The Welsh Ralph Horniman, however, could not be found. Suspicions were raised further, when, on searching his place of work and his home, no vestige of his possessions could be found either.

Alice, of course, felt fully justified. She had, by her actions and clear-thinking, saved an innocent man from a terrible injustice, and also led the police to search for the real criminal. It only remained for the real Ernest Sallow to be located.

Could Mrs Sallow's statement that the prisoner was not her husband be trusted? Had she intentionally misled the authorities? Or was it possible that Sallow had altered so much since she had last seen him that she did not recognise him, even though it was he? For here the mystery deepens; a photograph of the Welsh Ralph Horniman was located and brought to Rye for Mrs Sallow to look at. She stated that there was a "kind of similarity," but added, "this is definitely not my husband!"

CHAPTER SEVENTEEN

Charles Johnson sat in his flat in Willesden staring at the wall. He was thoroughly disillusioned with life; things had not gone according to plan. Though, and here he congratulated himself a bit, no one had actually asked why he had changed his name to Ralph Horniman before establishing himself in the hotel business.

As far as the other Ralph Horniman was concerned, not a trace had been found, and his friends were concerned about what might have happened to him. Of course, his part in these events was over, for it seems that he was not Ernest Sallow, unless, again, Mrs Sallow had been mistaken. But no! The Welshman was not Sallow. He had secretly upped sticks for his own reasons and sneaked out of Machynlleth taking all his belongings with him. He had been making himself rather too familiar with the landlady of his local pub, and the landlord had become quite unpleasant about it. Not only that, but the landlord owned the freehold of the bookshop that he leased and was making his life a living hell. He did not go far, though. Merely over the English border to Ludlow.

It had now been established that Ernest Sallow had changed his name to Ralph Horniman, and also that there were only two men in the whole of Britain calling themselves by that name, neither of whom, it now appeared, could be the long-missing murderer.

For some weeks the newspapers had continued speculating on the matter, until it became old news, dropping, eventually, from their pages altogether. All returned to normality, though, what "normal" means is a matter of opinion.

It was 1936. Three-and-a-half years had passed. Johnson had been given a small amount of compensation by the government and was living frugally, but without working. He thought of getting a job, but much of his joie de vivre seemed to have been sucked out of him, and he could hardly bear to walk out of his front door. He toyed with joining the march through Cable Street scheduled for Sunday 4 October. It wasn't that fascist ideals appealed to him, but an increasing longing for action made him think about how he might find a cause to fight for. Not that he was a fighting man—he had managed to avoid getting involved in any fighting for years now... but he mustn't think about that. Those thoughts could lead him to betray himself in a way that he did not want...

And so it was that on that Sunday, Charles Johnson took himself to London's East End, joined the British Union of Fascists and marched towards Cable Street singing the anthem that, at one time, he had hated. Things did not go quite as he expected. In his own mind, he had thought of a gallant march with Oswald Mosley as a glorious leader. However, reality soon kicked in, and the rioting was enough to make him turn away before he reached the ensuing melee.

As he turned away, he heard a voice call, "Well, if it isn't Ralph Horniman." He turned and, suddenly, found himself face-to-face with the last person he wished to see: Stephen Giddins.

Stephen looked as though he was prospering. He was smartly dressed in a suit of clerical grey; a bowler hat sat on his head, and he held a copy of the *Sunday Times*.

Charles Johnson looked at him, trying to appear nonchalant, as if this meeting meant nothing to him, though the circumstances of their last conversation still rankled.

"Hello, Stephen, you look like a stockbroker, why on earth are you dressed in business clothes on a Sunday?"

"If it comes to that, why are you dressed like a tramp?"

Stephen's remark, though unkind, was not too far from the truth. Charles Johnson was rather shabbily dressed. His shirt was un-ironed, and the shirt collar showed signs that indicated said item had not been washed for some time; his hat was a rather battered trilby.

He turned roughly away from Stephen Giddins, but he had only taken one step when a hand was placed firmly upon his right shoulder, and he was spun round to face him once more.

"Keep your hands off me!" he said through gritted teeth.

"Or what?" came the reply. "You're in no condition to deal with me. Look at you! What a state, what a come-down, eh? And you, always so high and mighty till you got in too deep with other peoples' money."

"What do you want? Mind, I don't have any money to give you."

"Yes, you owe me quite a sum. Still, we won't say anything about that—not if you do what you're told. By the way, I suppose I have to call you Johnson now."

"It's my name, damn you!" said Johnson sullenly.

"Well, I have a job for you, and, unfortunately, you're the only person qualified for it."

"I have no idea what you are talking about."

"No? Well, I don't suppose you could have. Come on, we're off for a little chat somewhere more private." This last remark was made with a gesture of some annoyance on Giddins's part, for two men standing not far away had suddenly become interested in what he had been saying.

The following morning saw Giddins, still dressed smartly, and Johnson, still shabby, though he had made some attempt to smarten himself up (even to the extent of washing his face), on a train southbound from Victoria Station to—and let this not come as a surprise—Paunceton Muffet.

"What's all this about?" asked Johnson once they were seated.

"You'll see. Now keep quiet, I have some thinking to do."

That Stephen Giddins was concocting a plan to obtain money by dishonest means was never in doubt. Johnson had no real objection to dishonesty—life had taught him a sharp lesson, namely that he needed to use his wits to survive. However, he did object to being in the power of a man like Giddins, and there was no doubt that he was in his power, for Stephen Giddins knew Johnson's secret: knew for a certainty that Charles Johnson, one-time hotel manager known as Ralph Horniman, was indeed Ernest Sallow. This in itself might seem to hold no danger for him, for once acquitted a person could not be retried for the same crime. However, there were, in this case, two problems with this rule of double jeopardy, which Giddins made clear to him. Firstly, Johnson's pardon depended on his lack of identity with Sallow, and if it should come to light that the pardon was incorrectly given, it might very well be revoked. Secondly, should that not prove enough to ensure his compliance, since the crime was committed in France, might not the French authorities be interested in extradition and a trial on their own terms?

These were abstract points of law, and the criminal knew this, being an intelligent man, but he did not care to test the matter, and so his compliance was unwillingly given.

INTERLUDE

Notes from The Lift Operators' Manual (1922)

English electric lifts are often wainscotted with hardwood panels (oak, mahogany, or teak), to 4 feet or so, topped with wrought iron, sometimes ornamental. Some lifts have mirrors for the convenience of passengers. Other lifts are constructed with steel frames with wire panels. These are incombustible and preferred on occasion. Occasionally, glass panels may be seen. Seats are sometimes fitted in larger lifts, but these have, in recent times, fallen somewhat out of favour. Lifts in enclosed shafts are sometimes fitted with emergency call bells, or even telephones, so that the lift operator is able to summon assistance should it be required. Electric light fittings are often installed at extra cost. The floors of most lifts are made of either linoleum or cork.

Older lifts have collapsible gates made of half-inch steel bars, together with tracks at the top and bottom, and are so configured that the lift may not move unless both inner and outer gates are shut.

They are sometimes referred to as 'scissor gates'. The more modern lift may not use collapsible gates, but instead be fitted with sliding doors.

These are usually deemed to be safer.

Passengers should not, for their own safety, get in or out of a lift while it is in motion, enter if the lift is too full, stand too near to the entrance, touch the operating controls, or talk to the operator.

A friction safety mechanism is the most usual way of ensuring that the lift cannot fall down the shaft should there be a problem with the ropes or cables. A counter-weight balances the moving lift. In the event of emergency, a crank handle is usually fitted, by means of which the lift attendant can wind the lift to the nearest floor level.

Lifts must be regularly serviced to see that all is in working order and that the guide rails are well-lubricated. Modern lifts contain reservoirs of lubricating oil, keeping the rails oiled during operation, but these will need filling from time to time. There was a time when rails were greased by hand, and lift attendants were known to climb the lift shafts to do this, a method known to be dangerous.

Lift controllers must be able to start the lift from rest, accelerate smoothly to full speed, and then slow down to enable the lift to stop at the right place, and then hold its position. The attendant selects the direction, up or down, and also controls the speed. The equipment supplied is as follows:

The operating device (rope, switch, lever or buttons), a magnetic brake control, and the door or gate locking mechanisms.

When a lever or handle is used to operate a lift, it is usually of the dead man type, so that if the attendant lets go, the lift will immediately come to a stop. This handle is invariably detachable and carried by the lift attendant so that, if a lift is unattended, no passenger will be able to start it moving.

More modern lifts are being designed which eliminate the need for a lift attendant. The passenger selects the floor by pressing a button and the lift moves automatically. Some passengers have been known to be rather reticent about travelling in these, and some buildings still employ lift attendants to operate the lifts even when they are operated in this fashion.

Notes for Lift Attendants

1. Do not hurry your passengers.

2. Insist politely that passengers stand back from the entrance so that they cannot be caught by the closing doors.

3. Close the outer and inner doors before starting the lift, making certain that all passengers are clear of them.

4. Do not allow passengers to leave if the lift is in motion.

5. Do not allow more passengers into the lift once it is at capacity.

6. Always try to make a perfect landing; ensure that the lift floor is level with the landing floor, and without making any bumps.

7. Never leave the lift without taking your lever or starting key with you.

8. When the lift is moving, never remove your hand from the control.

9. Make sure the lift has fully stopped before reversing direction.

10. Remain calm if there is an emergency and follow all safety regulations.

PART 3
ALICE AND THE LIFT

From Flowers of History by Roger of Wendover (died 1236) —Translated from Latin by J.A. Giles, D.C.L.—1849

Of the death of John, King of England—A.D. 1216

...John with a large force had been committing terrible ravages in the counties of Suffolk and Norfolk. At last, he took his way through the town of Lynn, where he was received with joy by the inhabitants, and received large presents from them. He then took his march towards the north, but in crossing the river Wellester, he lost all his carts, waggons, and baggage horses, together with his money, costly vessels, and everything which he had a particular regard for; for the land opened in the middle of the water and caused whirlpools which sucked in everything, as well as men and horses, so that no one escaped to tell the king of the misfortune. He himself narrowly escaped with his army, and passed the following night at a convent called Swineshead, where, as was thought, he felt such anguish of mind about his property which was swallowed up by the waters, that he was seized with a violent fever and became ill; his sickness was increased by his pernicious gluttony, for that night he surfeited himself with peaches and drinking new cider, which greatly increased and aggravated the fever in him...

CHAPTER ONE

The Daily Standard—Monday, October 5, 1936

> *HOTEL MANAGER REQUIRED*
>
> *FOR LARGE FAMILY AND COMMERCIAL HOTEL in PAUNCETON.*
>
> *Must be thoroughly experienced and good disciplinarian. References must bear the strictest investigation.*
>
> *Apply, by letter in first instance, to X435.*

Mrs Garthwaite sat in the lounge of the Hotel Splendide writing a letter to her sister. She had, she wrote, decided to advertise for a new hotel manager, no longer wanting to continue in that role herself. To tell the truth, her time as manager of the hotel she owned had been something of a disappointment, and she felt disillusioned with the whole thing. It was not that she had done badly—far from it; the hotel had prospered and gone from strength to strength. It was just that she found that she was not enjoying the direct reins of power, whereas she had enjoyed operating things from behind the scenes. Her sister, she knew, would sympathise and understand. At that moment, there were a number of renovations planned in the hotel, and it was operating with fewer guests and staff, so this seemed the ideal time to break in a new manager.

Three-and-a-half years earlier, she had attended the final day of the trial of the hotel's ex-manager at the Old Bailey with mixed feelings. She had been interviewed by the police—a distressing meeting—but had been assured that there would be no need for her to give evidence at the trial itself. She felt a sense of horror mixed with shame, upset and sympathy, but mostly it was the feeling of shame that dominated: shame that she had allowed a man such as this to have been given a senior position in her hotel. The Guilty verdict gave her no relief, as she felt she had been thoroughly betrayed by this man. The death sentence had made her feel ill. The reprieve and release had sent her into floods of tears, though whether from anger or relief even she could not say. Her sister had visited her at that time and had given what comfort she could.

She rose from her chair, letter in hand. Then, looking up, she saw standing before her the trim figure of Alice Winsome.

"Alice, how lovely to see you. What are you doing here?"

"I came down on the train this afternoon—only got back from France on Saturday. I've been travelling. London, Paris—shopping mostly."

"How wonderful you look! Paris fashions? Marvellous!"

"Yes, they really know how to dress there. I haven't been home for ages; my parents will be really surprised when they see me."

"I'm sure they will."

Mrs Garthwaite called over a waiter, who was clearing away some things from a nearby table and ordered afternoon tea for two.

"Are you still using your married name?" she asked Alice.

"Yes, the divorce can't happen for a couple of years, and Arthur has been making things a bit awkward, but actually I quite like my surname, it's nicer than my maiden name."

"Well, I know your father is Lord Tongue, but is that the family name?"

"Good heavens, no! That would be dreadful. Alice Tongue! No, the family name is Tingey, which isn't so bad until you put Alice in front of it, and then it sounds as if I'm mean with money."

The conversation continued for a while, and then the tea arrived.

"By the way," said Alice interrupting herself in the act of biting into a dainty sandwich, "I saw your advertisement in The *Daily Standard*. Are you really going to give up managing the hotel?"

"Only in appearance. I'll still be pulling the strings behind the scenes—or from above, if you prefer, rather like a puppeteer with a marionette."

"That will annoy the new manager, though, won't it?"

"Possibly. Anyway, are you staying with us tonight? We have some nice rooms available."

Alice arranged to stay for a week. Life can be one permanent holiday for those who are rich enough, so it would seem. Secretly, though, she thought that she still had a certain amount of unfinished business to complete. She wanted to take her time exploring the passages and tunnels that lay behind and beneath the hotel, and it was this that had brought her back. She decided that she would begin the following morning after breakfast.

There had been a change of personnel in the hotel staff. In particular, Andrew, Mary, Ben and Angela had all left. There were now only two lifts in operation, the others having been decommissioned temporarily since plans were afoot to convert them to automatic lifts, which would require no one to work them. The working lifts were operated on a rota by three pageboys, all smartly dressed, and all saucy enough in their manners to be able to earn large tips from the guests.

Night came, and while the hotel slumbered under the clear but cold October sky, a taxi arrived at that seedy part of town where Stephen Giddins still owned a house. The two men who left the taxi and went into the house were, of course, Giddins and Johnson. Stephen Giddins turned on the hall light, and then entered the front room followed by Charles Johnson, who did not have particularly good memories of that house and would rather have been elsewhere. The light from the hall cast strange shadows into the room, but Giddins did not turn on the light.

Charles Johnson, though, had had enough of mysteries for one day, thank you very much! And he went over to the light switch by the door and flicked it on.

"What do you think you're doing?" said Giddins, quickly closing the curtains.

"I like to see what's going on, I've had just about enough of this!"

"All right, keep your hair on. I've got something to show you." At which point, Giddins showed Johnson a copy of *The Daily Standard* folded so as to show Mrs Garthwaite's advertisement. "The old dear's been running this ad for a week, and I have a plan that involves you."

Johnson looked puzzled, but Giddins continued,

"You know the hotel as well as, or better than, anyone. You're going to apply for that job."

Johnson started to protest, but Giddins held his hand up and stopped him.

"I know you're going to say that they'll all recognise you, but they won't once I've finished with you. We're going to change your appearance so that no one'll know you: smarten you up a bit, change your voice. She hasn't found anyone for that job yet, because she can't make up her mind to it, whatever she says. But you're going to change her mind with your winning ways, oh, yes."

"But why?"

"Because there's something hidden in that hotel that I want, and you are going to get it for me."

CHAPTER TWO

The Paunceton Guide Book, Pub: Adam and Charles Black, 1910

Upon descending the hill that lies between the towns of Paunceton Muffet and Paunceton-sur-la-Mer, we see behind the rising promontory to the south-west a view of the ruins of the Anglo-Saxon fortified monastery, thought (somewhat paradoxically by the more romantically minded) to have been dedicated, in antiquarian times, to Saint Edgar the peaceful.

The ruins are private property, and there is some difficulty in procuring permission to view them. During the excavations there in 1850, a number of coffins were discovered, though from a later period, apparently those of Guy de Muffet and his wife Beatrice.

During the reign of Henry II, the revenues of the monastery have been estimated at a sum equal to £20,000 of the present currency. The grounds included a pigeon-house, fish-ponds, of which traces can still be seen, and a grand refectory, long since demolished. The monastery prison, a circular underground building, still exists, though the entrance is difficult to find and rather dangerous to access.

The Paunceton Guide Book, Pub: Adam and Charles Black, 1910

MEMORABLE PLACES and HOUSES—The Hotel Splendide (once known as the Star Inn), which stands facing the sea front, with its back against the cliff wall, once contained a fine old staircase of carved oak, now sadly replaced by a modern staircase of grand proportions, dividing into two branches, each leading upwards to one of the two wings of the hotel. The visitor to the hotel will at once discern that little of the old Star Inn now remains, the building having been greatly remodelled and enlarged in 1894. However, the corridors on the third floor of the hotel are known to have access to further passages which are said to lead to a complex series of tunnels burrowed through part of the promontory to the prison of the fortified monastery.

The Hotel has four passenger lifts, or elevators, all beautifully decorated and rapid in motion. In the eastern or left-hand wing, on the ground floor, are situated some handsome apartments, consisting of the Ladies' Drawing-room, General Sitting-room, and Ladies' Music-room containing a Collard and Collard grand pianoforte. The Dining Hall is a noble apartment, 120 feet in length by 47 feet in breadth, beautifully and richly decorated with columns of imitation marble, extending the whole length on either side, with lofty windows lighting it from the south. In the west wing are situated the Smoking and Billiard-rooms, each in itself well worthy of viewing. The corridors on the ground floor are remarkably light,

The Paunceton Guide Book, Pub: Adam and Charles Black, 1910

cheerful and well-ventilated; and the lavatories at the south end of the west corridor are on a very commodious and elaborate scale. Behind the hotel is a small auditorium used for business presentations.

Below the ground floor, reached by stone stairs, and only known to the officially initiated visitor, stretch the subterranean apartments of the vast building, in which the visitor is introduced to what may very properly be termed the working hive of this vast establishment—the kitchen and larders, the bakehouse, wine-cellars, engine-room & more.

There is a legend that the crown jewels lost in 1216 by King John are hidden somewhere in the tunnels that lie between the old Star Inn and the fortified Monastery of St Edgar the Peaceful. The first mention of this is contained in a 15th century manuscript, Gemmae occultae Angliae, now stored in the British Library. There have been a number of attempts to search the passages, the last serious one being made in 1901, the year Edward VII visited Paunceton, but no evidence of any hidden treasure has ever been found. Later, unofficial searches have been made, all fruitless. There is a story that the jewels are said to give a dreadful power over life to their owner, but this is an old wives' tale told to discourage children from searching the tunnels, which are dangerously unstable.

Alice sat in bed reading the Paunceton Guidebook. It was an old copy that she had found on a high shelf in the hotel library, almost hidden among old volumes of Law Journal Reports. The language was archaic in style, but far more interesting than the modern guides of the town, which gave few historical details and were full of advertisements for guest houses, local photographers and sun cream, and which concentrated on local restaurants, shops and excursions. She had pulled out many of the old volumes in the library, particularly those with no information on the spines, in order to see what they were, and had carried three of them to her room. Her eyes lit up when she read of King John and the crown jewels. Surely here was a mystery worth investigating, and who better to investigate than she?

The following morning, she showed the book to Mrs Garthwaite and told her of her intention to explore the passages at the back of the hotel. Mrs Garthwaite pooh-poohed the idea with a downward wave of a hand.

"Huh! That's an old story. My late husband took part in the last proper search of the tunnels. I can assure you there's absolutely no truth in it. Every so often someone starts up about it, and we have to stop them from trying. The last person who tried got lost, and it took nearly a day for him to find his way out. A pretty sorry sight he was too. We had to send search parties to find him. You remember Zoë? It was her brother. He turned out to be rather a bad lot, I'm afraid. His parents practically disowned him."

"Still," said Alice, "I should like to try."

"Well, I shan't stop you," said Mrs Garthwaite, "but I suggest you take someone with you and that you go properly equipped. Actually, it's rather exciting. I'd go myself, of course, but, well, I'm getting a bit old for that kind of thing."

Alice secretly agreed but refrained from saying so. One of the young lift boys was summoned to see Mrs Garthwaite, and a few minutes later, there was a knock on the office door. On being invited in, the lad entered and was introduced to Alice as the most sensible of the young scallywags who currently worked the lifts.

In the meantime, Stephen Giddins and his girlfriend were preparing Ernest Sallow/ Charles Johnson/Ralph Horniman for the task ahead. His hair was cut and dyed, his chin, jaw and upper lip were shaved, he was dressed in a clean suit, not new, but well-ironed.

Underneath the suit, he wore a corset in an attempt to disguise his flabbiness.

After Giddins's girlfriend had left the room, the complaining began.

"I feel like a trussed turkey."

"Yes, and you look like one. Can't you relax a bit more?"

"It's this wretched corset, it's too tight. Look here, I'll have to take it off, it's digging into my ribs." He undressed, and the corset was removed.

"You'll have to be a bit more enthusiastic if we're to get access to what I'm after."

"Is that what this is all about? You're on a search for King John's hoard? What a load of rubbish! You already tried that, that's what I heard. Got a bit lost, too. There's nothing there. What makes you think I know anything about it? If I knew how to find the hoard, don't you think I would've done it years ago? I had plenty of opportunity."

"You're really on the wrong track. That's kid's stuff. No one but a child believes that there's anything of value hidden in those tunnels."

"Then what about your search?"

"I was young. I got lost and gave myself a fright. No, my friend, that's not the reason I want—need to get into the hotel."

"I'm not your friend," snarled Johnson scornfully.

Giddins ignored him and continued:

"Let me tell you a story. Some years ago, the then manager-"

"-Mr Garthwaite?"

"Yes, old Garthwaite... decided to go into a rather interesting side-business of his own making. Not honest, but profitable, oh yes, very. Can you guess what that business was?"

"I can't imagine what the old boy could have got up to. He was honest as far as I know."

"Then you don't know much. In 1919, just after the war, five robbers in British uniform stole one-and-a-half million marks from a Reichsbank branch near Bonn. They gagged the bank officials and made off towards Cologne in British motor-ambulances. That money was never recovered, but I know where it is."

"Garthwaite wasn't in Germany in 1919."

"No, but he received the money and hid it."

"Can't be worth much now. Not enough to make it worth going after."

"That wasn't the only money he took. There's much more."

"Then why haven't the thieves gone after it themselves?"

"Because they don't know where it went, do they? They carried on looting and stealing, but they were too trusting, and their 'banker' ran off with the lot, left it with Garthwaite for safekeeping, and then got killed in a car crash."

"And you know this because…"

"My goodness, you're slow," said Giddins. "I explored the hotel and got lost, remember. But I know what I saw. Old Garthwaite taking the money and promising to look after it—for a cut, of course. But Garthwaite himself didn't last long after that."

"And what have I got to do with it?"

"You know that hotel well, I suppose?"

"Yes."

"Then you will know where best to look for it all. But you need to have easy access to the place."

"Suppose I don't want to get involved?"

"Remember what I know about you."

"Yes, I remember."

"The old biddy's interviewed a few already, but none of them has got the job. I sent an application on your behalf. You better mug up on these. By the way, your new name is Maxwell Cruickshank, I hope you can do a convincing Scottish accent."

Giddins gave the newly named Cruickshank a sheaf of papers containing copies of the letter and the references he had sent to Mrs Garthwaite.

CHAPTER THREE

Alice and the young lift operator began their exploration of the tunnels, while Mrs Garthwaite prepared to interview yet another candidate for the position of manager. At two o'clock that afternoon, the gentleman in question was shown into her office. They shook hands and moved towards the desk.

"Mr Cruickshank, please take a seat," said Mrs Garthwaite, as she settled herself into the chair that Mr Horniman (now called Cruickshank) had once occupied.

It need hardly be said that Cruikshank's Scottish accent was bad enough to freeze the marrow of any Scotsman from any part of that country. He tried to model it on Harry Lauder, having seen him perform years before at the London Pavilion, but it was a poor imitation.

Fortunately, Mrs Garthwaite had never been to Scotland, indeed, she had never been further north than Nottingham, so his accent seemed perfect to her.

Cruikshank, which is what we must call him now, sat and looked up at his former employer. "If, y'don't mind me saying so, Mrs Garrrthwaite," he sang, trilling almost every letter r, "y'r office shows wonderrrful taste." This was, in fact, more a reflection of his own taste, since little had been altered since he himself had organised the room's layout and decor.

"You are very kind. I've been looking at your references and your curriculum vitae, and I must say they are most impressive. They do beg the question as to why you wish to locate to the south coast, such a long way from your home. I did, of course, write to the hotel in Inverness, and they were most enthusiastic about you."

"Ma wife died, and I really needed a change of scene."

"I'm sorry to hear that. Now then, perhaps we can get down to business."

The interview proceeded most satisfactorily, and there was little doubt that Mrs Garthwaite was suitably impressed by the brisk, yet personable, character of Maxwell Cruikshank. He talked about his childhood in India as the son of an army sergeant major, he listed, most casually, a number of well-known people he had met, and generally demonstrated such ease of demeanour that there was no doubt that he would talk himself into the job with little difficulty.

It is not the intention to demonstrate a Scots dialect, especially an imitation one, for that could only irritate, so you will have to imagine it, though the unusual turn of phrase that Cruikshank adopted will not be avoided. Perhaps the fact that Mrs Garthwaite did not recognise him might come as a surprise, but he revelled in playing different characters, often feeling that he should have been on the stage. After all, he had adopted a number of identities at one time or another, mostly with some measure of success, and this was merely another to add to the collection. Mrs Garthwaite showed him round the hotel and introduced him to the staff; Cruikshank was polite and affable to all.

It was agreed that Mr Cruikshank would take up his position as manager the following day, and the rest of the afternoon would be his own so that he would have time to move into "Horniman's" old apartment.

The conclusion of the interview coincided with the arrival of Alice and her new young friend into the foyer. Cruikshank was taking his leave of Mrs Garthwaite and was about to step into one of the lifts in order to go up to his apartment on the top floor, but as Alice and young Frank came into view, Mrs Garthwaite called him back, and the lift ascended without him.

"Mr Cruikshank, I'd like you to meet a good friend of mine, Mrs Winsome, whose great perspicacity has been of considerable help to me. (Frank, can you find out why only one of the lifts is working?) Mr Cruikshank is our new manager."

"Pleased to meet you, Mrs Winsome," said Cruikshank, in a rather wheezy falsetto-his attempt at a cultured Morningside accent. Then, he cleared his throat and continued in a baritonal Glaswegian, "Are you stayin' here with us?"

"Yes, indeed," said Alice, staring at Cruikshank through her glasses, which she now wore most of the time, having abandoned Vanity for Clarity.

"I hope you're having a grand time." As Cruikshank uttered those words, he knew they had sounded more Lancashire than Scotland. He cleared his throat again, and continued hurriedly, "As they say at home where I come from, 'You're welcome here.'"

Alice was puzzled; she could not say why, but there was something about this man that she distrusted. Mrs Garthwaite, on the other hand, was becoming even more certain that she had made a fine choice. Cruikshank, though, was looking flushed, and small beads of sweat formed on his forehead. He dabbed away with a large white handkerchief that he had fished out of his jacket pocket. He cursed the day he had agreed to go along with this deception, though he had no intention of following any instructions given him by Stephen Giddins, preferring to work this game of "Hunt the Thimble" on his own behalf. Nevertheless, he felt that he had been placed in a most embarrassing situation, made all the more ridiculous by his enforced adoption of a Scottish accent. Well might he have agreed with Sir Walter Scott's saying,

Oh what a tangled web we weave, When first we practice to deceive.

He felt himself to be in dire straits and longed for a lifebuoy, but none could be seen. Just as he was about to launch himself once more upon the uncertain waters of his fake accent, the lift doors opened again, and a young couple walked out of the lift.

"Excuse me, ladies," he said to Mrs Garthwaite and Alice. He walked into the lift, the doors closed, and he was mercifully saved by an ascent to the top floor.

"And now, Alice," said Mrs Garthwaite, "you must come and tell me all about your exploration." And she whisked Alice away to her private sitting room for a cosy chat. Alice, despite the feeling that something was not right, followed and was soon telling of her wanderings with Frank in the corridors behind the Hotel Splendide.

CHAPTER FOUR

Only one lift was operating. Frank walked down to the hotel kitchen where he expected to find his colleague Neville. His expectation was realised. Neville was seated on a wooden chair under a staircase eating a cake. It was a beautiful cake, or, at least, it had been once. Now, most of it was inside Neville, and Neville was not looking too happy about it, even though he was still eating.

"Mrs G wants to know why you're not in your lift," said Frank.

"What's the time?" asked Neville.

"You look awful," said Frank ignoring the question.

"I feel sick."

"Well stop eating and get back to work."

But Neville got up and rushed off to the nearest toilet.

"You can do my shift later," called Frank after him.

Frank shrugged and walked back to the foyer where he got into the lift that Neville was supposed to be operating. The other lift was by that time delivering Mr Cruikshank to his rooms. Thomas, the other lift operator, started his descent, yawning as he did so, for while Neville was always eating, Thomas was always sleeping or lying down. Frank found their behaviour extremely irritating.

All three lads were in their fifteenth year, and Frank was aware that he was the only one who pulled his weight. He felt under- appreciated, and, always on the lookout for bettering himself, showed an eagerness to please that sometimes startled those he was helping.

Having dealt with the characters of the three lift boys, we can now turn to the tale that Alice told Mrs Garthwaite.

Alice liked tea, of that there was no possible doubt whatsoever, although she did not like to drink it quite as often as Mrs Garthwaite. The teacups were Japanese: beautiful, dainty things painted with colourful scenes on them. They were so pretty that it was a joy to drink out of them, and Alice, therefore, felt duty-bound to show her appreciation by drinking copious amounts of tea, though she rather wished that Mrs Garthwaite would stop insisting that she drink up, before pouring more. Mrs Garthwaite, on the other hand, seemed to have an endless capacity for the intake of liquid, showing no signs of discomfort.

"Tell me all about it."

"Well," said Alice, "Frank and I started in the corridor where I originally began my wandering all that time ago, and we followed the same route, until eventually, we got to that room where I found Zoë."

"Oh, yes, Zoë," said Mrs Garthwaite, who was easily distracted from any subject, "dear child, I wonder what happened to her." She spoke as if she believed she thought of Zoë as a 'dear child', forgetting her antipathy to her.

Alice did not want to lengthen her tale by following digressions onto other matters, she liked to keep things succinct and, at that moment, felt that she must excuse herself for "a quick visit," as she put it.

"Of course, dear," said Mrs Garthwaite. Alice left the room, returning shortly afterwards feeling far more comfortable, but rather dreading the thought that Mrs Garthwaite would begin filling her teacup all over again.

Alice and Frank walked the mysterious passages without speaking much for some time. Alice began to feel excited once she found herself back inside the large and unused reception room with the deep carpet patterned with the snake motif. Once more, all sound from outside was suddenly cut off. Frank began to speak, but Alice held up a hand to cut him short. The snake- like pattern, she now realised, reminded her of her home and the way that the moonlight played on the carpet in the hallway there as it streamed through the round window above the front door. For a moment, a feeling of great nostalgia washed over her, but she dismissed it and began to study the oil painting of the bald-headed, bearded man that was fixed to the wall above the marble fireplace. There was no doubt he was an impressive figure: stout and rather intimidating. There was, however, still something that troubled her about the portrait, but it eluded her. She was just about to turn away from it when Frank, who had been standing next to her looking at it with his head slightly tilted to one side said,

"His eyes are different colours."
"What do you mean?" said Alice.

The room was dim, and even with her glasses on, she could not see that one eye was any different to the other.

"Yes, they're different colours, well, slightly, and the left eye is a bit bigger than the right one."

Alice began to see that there was a difference but was unsure if there was any significance to it.

"I wish we could get closer to it to see," she said.

Frank was already burrowing under the sheet that covered the chandelier on the floor at the far end of the room.

"There's a step-ladder here, Mrs Winsome," he said. "Look, I'll get it out, and we can look better at the picture."

Clouds of dust billowed out from under the sheet as Frank pulled at the ladder, which had been lying on its side. He coughed and spluttered and eventually emerged, covered in cobwebs and with his hair in a fearful state. Alice couldn't help but laugh, and the good-natured Frank joined in with her. He brushed himself down and then walked over to her carrying the ladder.

It was a rickety wooden affair that could be pulled out into a triangular form with a small platform on top. Frank set it up in front of the fireplace.

"Shall I go up first, Mrs Winsome?" asked Frank, who was enjoying the adventure and really wanted to take the lead.

"No, I'll do it. Hold the ladder for me."

And Alice ascended. She stepped onto the platform at the top, rather nervously and, using the wall to keep balance, found herself staring into the face of the bearded, bald man.

"Hold the ladder steady, Frank," she said in a worried voice, for it had begun to wobble rather alarmingly. Frank gripped the sides of the ladder more firmly, and Alice continued her examination.

"What can you see?" said Frank.

"Well, it's very dirty, and there's a cobweb over a corner of the frame."

"What about his eyes?"

"Yes, well, one of them has a brown smudge over it, and I think that's what makes it look different to the other. But the other one is a bit bigger. Hm, interesting! I wonder why..." Alice touched the portrait with the index finger of her right hand. "It's been painted on wood, and... my goodness! It's a button painted to look like an eye."

She pressed the button, which moved inward by a quarter of an inch or so. There was a soft rasping sound from below.

"Mrs Winsome, you should see this," said Frank.

"Wait a moment, I'm coming down, keep holding the ladder."

Once back on the floor, Alice looked at Frank, who pointed to the fireplace. "There's a small hole there which just opened," he said.

Just inside the fireplace, where the marble ended and brickwork began, a hole the size of a farthing had appeared. They both looked at it.

"It's a keyhole," said Frank. "I wonder where the key is."

Since neither knew where the key might be, they continued the exploration till they came to the room where Zoë had been found. Then Alice led the way back to the manager's office, following the route along which Jack Jackson had led her and Zoë five years earlier.

"This place is huge," said Frank as they passed a corridor that led off to the left, "it would take days to check it all."

"I think these passages are well-documented," said Alice. "What I want to know is what that keyhole is for."

CHAPTER FIVE

Alice finished telling Mrs Garthwaite about the discovery of the keyhole, adding,

"It's quite a mystery. It must open something, but I couldn't see a door, or anything that might be opened by a lock. There was no handle or knob. I do wish I knew the answer."

Mrs Garthwaite was looking at her curiously.

"I wonder," she said, "yes, indeed I do."

"What do you wonder?"

"When my husband died, I went through all his things carefully and made certain that everything was in order. There was a keyring with a few keys that were of no particular significance, though the fob was quite unusual. All the keys were duplicates of others that are used in the hotel. But one of them seemed to have no use at all."

"What did you do with it?"

"Well, it's in the office, I think. Let's go and look."

They both walked to the office (which the next day would become the sanctum of Mr Cruikshank), and Mrs Garthwaite easily found the keyring, which was hanging with the others in full view.

"Have a look," she said, handing the bunch to Alice. It consisted of a metal ring with four keys on it and a dark green glass fob.

Alice was taken aback somewhat when she noticed that the design of the fob was very similar, if not identical, to the snake pattern on the carpet in the hall where the portrait hung.

"That's the strange key," said Mrs Garthwaite, pointing to it.

"I think I'll go back there now," said Alice.

"Now?"

"Right away."

"Then I'm coming with you," said Mrs Garthwaite with uncustomary boldness.

"Should we take Frank?"

"No, he's working the lifts now."

Mrs Garthwaite followed Alice timidly along the corridors to the dim reception hall with the portrait. Alice herself felt strangely alert as they went. She seemed to have a heightened sense of awareness. Every sight seemed magnified, every sound clear and distinct. But, when they finally reached that place, all sound was suddenly cut, as if it had been turned off.

A heavy, musty smell filled the atmosphere, and the dim light cast by the two exposed lightbulbs suspended from the ceiling seemed to make every object appear to be further away than it actually was.

"What is this place?" whispered Mrs Garthwaite.

"I thought you knew," said Alice, trying to make her voice sound as normal as possible, though she was aware that it sounded muffled and nebulous.

They walked to the fireplace.

"Who is that?" asked Alice.

"I have no idea. It looks a little like my husband, though it isn't him. How strange." The keyhole was no longer visible, and so Alice went back up the ladder while Mrs Garthwaite held it. Once at the top, Alice pressed the button in the eye, and as before, there was a slight rasping sound as the keyhole was exposed.

Alice had the keyring in her handbag. She climbed back down the ladder and took it out. The fob could clearly be seen to match the pattern on the carpet. Both she and Mrs Garthwaite felt greatly excited as Alice took the key and went to insert it into the lock.

It did not fit!

"Let me try," said Mrs Garthwaite, certain that Alice must have been going about things in the wrong way.

Alice passed her the key, and Mrs Garthwaite did her best, but it was obvious to both that the key was far too large.

"How frustrating," said Mrs Garthwaite with some annoyance, as she had been feeling quite enthusiastic about finding out what might be revealed. She felt as if she were a ten-year-old girl all over again. She opened her handbag to put the keyring into it but fumbled and dropped it onto the marble hearth instead. There was a sour clinking sound as the front of the fob shattered.

"Damn and blast!" exclaimed Mrs Garthwaite. "Oh, excuse me," she said holding a hand over her mouth. "Naughty!" she said, slapping her own hand. Then she giggled slightly.

But Alice was picking up the keys from the floor.

"There's something inside this," she declared.

It was true. Hidden inside the now broken keyring fob was another key.

"It can't be!" said Mrs Garthwaite.

But it could! Alice inserted the key into the lock and turned it. A small panel in the marble was revealed. It opened easily, and behind it, there was a handle that, when turned, opened a very narrow door to one side of the fireplace. Beyond could be seen another passage that turned immediately to the left.

Alice began to go through the door, but Mrs Garthwaite held her back.

"Wait a moment, I'll never fit through there, I'm too well-built."

For the first time in her life Alice felt that her slim figure would be a real advantage.

"That's all right," she said, "I'll fit through easily."

"Maybe we should go back and get help," said Mrs Garthwaite. "I could get Frank." But it was too late. Alice had gone through the opening and was already out of sight.

Fortunately, she had supplied herself with an electric torch, and she fished it out of her handbag as she walked slowly along the passage.

"What can you see?" called Mrs Garthwaite.

"Not much," said Alice. "There's another door." She opened it and walked through.

The door had a spring mechanism closing device. It shut after her, and then there was no turning back for there was no way to open it from her side. Mrs Garthwaite, still standing by the fireplace called again, but there was no answer from Alice.

"Damn and blast!" said Mrs Garthwaite again. As she said this, the door by the fireplace shut with a click, the small panel closed, and the lock was also covered once more. Mrs Garthwaite had just made her mind up to climb the ladder in order to press the eye so as to reveal the lock, when she realised that Alice had the key, and that the door would be impossible to open. "I'll go and get help," she said.

CHAPTER SIX

While Alice and Mrs Garthwaite were beginning their examination of the fireplace in the large hall, Maxwell Cruikshank was entering the office he would soon claim as his own dominion. In his hand, he carried a black leather Gladstone bag. A feeling of nostalgia swept over him as he looked at his old chair and desk, but he had no difficulty turning his attention to the matters in hand. Had Mrs Garthwaite been in the room when he went in, he had been fully equipped with a reason for his visit, but the room was empty, which meant he could start his search.

Cruikshank knew the hotel and its layout well, including the passages that lay behind, but he did not know about the narrow door by the fireplace. He turned his attention to the office first, imagining how the late Mr Garthwaite would have behaved if he had had something important to hide. There were a few possible hiding places, and he began to search quickly but methodically, always replacing anything he moved in order to leave no clues that anything had been disturbed.

He had decided to cut Stephen Giddins from the proceeds of anything he might find. That would teach him a lesson! Then, after he had found what he was looking for, he would slip quietly away.

It was frustrating work, and he knew that his time might be cut short if Mrs Garthwaite were to enter the room. He wanted to find Mr Garthwaite's hoard as quickly as possible, certainly before Giddins could start putting his nose in.

One by one, he removed all the books on the bookshelves to check behind them. He already knew that neither the mantlepiece nor the large carriage clock that stood on it were worth searching. He thought of looking up the chimney but remembered that he had done that once before when he was Ralph Horniman, straight after the chimneysweep had visited and shown him just how clear the chimney was. He looked through all the keys kept in the office, but found nothing out of the ordinary—hardly surprising, since the one key that might have given him pause for thought was in Alice's handbag.

It suddenly occurred to him that the green leather sofa was something at which he had never looked closely. He felt all over the seat and the back, then dragged it away from the wall with no little effort. The sofa was very heavy, and he twisted himself into an uncomfortable position to move it. A sudden pain shot through his back, and he lay down on the sofa for a few seconds, stretching his arms and legs into all sorts of positions in a vain attempt to cure the muscle he had pulled. Eventually, he sat up and, bending forward, curled himself down, while still seated, to try to look under the sofa. This was a thoroughly ridiculous thing to do. He hoped it might stop his back from hurting, but it made the pain worse. Not only that, but it was impossible to see under the sofa from that position, and it was also impossible to turn it over without help.

"If I can't move this thing, then Garthwaite probably couldn't either." And he dismissed from his mind the sofa as a possible hiding place.

Then another thought occurred to him. If old Garthwaite had hidden something in the passages behind the hotel, it would certainly be accessible from the entrance to them, which lay in the false cupboard in the office toilet. But where? Although he knew those passages well, he could not think of an effective place to hide anything. Still, it was worth a try. And so, Maxwell Cruikshank entered the maze of corridors using that entrance.

As soon as he had closed the "cupboard" door after him, Mrs Garthwaite entered the office, looking rather flustered. She was followed by Frank, whom she had summoned from his lift duties on her way back from her abortive expedition.

CHAPTER SEVEN

Alice walked slowly along the corridor. The only light came from her torch, though she thought she could make out a greyness up ahead, which implied there must be a little light further on. Moreover, at one moment, a soft breeze of somewhat rather stale air wafted towards her. She turned the torch off and stood still. There was silence. No, not silence; a gentle tapping sound could be heard. She walked on, and soon found herself in a small lobby area in which a dusty, old desk had been pushed up against a wall. Opposite that was a lift shaft with an old scissor gate. The stale breeze and the grey light emanated from there, and a small piece of wood attached to a hook by a piece of string swung idly in the breeze, tapping gently against the wall by the lift. Alice pulled the piece of wood down and looked at it. It had something written on it, but she had to turn her torch back on to see that it read Basement. The desk had little to offer. There were a few sheets of blank paper, yellowed with age as far as she could tell, and two pencil stubs. She went over to the lift shaft and pressed the button to summon the lift. There was no movement. Alice peered through the lift gates and realised that the lift was actually there behind them, only it was so dirty she had thought it was an empty shaft. She pulled the outer gates open and then the inner ones, then turned and shut them. Torch on, she examined the lift to see if there was any way of finding out how to operate it.

"It's an old service lift for the staff, I expect. I wonder how long it's been since it was last used."

She was standing facing the small lobby. There were no instructions inside the lift, but to her left was a lever attached to a round hub such as she had seen lift operators use. She had never operated one before, of course, but she decided that now was her chance. One side of the hub was marked with the letter D, the other with the letter U.

"D for down, U for up, I suppose." She took hold of the lever and gingerly moved it from its upright position forward towards the letter U. The lift gave a shudder and a groan and, with a clanking sound, began to ascend.

A dirty brick wall passed before her eyes, seeming to move in a downward direction as the lift rose. Alice discovered quite quickly that she could control the speed of the lift by moving the lever back, and she slowed it down, not wanting to miss anything—not that there was much to see. She passed by another external scissor gate and stopped the lift, though it was almost three feet too high.

Alice squatted down and looked into the room at which the lift had arrived. It seemed to glow with an orange light, and she could see that it was full of machinery. She stood and, by careful manipulation (and a couple of false starts), managed to get the floor of the lift to a position where she could comfortably step out. She opened both sets of scissor gates and walked into the room.

It was a boiler room, and not particularly interesting at first sight. Nothing there seemed to be in use anymore. There was a door to one side of her with a frosted orange glass window, but it was locked shut. Light shone from the next room, lighting the boiler room, but it was impossible to see what lay beyond the door. There was a mirrored cabinet on the other side of the room, and it was so strangely incongruous there that Alice felt drawn to it. Feeling rather like a famous Alice of old, she might have muttered, "curiouser and curiouser," to herself as she opened the cabinet.

Inside was an old leather bag that was closed with three straps down the front. A fourth strap was conveniently placed for carrying it. Alice hauled it out and carried it closer to the orange window to examine it more closely.

"Well, this certainly doesn't contain King John's crown jewels, but I wonder what's inside."

The metal buckles that fixed the straps in place were too stiff and the straps too thick for her to open the bag, and after trying for a few minutes, she gave up and carried it back to the lift. The bag itself was in quite good condition, though it showed signs of having been well used. It was fairly heavy and obviously very full.

Once back in the lift, Alice manoeuvred the lever, and the lift rose once more. Steady upward progress was suddenly brought to an end with a loud grinding noise and a jolt that knocked Alice off her feet. She held out her hands to avoid colliding with the lift gate and, as a result, grazed her palms badly. The lift had stopped between floors, and Alice was trapped with no way to summon help. She bit her lip with anxiety, but though her head flushed, and her heart pounded, she decided not to panic. Not yet.

She looked to see if there might be a way of opening the lift doors and squeezing herself into the lift shaft, but she quickly realised that the space between gate and wall was far too narrow, and that, in any case, a venture of that sort would be far too dangerous. However, when she looked up, she noticed that there was a small hatch in the ceiling. There seemed to be no way to reach it, but, even at the cost of the pain it gave her hands, she started to climb the scissor gate, using it as a ladder, after first wrapping the straps of the old leather bag and her own handbag around her shoulders. The gate made a poor sort of ladder! She slipped and hurt herself more than once, but finally, and with very sore hands and aching back, she reached the lift's ceiling. Then it was a question of how to reach the hatch, which was not conveniently placed. She tried to arch herself backwards, holding on with one hand while reaching up with the other. The leather bag suddenly slipped from her shoulder, and the strap fell into the crook of her arm. With the impact of this, she began to fall, and so, with a great leap, she pushed herself back and landed once more on the floor of the lift. Sweat dripped into her eyes, and she mopped it away with her sleeve.

Looking very dishevelled, she tried again, but this time, once she reached the top, she swung herself out with one hand holding on and one foot balanced on part of the gate. This was more successful, and she was able to reach the cover of the hatch and push it. It slid slightly to one side, and Alice curved her free hand over the lip of the hatch and held on tightly. Then, with a great effort, she pulled herself up so that the other hand was also holding on to the opening. Now came a difficult move, for her left shoe was stuck in the gate, and no matter what she did she could not free it. She was tired now, and the problems had multiplied, for the bags she had round her shoulders felt heavy, but if she let go with her hands, she would fall in an extremely awkward way as her foot was trapped. Almost blinded by sweat, she tried to pull her left foot towards herself, and was finally rewarded when, with some difficulty, she managed to wriggle it out of the shoe. She hung there for a few moments, and then, by some miraculous effort, managed to drag herself upwards so that her head and elbows were above the hatch and resting on the roof of the lift. She remained there for what seemed like hours, but was in reality only five minutes, and then pulled the rest of herself through the hatch.

  The first thing was to wipe her eyes. One of the lenses of her glasses was cracked, and she could not work out how that had happened. She slid the hatch cover back into place, not wanting to risk falling back down, and then looked around to see what she could see. The walls were dirty, and the air was musty, but cold. The lift shaft yawned away above her, and she could see the dim light cast by the openings of higher floors. On the wall opposite the floor openings, about a foot higher than the lift roof, was a strange-looking door with a snake-like handle. She climbed up walked over to it, opened it, and clambered through. Beyond was a corridor with a floor as wide as the walls were high, giving the effect of looking through a long, upright square. There was suddenly a huge grinding and clanking noise behind her, and she turned and looked through the door she had just entered by. The lift had begun a rapid descent, and, with a loud report, it landed at the foot of the shaft sending billows of dust upwards. Alice drew back immediately. "I might have been inside that," she whispered.

For now, though, it was time to continue her journey through this weird, new world.

CHAPTER EIGHT

Alice removed her right shoe, and holding it in her hand, began to walk along the slippery linoleum floor of this latest corridor. After a few moments, she realised that a single shoe was of no use without another that matched, so she discarded it. There was a background aroma of floor polish, or perhaps disinfectant, that made her stop in order to distinguish exactly what it was. It was vaguely reminiscent of hospitals, and for some reason, she found this more than a little disturbing.

There was enough light to make everything clear, though some of the bulbs flickered and buzzed. A staircase opened out to her left, and she walked up it, constantly alert for any sound. Her stockinged feet made no noise as she walked, but she was rather out of breath, and her heart was pounding.

What Alice could not know was that, at the very moment that she began to walk up the stairs towards the next level, Maxwell Cruikshank had entered the corridor on that level from the far end and was walking towards her. Cruikshank too was unaware that he would soon be brought face-to-face with anyone else. He had entered that region by a different route to Alice and was continuing to look for anything out of the ordinary that might indicate a hiding place he had previously missed.

Both were shocked when they almost collided at the top of the stairs. Alice clutched onto the handrail to steady herself, while Cruikshank suddenly sat down on the floor with a bump.

"Mrs Winsome, what on earrth arre you doing here?"

"Mr... Cruikshank?"

Cruikshank stood. The scowl on his face told Alice that he was probably not best pleased to see her. "I don't think you should be wandering alone here, you might get lost," he said.

"Don't I know you?"

"Aye, Mrs Garthwaite introduced us."

"I didn't mean that. Haven't we met before?"

"I think not," said Cruikshank, trying to hide his face.

"I do know you," said Alice, "your name isn't Cruikshank, you're Ralph Horniman."

"You think so?" said Cruikshank/Horniman with a menacing look, "Then I think you know a bit too much."

Alice backed away but slipped and fell. Horniman bent over her, grabbed her arm and hauled her to her feet.

"You'll kindly do as I say," he said as he propelled her and the bags she held through an open door and into a room with desks and chairs arranged like a classroom. "And you will tell me what you are doing nosing around here," he continued with a wheezy voice. He snatched both bags from Alice, threw them onto the floor behind him, then pushed her onto a chair and raised himself to his full height.

Things did not look good for Alice as Horniman towered over her with glowering face. Then, as if by a miracle, a voice was heard from the doorway:

"Mr Cruikshank, what do you think you are doing?"

It was Mrs Garthwaite, and with her was Frank.

Alice called out, "He's not Cruikshank, he's Horniman," and as she did so, Horniman wheeled round to face Mrs Garthwaite. Frank gallantly stepped between them. Horniman looked unsure of himself for a moment, but quickly regained composure.

"My dear Mrs Garthwaite, Euphemia, how nice to see you again. It would be so nice to pick up where we left off all those years ago."

"Don't you 'dear Mrs Garthwaite' me! I don't even know your name. It's not Cruikshank, and it's certainly not Horniman. What is it?"

"Let's say Horniman for the moment, I quite liked being Ralph."

"And why, may I ask?"

"Because that is when I had the pleasure of first meeting you."

"Don't trust him," said Alice, "he's slippery as an eel."

"A fat eel, if you ask me," added Frank.

"No one did ask you," said Horniman.

"You are Ernest Sallow, aren't you?" said Alice.

"Once, but it was long ago. I made something of myself, though, and then it was taken away from me. Well, I'm not letting that happen again. You're all here now, and you're the only ones who know, and I know what to do with you."

"The man's raving," said Mrs Garthwaite.

"Raving? Raving? is that what you think? I'll soon deal with you!"

Violence was threatened, and Frank pushed Mrs Garthwaite back into the corridor and prepared to do battle. Horniman came towards him, and Frank stepped into the corridor where there was more room for a fight. Horniman came after him, and Alice followed only to be motioned by Frank to stand near Mrs Garthwaite.

And then came yet another surprise.

CHAPTER NINE

Stephen Giddins was not one to trust his associates. In particular, his latest creation, that of Maxwell Cruikshank, worried him. "He's a slimy devil, bound to search for the money himself and then leave me out of it if he can."

So it was that, while Mrs Garthwaite was interviewing Cruikshank, Giddins made his way to the ruins of the fortified monastery. Having parked his car in an out-of-the-way spot close to the narrow footpath that led there, he began to make his ascent. The way was steep, and the path overgrown and slippery. A cold wind whipped his hat from his head and sent it tumbling away into the distance. Giddins wrapped his coat tightly around himself and pulled the collar up. His thin, straw-coloured hair blew untidily in the wind, and a light rain began to fall. Above him, the grey sky gave warning of worse weather to come, and he could just glimpse a triangle of the dark grey sea. He slipped on the mud and only just saved himself from falling. The knees of his trousers were now very muddy, and his shoes squelched as he walked. Giddins clenched his teeth and ventured on.

When he finally reached the ruin, he stumbled about trying to find the entrance to the old cell. It should have been easy to find, although it had always been hidden by a growth of untidy bushes, but what he did not know was that, a few years ago, a group of well-intentioned locals had blocked it up with rubble.

When at last he located the spot, he cursed out loud. Bending down, he began to move the rocks, but it only took only a few minutes before he realised that his efforts were futile. He stopped and leaned back, stretching his aching body, with one hand against a wall and the other wiping away the rain from his face.

To one side of the blocked entrance, the ground dipped steeply into a hollow in which grew a large laurel bush. Giddins was looking down at it when, from the darkening sky, came a flash of lightning, and then another. Almost before he knew what he was doing, and certainly before the thunder followed, he was sliding down the slope, for something had caught his eye. He tore roughly at the bush when he reached it and was rewarded by seeing behind it a low arch in the stone wall. Without thinking too much about making himself wetter and muddier than he already was, he pushed himself through. The remnants of an iron grill, which had once blocked the arch, scratched him as he went, tearing a rent in his trousers just below his right knee, but in only a few minutes he was standing, as he had done years before, in the prison cell of the old monastery. He had not come unprepared; he took a flashlight from his inside coat pocket, switched it on, and began to look around. The entrance to the tunnels that ran beneath the monastery was not hard to find. Perhaps it had been made centuries ago by a prisoner attempting to escape captivity; the reason for its creation had long since been lost to time. Now, Stephen Giddins entered the maze of passages and began to search for a way down to the corridors that lay behind the Hotel Splendide.

Sometimes there were roughly-hewn stairs to climb down, sometimes there was only a slope, but whenever the way forked, Giddins made sure to choose only passages that led downwards. Before long, he was at the lowest level but hopelessly lost.

"This is not the way I came before," he muttered.

Giddins need not have worried. The luck of the devil was on his side, for he was closer to the hotel than he imagined; a way in was just around the next corner. He sat down on a low shelf, which projected from the wall on his right, and rested his aching legs. He stretched them out one by one and flexed each foot, and then began to search through his pockets for a cigarette. His eyelids lowered as he drew the smoke into his lungs, and he sat there for a full five minutes. Suddenly, he became aware of a noise from somewhere up ahead. His hand reached into his coat pocket, which contained a loaded gun. He smiled wryly to himself, threw the cigarette aside, and walked on.

On turning to the right, he found himself facing a closed door, behind which he could clearly hear the clanking sound as of working machinery. He had, in fact, come to a place beside the lift shaft with the old service lift in which Alice, not long since, had started her upward journey. He opened the door and found himself at the bottom of a narrow stairwell. On looking up, he saw that the stairs rose for several flights, and tired though he was, he began the climb. The first two levels he came to had doors that were locked. The door on the next level opened. Things looked more promising at first, and he was just about to pass through the door when he heard an awful scraping sound. This was followed by an immense crash and, though he could not know it, this was the moment that the lift had fallen to the bottom of the shaft and smashed. A little further along, another staircase opened to his right, and, since this looked more promising, he began his ascent. He was now heading almost directly for the place where Mrs Garthwaite and Frank were about to interrupt Cruikshank-Horniman (or whatever his name was) in the process of attacking Alice. As he ascended the stairs, he could hear voices reverberating down to him. Some in urgent, whispered conversation, others raised in agitation.

Stephen Giddins turned a corner at the top of the next flight of stairs and saw Frank squaring up to the menacing figure of Cruikshank, now re-established as Ralph Horniman, while Mrs Garthwaite and Alice stood behind Frank. Frank, who was considerably smaller than his opponent, was gallantly motioning the ladies to stay back while he dealt with the danger.

Giddins, not knowing exactly what was going on, rushed forward and sent both Horniman and Frank sprawling onto the floor.

Giddins drew his gun and pointed it at Frank.

"Stand with the ladies," he ordered. "Well, now, what's going on here?"

Mrs Garthwaite began to speak.

"Quiet," said Giddins, "I wasn't talking to you."

Horniman's eyes wandered to the room they had just left, and Giddins realised that something needed investigating.

"What's in there?"

"She was carrying two bags," said Horniman.

"Get them!"

And Horniman went in, emerging quickly with Alice's handbag and the large leather bag she had found.

"Pass them here, no, wait, open them."

Horniman opened Alice's handbag, which was now in a sorry state, scuffed and torn and with a handle that had come loose at one end. He showed the inside to Giddins who shook his head slightly. Horniman threw the bag at Alice who caught it clumsily. The contents went spilling out over the floor. This is not the place to discuss the contents of a lady's handbag, though there was nothing that might raise a blush inside it, but Alice was, nevertheless, both angry and mortified. She squatted down and began to scoop the items back into the bag.

"Stop that!" said Giddins, and she stood again. Meanwhile Horniman was struggling with the other bag.

"I canna open it," he said, forgetting that he no longer had to use a Scottish accent, although Giddins was as yet unaware that his identity was known to the others.

"You three, into that room," said Giddins.

Mrs Garthwaite, Alice and Frank went inside, and Giddins shut the door.

"Now," he said to Horniman, "hand it over, and stand back."

Horniman gave him the bag. Giddins instantly saw that the bag could not easily be opened, so he pushed it back to Horniman, instructing him to open it and then pass it over. Horniman struggled with buckles and straps, and eventually managed to loosen them enough to open the bag. He was, therefore, the first to see the contents, and he began to laugh. First of all, a sort of smothered wheezing, and then a great bellow. Even the threatening looks from Giddins could not stop his shoulders shaking, despite his best efforts to cease his laughter.

Giddins impatiently emptied the bag onto the floor. Bundles of paper cascaded out, but no money of any sort. Nothing of value seemed to be inside. Horniman knelt down and picked up some of the bundles.

"Bills," he said. "Invoices and receipts. Tax accounts and letters, and that's all."

Giddins, furious, opened the door to reveal the three still within the room. "All right," he said quietly, his face white with anger, "where's the real stuff?"

None of them had any idea what he was referring to, and Giddins realised that they could not possibly know about the stolen money. He rounded on Horniman who, he reasoned, must know the answer.

"You!" he cried violently. "You know something about this. You weren't in charge of this hotel all those years without knowing all about it, though God knows what you did with it all, you never had the brains to get rid of it, and you never had enough to pay your debts."

Everything now happened very quickly. Horniman backed up as Giddins got closer to him. He clenched his fists feebly and made an awkward attempt to defend himself, but Giddins lashed out, felling him with a blow to his face. His flailing arms tried to reach for a nearby shelf on the wall, but his hands missed their mark, merely pulling the shelf onto himself and breaking a nearby wooden chair as he fell. His head struck something on the floor, and momentarily stunned, he lay there, eyes shut. The others were dumbfounded at the sudden turn of events.

    Giddins looked down and saw a wooden box by Horniman's head. He picked it up and opened it. Inside was a black cloth, and beneath that was a once shiny object—a crown, hardly big enough for a man's head, but surely something of value. Mrs Garthwaite, meanwhile, had taken up a leg of the broken chair and, advancing towards Giddins, attempted to strike him with it while he was distracted by the crown. Giddins looked up at that moment and neatly avoided the blow, though dropping the box as he did so. Alice and Frank pulled Mrs Garthwaite to make her come away as Giddins advanced upon the three of them, gun in hand.

    At that moment, Horniman, who had recovered his senses, heaved himself to his feet and, holding the wooden shelf before him like a battering ram, charged at Giddins, knocking him off balance. Giddins tried to save himself from falling, but his efforts were in vain, and he fell against the lift doors behind him. Horniman dropped to his knees, while Giddins wrenched the doors open and stepped into what he thought must be a lift unaware that the lift lay in pieces several floors below. With a short cry, he slipped and disappeared down the shaft.

Frank and Alice immediately began to run down the stairs to the lower levels. Mrs Garthwaite began lumbering after them, and then remembered the box with the crown inside. She turned and went back to get it, only to find that Horniman, who had taken one look to size up the situation, had himself seized the box and was running in the opposite direction.

CHAPTER TEN

Horniman did not get far. He had fully expected to find his way back to the main part of the hotel with ease, but he mistook one corridor for another and instead found himself out of breath and facing a dead end. Mrs Garthwaite, whose shrieks for help had reverberated down to Alice and Frank, was not too far behind him, but she was even more physically unfit than Horniman, and had pulled up short, soon to be overtaken by Frank who rushed by her and managed to get to Horniman, who gave up the box to him on demand.

Alice had stopped by Mrs Garthwaite and was offering assistance to her. But there was no way they could force Horniman to accompany them back to civilisation, and so the three adventurers made their way back, without him, but with the box that held the crown safely in the hands of Mrs Garthwaite.

Horniman, who craved the crown for its life-giving properties, having persuaded himself that the legend might very well be true, was disappointed. He had not, though, questioned how it was that a crown of such value, one that had allegedly belonged to King John himself, had come to be where it was. That mystery would be partly unlocked by Alice.

Horniman crept away, and was not to be found by the police when they came searching for him.

Mrs Garthwaite rewarded Frank for his bravery. That evening, she and Alice met in the hotel office to discuss the events of the day. The police were investigating the scene of Stephen Giddins' death and had taken statements from the witnesses (those that could be found).

"I'll have to report the discovery of the crown," said Mrs Garthwaite. "Goodness knows how it came to be there. You know the story, I suppose."

"I read something about it," said Alice. "Do you suppose..."

"Heavens, no. But some people will jump to conclusions."

Alice thought hard,

"Might a guest have abandoned it, or lost it?"

Mrs Garthwaite handed her the wooden box, and Alice examined it. The crown itself was on the coffee table in front of the sofa on which they were both seated. The outside of the box was plain, but the inside had a brass plate fixed under the lid on which a faint inscription could just be read if one held the box at exactly the right angle near a not-too-bright light. It read: *Corona aurea hominess audaces facit.*

"What do you think that means?" said Mrs Garthwaite.

"It's Latin," replied Alice. "It means 'A crown of gold makes men audacious.'"

"How odd!"

"Wait, it's a poem. 'A crown of gold makes men bold.'"

"Ridiculous, who ever heard such a thing."

"It's not very good English—or Latin, if it comes to that."

"Did you learn Latin, then?"

"Mm, yes, a bit. It's a puzzle, though."

"I'll report it to the police."

"Yes, and I'll do some research."

The following day, Alice went to the local library to see what she could find in the way of reference books that might help her. The librarian suggested she try the Paunceton Museum of Antiquities, where interesting early documents and books might better be found, and so, half an hour later, she found herself knocking on the door of a high-walled, terraced building in a side street with a scrap of dirty paper fixed on it, on which were written in spidery, capital letters the words "OUT, BACK SOON."

Alice tutted impatiently when she saw the notice, but she need not have worried, as only a minute later a tall, elderly gentleman appeared from round the corner holding a bottle of milk in one hand and a bunch of keys in the other. He stared at Alice, rather surprised to see anyone standing there, so infrequently was the museum visited, but continued past her with key extended to unlock the door.

"Wrong key," he said after a moment. "Here, hold this will you," and he gave the milk bottle to Alice and began to search through the keys till he was satisfied he had found the correct one. "I always get them mixed up, you see. They're so very similar." He opened the door and stepped in.

"You could always label them," Alice said as she followed him.

"Eh? What's that?"

"Label them. So that you knew which was which."

"Which was what? Never mind, we're in now. Oh! you mean the keys, yes, I could label them but..."

"Yes..."

"I don't have any labels. Anyway, my name's Peters. How may I help you?"

"Well, Mr Peters, do you know anything about a lost golden crown?"

"You mean the King John story? There's no truth in that whatsoever, and I should know."

"No, I mean something quite different," said Alice. "What do you mean—you should know?" she added with a tone of puzzled curiosity.

"Aha!" said Mr Peters, searching through some dusty volumes on his desk, "here it is, my own copy." And he passed a slim volume to Alice. It was a copy of the Paunceton Guidebook, not the 1910 edition that Alice had read, but an older version.

"I really shouldn't have done it," said Mr Peters, but I was young and mischievous. And, well, since you're interested, it so happens that this book was first published in 1876. I was young... did I already say that? Yes, I did. Well, it was republished in 1910, I believe, and there you have it."

"What do I have?" said Alice feeling rather confused.

"Bless me, I've left out the most important part of the story."

"Yes, I can see that."

"Well, there wasn't really much of interest to say about Paunceton. I mean, there's the ruin et cetera, but I was not quite twenty. Oh, I should have said, I wrote the guidebook. Yes, and took the photographs for it as well. My father was something of an early enthusiast.

"Where was I? I lost myself. Oh, yes, the crown jewels—I made it up. That's all there is to that, but everyone seemed to like it. Of course, it was all a bit of a joke at first, though the vicar rather took me to task. The parish history was his little baby, you see, and I'm afraid he thought I was treading on his toes. He was not pleased at the local notoriety created by my including a bit of fakery about the history of the town. Still, it's all in the past, what? The 1910 edition was not my idea. In fact, I rather hoped the book would die a death. You see, after a while, I began to see that he was right, the vicar, you know. Right to tell me off like that. I wanted the history to be accurate and not to have that moment of nonsense included. Still, not many were sold, so that's a relief. Though quite a few people believed my little fiction to be true."

Alice listened to all this with a mixture of interest and amusement.

"Actually, that's not the crown I meant. We found one, you see. In the hotel, or rather, behind it. In a box covered with a black cloth. The box had a Latin inscription inside—Corona aurea homines audaces facit."

"Yes, I see," said Mr Peters. "Well, I hardly need translate that for you, I suppose, the meaning is quite clear. I'm certain that it has nothing to do with King John, though. What does it look like?"

"The crown? Well, it's gold, or gold-coloured, anyway. No hallmark, no jewels, though it is chased rather nicely with a leaf motif, and it's quite heavy. It's been reported to the police and sent away for valuation."

"Well, all the documents and books about important things in the town eventually find their way here, but I don't remember seeing anything about a crown. In fact, even the story I made up does not actually mention a crown, though perhaps 'crown jewels' might give rise to confusion. How strange, how very strange."

Alice left, feeling that she had, if not solved the mystery, at least shed a little light on connected matters. Perhaps the full truth would never be known.

CHAPTER ELEVEN

The Paunceton Gazette

TUESDAY NOVEMBER 10ᵀᴴ 1936   **2D**

60 Ft DEATH FALL

INQUEST ON PAUNCETON BUSINESSMAN.

A verdict of "Accidental death" was recorded at the inquest yesterday of well-known Paunceton businessman Stephen Giddins, who was killed by falling down a disused lift shaft behind the Hotel Splendide in Paunceton two weeks ago. In the opinion of Doctor Brown who examined him shortly after the fall, death was caused by his injuries and shock.

An inquiry as to the safety of the lift shaft conducted at the same time found that no blame could be ascribed to the hotel or its owners, as Mr Giddins had entered the lift shaft of his own accord while apparently not in his right mind.

The business methods of Stephen Giddins have been under scrutiny by this newspaper before, and it now seems that the police were about to arrest him on suspicion of fraud and forgery.

His family, who were out of the country, were informed of his death, and his father was present at the inquest but made no comment.

The Paunceton Gazette

TUESDAY NOVEMBER 10TH 1936 **2D**

THE CROWN OF PAUNCETON

The British Museum may be given the opportunity of acquiring the golden coronet discovered in the passages behind the Hotel Splendide.

If the museum does buy the coronet, the hotel proprietor will receive a percentage of the value, judged to be over £500. The coroner of East Sussex, Dr Hoare, after hearing the evidence of its value, declared the item to be Treasure Trove, and, therefore, the property of the Crown. Dr Hoare further ruled that the coronet must be sent to the Treasury, as is normal in these cases. The find was reported immediately, and Dr Hoare, after hearing the evidence of its value, congratulated the finder, Mrs Euphemia Garthwaite, owner of the hotel.

So that there should be no confusion in the minds of our readers, and since some have already jumped to incorrect conclusions, it must be stated that there is no truth in the rumour that this object forms any part of the lost crown jewels of King John.

The year is 1931. Newly married, Alice Winsome leaves her fortune-seeking husband and travels to a town on the south coast of England to stay at the Hotel Splendide.
But the building is not all it seems to be.
The dark secrets of the hotel staff slowly unravel to reveal a web of mysteries. And while the lifts go up and down, carrying guests from floor to floor, conspiracies and intrigue threaten Alice's peace of mind.

veneficiapublications.com

The crown, or coronet as it came to be known, was indeed bought by the British Museum and put on display among Anglo-Saxon artefacts, and many saw it there, though few took much notice of it.

One person who did take notice was a somewhat stout and rather flabby man in his late middle-ages who gazed wistfully at it through the glass case, wondering what he might have been able to achieve if only he had been able to hold it for a short while longer. But he knew now that it could never be his. A day later, he knocked shyly at the front door of a cottage in Rye. The lady who answered looked at him questioningly; he shook his head.

Mrs Dorothy Sallow scowled; her husband took a step back, and she calmly closed the door in his face.

CHAPTER TWELVE

Some three years had passed since Alice had last been to Mandible Hall, the big house in which she had grown up. Now, after all that time, she returned to the old place. It was a cold and wet November afternoon when she arrived at the tall iron gates; she lifted the latch and listened to the familiar screech as she opened them. The sound set her teeth on edge, just as it always had.

Alice walked up the drive without shutting the gates behind her. The wind sighed as if it was sorry to see her back in this dismal place that she used to call Home. She had no luggage: why should she need any? All her things would still be where she had left them.

When she reached the front door, she rang the bell and then turned to look back down the drive, trying to appear nonchalant to whoever should answer the door, whereas, in reality, her heart was already nervously pounding away.

The door opened, and she turned to see the tall and gaunt figure of Groves.

"Hello, Groves," she said casually as if she had never been away.

"Why, Miss Alice, that is Mrs Winsome, you've come back," replied Groves hoarsely in his deep voice. "This has been a sad place since your father died."

She walked in and stood in the dimly lit hall. Groves closed the door.

"I'll tell Mrs Townsend that you're here," he intoned. "She's the new cook."

But before he had taken three steps, a harsh voice suddenly called out,

"Who is it, Groves? Tell them to go away, I'm not in—to anyone!"

The lights were suddenly switched on, and the hall was miraculously bathed in garish colours: reds, greens and yellows.

"Well, who is it, who is it?" demanded the voice. "If it's Dr Petrie, tell him I'll see him tomorrow."

A figure appeared in the doorway at the end of the hall.

"Hello, mother, I'm back," said Alice.

"Alice, my love," said Lady Tongue gently, "how wonderful to see you."

Bryan Kesselman is the author of two previous books, Paddington Pollaky, Private Detective (a biography of a Victorian private investigator) and The Madness of Captain Mills (historical fiction based on real events).

Musical compositions include the operas Dreyfus: Prisoner of Devil's Island and The Time Traveller, and cantatas for choir and orchestra Zimbabwe Suite and Seven Ages of Man. He studied at the Guildhall School of Music and Drama and has sung a number of baritone roles for small professional opera companies.